Global Motivations

Honda, Toyota, and the Drive toward American Manufacturing

Jonathan S. Russ

UNIVERSITY PRESS OF AMERICA,® INC.
Lanham • Boulder • New York • Toronto • Plymouth, UK

Copyright © 2009 by
University Press of America,® Inc.
4501 Forbes Boulevard
Suite 200
Lanham, Maryland 20706
UPA Acquisitions Department (301) 459-3366

Estover Road
Plymouth PL6 7PY
United Kingdom

Library of Congress Control Number: 2007936544
ISBN-13: 978-0-7618-3930-9 (clothbound : alk. paper)
ISBN-10: 0-7618-3930-5 (clothbound : alk. paper)
ISBN-13: 978-0-7618-3931-6 (paperback : alk. paper)
ISBN-10: 0-7618-3931-3 (paperback : alk. paper)
eISBN-13: 978-0-7618-4206-4
eISBN-10: 0-7618-4206-3

For My Parents

Table of Contents

Introduction

In 1886, when German engineer Karl Benz tested his first gasoline-powered motor vehicle, a three-wheeled carriage propelled by a one-cylinder internal combustion engine, the era of the automobile dawned. Soon, engineers, inventors, and tinkerers throughout Europe and America were experimenting with motor vehicles of their own. Engines powered by electricity, diesel fuel, kerosene, and gasoline were attached to vehicles of all shapes and sizes in order to produce newfangled transportation devices. But in no place else did the idea of the automobile take hold as it did in the United States. With a landscape characterized by wide-open spaces and vast distances between settled communities, the U.S. was particularly well suited for the use of such an independent mode of transportation. The combination of technology, capital resources, geography, and an ever-growing consumer base destined the country to become the world leader in automotive production. The motorcar soon eclipsed its function as transportation and entered into the very fabric of American life.

In the early years of the Twentieth Century, hundreds of automotive producers were in business across the U.S., though many lasted only long enough to manufacture one or two finished vehicles. Ironically, as an increasing number of Americans were able to afford automobiles, the number of companies producing motorcars declined. Weaker and smaller firms either went out of business or were absorbed by their more prosperous competitors. As the winnowing process continued into the 1920s, a few great names emerged in the business. Companies such as General Motors and Ford already dominated, but firms such as Studebaker, Nash, Hudson, and Packard were also targeting customers from various walks of life. In time, however, from the ravages of the Great Depression to the industrial consolidation of the post-World War II

viii *Introduction*

economy, the field of American automotive producers narrowed further, leaving only a handful in business. Though manufacturers became fewer in number, American automotive producers competed for the business of millions of customers. Whereas in 1950 5.1 million cars were sold in the United States, by 2000 17.8 million passenger vehicles were sold, 8.8 million of which were cars, with the remainder being comprised of light trucks and sport utility vehicles.[1] By 1987, when Chrysler Corporation purchased the assets of the American Motors Corporation, the American auto companies collectively were known by the number that remained in business: The Big Three. Between them, the General Motors Corporation, the Ford Motor Company, and the Chrysler Corporation produced and sold the majority of automobiles in the United States. By the late 1980s, the size and scope of their industry was enormous. In addition to the numbers generated in sales and payrolls, the American automobile industry accounted for nearly $1 trillion annually when the activities of associated businesses supplying auto parts, financial services, and retail sales were taken into account.[2] What Karl Benz and Henry Ford had pioneered 100 years earlier evolved into some of the largest industrial enterprises the world had ever known.

To say that the Big Three were the only remaining automotive manufacturers in the United States by 1990, however, is misleading. Though they were in fact the only auto makers originally founded in the U.S. that were still in business, they had come to share the American automotive landscape with rivals from abroad. First, of course, was the competition posed by imported automobiles. During the 1980s, sales of imported motor vehicles accounted for approximately one-third of the American automotive market. In addition to the millions of imported cars, however, a new form of competition came to threaten the Big Three in their own backyards. In a seeming reversal of historical trends, the 1980s saw an increased number of companies producing cars on American soil. Unlike their earlier counterparts that had gone under, however, the new auto producers were not American. They were subsidiaries of the Big Three's foreign competitors, and their arrival introduced a new word to the automotive lexicon: the transplant manufacturer.

By 2005, there were ten transplant manufacturers dotting the American automotive landscape. Honda, Toyota, Nissan, Mitsubishi, Subaru, Hyundai, BMW, and Mercedes operated their own factories, while a joint venture between Mazda and Ford known as AutoAlliance, and another between Toyota and General Motors called NUMMI, rounded out the field. Taken as a whole, the new arrivals to American automotive manufacturing produced over 3.3 million vehicles in the United States in 2003, or 20.1% of total U.S. output.[3] Though their operations and activities in the U.S. were still overshadowed by the Big Three, the presence of transplants was noteworthy indeed. These were not small upstart ventures that were new to the automotive business. To the contrary, they were companies that had considerable experience producing motor vehicles in Japan, Germany, and Korea for both domestic and international consumption. That they had invested billions of dollars in order to establish manufacturing ventures in the United States was a development of historic proportion, and their arrival signalled in a new era in American manufacturing.

At the very time that transplant manufacturers were expanding their presence in the United States, the traditional American auto firms were struggling. General Motors, Ford, and Chrysler (which itself had been acquired by Germany's Daimler Benz in 1998) all had excess production capacity, and sales had to be bolstered by generous incentive packages. What emerged, therefore, was a novel phenomenon: vehicle manufacturing in the United States was doing rather well, but the most successful firms producing those vehicles were no longer American in origin. Foreign firms were hiring assembly line personnel and investing billions of dollars to manufacture in the United States at the very time that American companies were shedding workers and closing factories. The Big Three faced competitive pressure from all sides: imports continued to nibble market share, but increasingly the bigger battle was waged by the foreign nameplates manufacturing in the American heartland.

Although the Big Three firms held an edge in the production and sale of light trucks, their transplant competitors continued to gain market share in the car segment. To illustrate the point, in 2003 the top two car factories in the United States were Asian transplants: Honda's plant in Marysville, Ohio produced over 445,000 cars, and Toyota's Georgetown, Kentucky plant made over 435,000. By contrast, Ford's top factory was a light truck assembly plant in Louisville, Kentucky that turned out 367,000 units in 2003, whereas General Motors' top producer was a light truck plant in Moraine, Ohio that made 352,000 trucks.[4] Moreover, with new SUV, truck, and minivan designs rolling off of transplant assembly lines, even Detroit's long-dominant hold on the light truck segment was under threat.

While America's traditional automotive firms shed workers and downsized, it did not follow that the industry as a whole was in trouble. To the contrary, with nearly 12 million units being produced in the U.S., output was strong. Further clouding the picture were enormous productivity gains that had been made during the 1980s and '90s. Though the U.S. auto industry produced more than twice as many vehicles in 2003 than it had in 1956, it did so with fewer workers. Thus, if measured by a numeric workforce, the U.S. auto industry was declining, but if measured by output, then the industry as a whole was in pretty good shape. Indeed, such was the case throughout the spectrum of American manufacturing. As a percentage of the total workforce, industrial employment in the United States had been slipping steadily since the 1950s. For example, in 1950 the manufacturing sector accounted for a little more than 30% of all non-farm employment in the United States, but by 2002 that figure had declined to 11.5%.[5]

This is not to say, however, that manufacturing had declined in importance to the American economy. Since the late 1940s, manufacturing's share of the Gross Domestic Product (GDP) ranged from between 16 and 19%.[6] Since the actual number of industrial workers has remained fairly consistent over time, it follows therefore that productivity soared in the second half of the 20th Century. Like general trends would indicate, some of those productivity gains came in the U.S. auto industry. Developments in automation, labor-saving machinery, and product engineering reduced the demand for workers. Still, despite growing efficiency in the U.S. auto industry, the new transplants were even leaner and more productive.

THE SUBJECTS

To better grasp the activities of transplant manufacturers in the United States, this book considers the arrival of the two most prominent companies, Honda of America Manufacturing, Inc. and Toyota Motor Manufacturing, U.S.A. By the early years of the 21st Century the two were distinguished as the leading transplant producers, with Honda (including its Accura division) producing over 593,000 cars in 2003 at two facilities in Ohio, and over 252,000 trucks at two plants in Alabama. As for Toyota, it turned out over 435,000 cars at its Georgetown, Kentucky plant in 2003, and 291,000 trucks from its Princeton, Indiana plant.[7] In addition, NUMMI, the joint venture between Toyota and General Motors, produced over 233,000 cars at its Freemont, California facility.[8] Impressive though the data may be, however, there were other characteristics that single them out for study. Honda and Toyota are two very distinct companies that approached transplantation to the United States in different ways. Although the popular media often paints Japanese firms with a broad brush, the marked contrast between Honda and Toyota merits consideration.

Although both Honda and Toyota had been marketing vehicles in the United States since the late 1950s and early 1960s, this work is primarily concerned with their arrival as independent vehicle manufacturers. Thus, while Honda and Toyota had well-established sales and distribution arms in the U.S. by the 1960s, the activities of those enterprises are not included in this study. The reason for this is simple; though both firms engaged in sound sales and distribution practices, neither pursued them in a fashion that was uniquely relevant to their activities as transplants. This study also does not focus upon other manufacturing that Honda and Toyota conducted in the United States. While Honda produced motorcycles and Toyota had an interest in NUMMI with General Motors, both ventures will be shown to be precursors that led to the decisions to become independent transplant automotive manufacturers. Likewise, Honda's U.S. marine engine, lawnmower, and generator production is also not included in this study.

Notable among the differences between the two firms was the timing of each company's decision to establish their automobile facilities in the U.S. Honda, a significantly smaller company than Toyota, became the first Japanese auto maker to open and operate a manufacturing facility in the United States. As such, it took risks where no other Japanese car company had ventured before. Honda's early commitment to American production was central to its later corporate development. Toyota, on the other hand, was remarkable for its relatively late arrival as a transplant in the U.S. As Japan's largest automobile company, Toyota was considerably more conservative than Honda in its approach to manufacturing outside Japan. Therefore, Toyota's eventual decision to operate a production plant in the United States signaled that transplantation was not a passing fad. While one company thus ushered in the phenomenon, the other lent it credence.

In considering the establishment of Honda of America Manufacturing's facilities in the State of Ohio and those of Toyota Motor Manufacturing in the Commonwealth of Kentucky, this study first draws a general history of the two firms in Japan. Both companies developed along distinct lines under the vision and leadership of very different people. The result of their histories can be seen in their respective corporate cultures that ultimately affected their arrival in America as transplants. This study examines how corporate culture influenced investment decisions in the U.S., and also looks at how the twin crises during the 1970s in the international currency and energy markets had an impact. Though both events were beyond the control of Honda and Toyota executives, they made a profound impression upon the way each firm conducted its business.

Of significant concern to this study is the process by which Honda and Toyota came to settle in Ohio and Kentucky. Though the Big Three operated auto plants in both states, neither Honda nor Toyota opted to construct their facilities in close proximity to them. Both chose relatively rural locales that were unaccustomed to the rhythms of heavy industry. In explaining what factors attracted the automakers to these sites, this study considers the role that state-sponsored promotion played in the decision-making process. It is striking that Honda and Toyota were investing billions of dollars in seemingly untested locations at precisely the time that the Big Three car companies were closing plants in America's industrial centers. This being the case, the matter of site selection warrants scrutiny.

Of equal interest is the work force that Honda and Toyota set out to hire. Much had been written during the 1970s and 1980s decrying the quality of American labor and the state of labor relations. Both companies, given media reports, were understandably leery about American workers. Moreover, since new hires in their Japanese plants usually came by way of referral from current employees, Honda and Toyota were in the unfamiliar position of having to hire an American workforce from scratch. If either firm had any hope of succeeding in its transplant ventures, dedicated and productive employees would be required. Given the negative attributes often assigned to American labor, both companies pursued strategies aimed at thwarting the problems that appeared to characterize the work forces of their American competitors. This study therefore considers the employee profile each firm sought, the hiring practices each used, relations with American labor unions and government agencies, and the criticisms that each came to face.

Given the multi-billion dollar investment that both Honda and Toyota have made, their collective commitment to manufacturing in the United States is clear. And why shouldn't it be? The American manufacturing operations of both firms are profitable, and consistently strong sales figures demonstrate that their products are popular with the car buying public. Moreover, since both firms also have begun manufacturing minivans and trucks in the U.S., they have an additional opportunity to take further market share from their competitors. Though it is premature to predict just how sweeping their presence will become in the United States, at the very least it is clear that the presence of Honda and Toyota is not a passing phenomenon.

By 2005, it was obvious that much had changed in automotive manufacturing. On a global basis, Toyota had surpassed Ford to become the world's number two automaker behind General Motors, and few doubt that it will soon surpass G.M. as well. While both Honda and Toyota were considerably more profitable and efficient than either General Motors or Ford, that the two had become established fixtures in American manufacturing was no mean feat. Honda and Toyota chose different paths, formed different links with the communities in which they located, and had different solutions for building their respective work forces. Although this study will show how very different they are from one another, it will also demonstrate that both firms are similar in that they are profitable, their American workforces are well paid, and their products are of superior quality. Indeed, Honda and Toyota have proven that American automobile manufacturing is healthy in the 21st Century; it's just that the firms that are most successful at it are no longer headquartered in Detroit.

NOTES

1. *Ward's 1974 Automotive Yearbook*, (Detroit: Ward's Communications, Inc., 1974), 138; *Ward's 2004 Automotive Yearbook*, (Southfield, MI: Ward's Communications, 2004,) 242–243.

2. Peter Kastil, "Europe's Safe for American Hondas, " *The Wall Street Journal*, September 01, 1989, A6.

3. *Ward's 2004 Automotive Yearbook*, (Southfield, MI: Ward's Communications, 2004,) 242–243.

4. *Ward's Automotive Yearbook*, (Southfield, MI: Ward's Communications, 2004,) 224.

5. National Association of Manufacturers, *The Facts About Modern Manufacturing*, 6th Edition, 7.

6. National Association of Manufacturers, *The Facts About Modern Manufacturing*, 6th Edition, 7.

7. *Ward's Automotive Yearbook*, (Southfield, MI: Ward's Communications, 2004,) 26.

8. *Ward's Automotive Yearbook*, (Southfield, MI: Ward's Communications, 2004,) 225, 232.

Chapter One

From Whence They Came

On 8 April 1988, the one millionth Honda produced in the United States rolled off the company's assembly line in Marysville, Ohio, marking a momentous occasion for the people at Honda.[1] Theirs had been the first Japanese auto manufacturer to establish production facilities in the U.S. and, as the millionth car attested, it had been a successful venture. Combined sales of American and Japanese-made cars gave Honda a nearly ten percent share of the U.S. auto market.[2] By November of 2003, when the ten millionth Honda made in the U.S. came off the Marysville line, it was clear that Honda had come a long way since its first car was tested in 1962.

1988 was a benchmark year for the Toyota Motor Corporation as well. In May of that year, Toyota's first American-made Camry sedan was driven off the line at the firm's Georgetown, Kentucky plant. Although it had been manufacturing cars in the U.S. since 1985 at the NUMMI facility, a joint venture between Toyota and General Motors, considerable pride was taken in the company's wholly owned factory in Kentucky. Yet another chapter was unfolding in the firm's history, and with the addition of its Georgetown plant, Toyota operated factories on every continent in the world. This too was quite an accomplishment for a company that barely rose from the ash and rubble of World War II.

Leading up to those heady days had been decades of uninterrupted sales successes for Toyota and Honda in the United States. Between 1958 and 1970, Toyota had sold 250,000 vehicles in America, while Honda sales totaled less than 4,000 cars through the 1970 model year.[3] Theirs were cars sold at the fringe of the marketplace, known only to a handful of auto enthusiasts or those who wanted to drive something different or unusual. But then came the oil crises of the 1970s. Toyotas and Hondas that had once been derided for their small size and underpowered engines suddenly became attractive

1

compared to the gas-guzzling behemoths rolling off of Detroit's assembly lines. Concerns over the quality of American autos further bolstered sales as consumers refused to tolerate the idiosyncrasies associated with domestic nameplates. Though few Americans knew or cared much about either Toyota or Honda, they liked what they saw in their products, and gave their vote of confidence in the dealer showroom.

Throughout the 1980s, roughly 25 percent of all cars sold in the U.S. were Japanese.[4] Combined with the veritable explosion of Japanese consumer goods on American shelves, much of what was being bought in the U.S. appeared to have come from the island nation. Analysts and commentators came out of the woodwork to voice their opinion about Japan and its manufacturing economy. To the country's admirers, nearly all things Japanese had to be quickly imitated lest America became wholly uncompetitive. To its critics, Japan was simply an unfair trading partner bent on world domination, a nation from which American business and labor needed protection. Opinions on both sides of the argument were strong, with little room for compromise inbetween.

Despite their sharp divisions, commentators in the popular media invariably painted Japan and Japanese business with a broad brush. Little distinction was made between Japanese firms or the way in which they conducted their affairs. They were simply Japanese, and as such were assumed to be somehow monolithic, all part of a larger Japan, Inc. It became common to read of the "Japanese management style" or "Japanese manufacturing techniques" as if every enterprise shared the same set of operating procedures. In reality, Japanese firms were as varied as their American counterparts. While superficially they may have appeared similar, however, closer scrutiny revealed their individuality.

Toyota and Honda exemplified variety among Japanese firms; though they enjoyed roughly the same position in the U.S. auto market, they were in fact very different companies. Toyota, then the world's largest auto manufacturer behind General Motors, was among Japan's oldest vehicle manufacturers. Its main factories and headquarters are located in Toyota City, a place once known as Koromo. By all accounts it was an "establishment" company, defining the paradigm of Japanese industry as General Motors once had done in the United States during the 1950s. When American commentators discussed Japanese business practices, it was usually a company such as Toyota that they had in mind. It was large, prosperous, and influential. Honda, on the other hand, was much smaller and unconventional in comparison. It was a distant third in sales to Toyota on the Japanese mainland, commanding a 10.4 percent market share compared to Toyota's 40 percent share.[5] It was widely perceived as an upstart company whose future was not altogether secure. Despite its phenomenal success in the U.S., young Japanese managers remained leery about joining an auto firm that was a mere 30 years old.

Before turning to their respective operations in the United States, it is important to briefly consider the histories of Toyota and Honda. Their different corporate cultures, business activities, and investment strategies can be attributed to the ways in which the two firms evolved, and thus it is critical to explore this context.

GETTING STARTED

Like many of its competitors the world over, The Toyota Motor Corporation was born of one man's dream to build automobiles. And although he never lived to see his dream come to fruition, it was on account of his inspiration, and his initial capital investment, that Toyota came into being. That man was Japanese inventor Toyoda Sakichi.

A tinkerer by trade and temperament, Toyoda Sakichi made his fortune in the spinning loom business. Toyoda introduced his first wooden spinning machine in 1894 at the age of 27. Three years later he introduced Japan's first steam-driven power loom, which he continued to perfect over time. Since sericulture and, by extension, the silk textile industry were cornerstones of Japan's early 20th century economy, Toyoda's efficient looms found a ready market. His customers ranged in size from small "Mom and Pop" shops to the country's largest mills. Eventually Sakichi became both supplier and competitor when he established Toyoda Spinning and Weaving in 1918. Shortly before his retirement, Sakichi founded Toyoda Automatic Loom Works in 1926 as the central company of his various enterprises, known collectively as the Toyoda Group. Though he lacked a formal education as either an engineer or a businessman, Toyoda Sakichi nevertheless had secured international recognition for his life's work.[6] His achievements were later recorded in the Japanese grade school textbook immodestly titled, *Toyoda Sakichi: King of Inventors*.

In his quest for better machinery and technology, Toyoda Sakichi traveled abroad as he built his empire. In an era long before international business travel was common, Toyoda's journey's exposed him to ideas and processes that he would later put to his own use. On one such four-month trip to the United States in 1910, Sakichi was captivated by the automobile and its manufacture.[7] He took to the vehicles immediately, though it would be some years before he entertained the idea of manufacturing them in Japan. Indeed, it was not until Ford and General Motors began assembling autos in Japan in the

1920s that Sakichi was persuaded that there was a market for motor vehicles amongst his countrymen.

It did not take long for the Japanese subsidiaries of Ford and G.M., founded in 1925 and 1927 respectively, to dominate Japan's auto market. Seeing their success, Toyoda set his eldest son, Toyoda Kiichiro, on the task of studying automotive technology. Having earned a degree in mechanical engineering from Tokyo Imperial University in 1920, Kiichiro had spent his early career developing motors for his father's loom company. The time had come, according to his father, for him to turn toward automotive research. To that end, Sakichi provided Kiichiro with an initial capitalization of ¥1 million ($460,000), the tidy sum that the Platt Brothers of Great Britain had paid him in 1929 for the use of his loom patents outside Japan, the U.S., and China.[8]

Though he was eager to study automobiles, which at the time meant buying American cars and disassembling them to see how they functioned, Kiichiro was less than enthusiastic about fabricating them. He believed that Ford and G.M. so dominated the Japanese auto industry that there was little point in actually challenging them. In this opinion he had good company, as no major Japanese combine had risked capital in producing domestic vehicles.[9] On his deathbed in 1930, Sakichi reiterated his desire that Kiichiro continue his work with autos, in the hope that someday his son would enter into the business. Whatever personal reservations he may have harbored, the dutiful Kiichiro vowed to honor his father's last wishes.

Despite his filial commitment to his father, Kiichiro was unsure what direction his work with autos would take. Would his research lead to manufacturing vehicles, or would it leave him believing such a venture impossible? The only matter of which he was certain at the time was his need for more capital if his work was to continue. The original money given to him by Sakichi was nearly exhausted by the early 1930s, and Kiichiro needed the Toyoda Group to provide further resources. In successful family businesses such as the Toyoda's, Kiichiro would traditionally have had little problem arranging finances. After all, as a matter of primogeniture Kiichiro would have inherited his father's business upon his death, thereby leaving him in control. As Kiichiro well knew, however, he did not enjoy this traditional arrangement.

When he retired, Sakichi named his son-in-law, Kodama Risaburo, as the president of Toyoda Automatic Loom, with Kiichiro as his subordinate. Although Kiichiro was his eldest natural son, Sakichi had adopted Risaburo in 1915 when he married Sakichi's daughter. Technically, this made Risaburo, who was ten years older than Kiichiro, Sakichi's eldest son. The reason behind Kodama Risaburo's adoption was that he was the younger brother of Kodama Kazuo, the head of Mitsui Trading Company's branch in Nagoya. Sakichi had become indebted to Kazuo when Mitsui Trading financed his move in 1914 into cotton spinning using a machine he had invented; Risaburo's adoption the following year attested to the strong ties Toyoda had made with Mitsui through Kodama.[10]

Since Kiichiro was unable to direct Toyoda Automatic Loom's resources on his own, in 1933 he had to petition the company's board of directors. Risaburo initially objected to further capitalizing auto research since he saw little point in the venture. He believed that Kiichiro's progress was insufficient for the company to challenge Ford or General Motors any time in the near future. Nevertheless, since Toyoda Automatic Loom was essentially a family business, Risaburo had to consider factors aside from what might otherwise have been good business sense. His wife, Kiichiro's sister, reminded him of their father's desire that Kiichiro enter into the auto business. Giving into her pressure, and perhaps into his own sense of obligation, Risaburo dropped his earlier objections and authorized Kiichiro to move ahead. That August, Toyoda Automatic Loom Works created an automotive division.

Once committed, Risaburo gave Kiichiro the company's full backing. He lowered corporate dividends and tripled Toyoda Automatic Loom's capitalization to ¥3 million in 1934, doubling it again to ¥6 million in 1935, with ¥4 million of the new funds going to the automobile department. In 1936 the automobile department was made its own entity, the Toyota Motor Company. The new company's name came from a contest to find a suitable logo to replace "Toyoda" which means "abundant rice field." From 27,000 suggestions, Kiichiro and other members of the automobile department chose "Toyota," an alternate reading of the two ideographs that make up the family name.[11]

From 1933–1936, Kiichiro's automobile department continued the research it had begun earlier, except on a larger scale. American automobiles were dissembled and scrutinized. When the company's engineers designed the first Toyota vehicle, a light duty truck, its major components were derived from Ford, G.M., and Chrysler products. The biggest hurdle facing Toyota was not design, however, but rather securing a reliable and consistent source of parts. Though some Japanese firms claimed they could supply Toyota, the truth was that their wares were often undependable and shoddy. Parts had to be imported from the U.S., adding considerable expense for the nascent automaker. Toyota made as many parts as it could in-house, but this solution was still far from efficient. In the final analysis, it was only by virtue of government intervention that Toyota was able to compete with its international rivals.

During the course of the 1930s, Japan embarked on its ill-fated course of imperial expansion. The Japanese sphere of influence was spreading throughout

China, and would soon extend throughout the Asian Pacific. Military planners and bureaucrats in the Ministry of Commerce and Industry (MCI), predecessor to today's Ministry of Economy, Trade and Industry, believed that Japan's imperialist ambitions would be threatened if the country did not have its own motor vehicle industry. Should American subsidiaries in Japan choose not to supply the government with vehicles suitable for military use, Japan's expansionist desires would be hampered. Thus, in 1936 Japan's National Diet passed a measure known as the Law Concerning the Manufacture of Motor Vehicles that was designed to hinder foreign automakers, especially Ford and G.M. Among other stipulations, the legislation stated that companies manufacturing more than 3,000 vehicles annually within Japan had to be licensed by the government. Moreover, a majority of the stockholders in such companies had to be imperial subjects. Since the government would not license either Ford or General Motors, and since neither firm met the shareholder criteria, Toyota could fill the void.[12]

With the government providing a measure of protection, Toyota pushed ahead with the construction of its first large auto plant. Located in the rural town of Koromo, later renamed Toyota City in 1959, the facility was designed to manufacture 1,500 vehicles per month. Military procurement for Japan's war in China helped ensure that the new company had a steady flow of orders. Though Kiichiro had hoped to manufacture both cars and trucks, the military demand for trucks was such that Toyota needed to concentrate its early efforts on filling those orders. In 1939 the Japanese government forbade the manufacture of passenger cars anyway, further delaying Kiichiro's desire to broaden Toyota's offerings. Perhaps even more significantly, though, as a result of the new legislation both Ford and G.M folded their Japanese subsidiaries.

Although by the late 1930s Toyota found more domestic sources for parts, it still had to rely on foreign manufacturers for many sophisticated components. This situation presented the firm with real difficulties once the war with the United States began in 1941. Toyota filled its military orders as best as could be expected, but their vehicles often came without features that they had before the war. For example, supply difficulties resulted in trucks being shipped with a sole headlight, or brakes installed on the rear wheels only. The company also came to experience severe labor shortages as the war progressed and able-bodied men of all ages were conscripted for military service. By the war's end, Toyota employed disabled military veterans, schoolchildren, nuns, geishas, and even convicted criminals.[13] Although Toyota officials knew that all Japanese manufacturers suffered from similar difficulties at the time, they nevertheless were disappointed and frustrated with their state of affairs.

With the cessation of hostilities in August 1945, Toyota executives briefly paused to take stock of their company's situation. Looking back on the days following Japan's surrender, former Toyota president Toyoda Eiji, then a young director of the firm, noted that his company could have sustained far worse damage than it had. According to Toyoda,

> The last bombing raid came on 14 August, in the afternoon. Three B-29s each dropped a large bomb, either 500-kilo or one-tonners, I don't know which. The first bomb fell right next to the company housing complex, leaving a large crater. The second fell harmlessly into the Yahagi River nearby. But the third bomb fell right on the money, leveling about a quarter of the plant.

> After Japan's surrender on August 15, a bombing survey commission came to the plant to check on the effects of the air raid. They brought with them photos showing excellent aerial views of the plant. When I saw those pictures, I realized that there had been no way of evading an attack. The American forces had not bombed at random; they had taken careful aim.

> I was horrified when I took a look at the bombing schedule the commission had with them. Toyota City was to have been bombed and burned to the ground exactly one week later, on 21 August.[14]

Compared with most other Japanese manufacturers, Toyota had been quite lucky.

THE CRITICAL YEARS

If the end of World War II meant peace for Japan, it did little to immediately restore the country's prosperity. After years of fighting abroad, and later suffering aerial raids on its domestic facilities, the nation was exhausted and largely destroyed. American fire bombings and raids on military installations caused nearly 700,000 casualties on the Japanese home islands. Close to nine million people were left homeless, and food and medicine were in short supply. The two million civilians and three million soldiers who were repatriated further strained the country's scarce resources. Prospects for the future looked grim.[15]

Although Toyota had sustained only limited bomb damage in the final days of the war, it still had nothing with which to build vehicles, let alone customers to buy them. Economic activity had ground to a halt.[16] Toyota tried to stay solvent by doing auto repair work and even experimented with dry cleaning, chinaware production, and canning fish paste. Though Kiichiro hoped that such activities would provide his workers with something to do, he knew that ultimately the firm would only survive if it could return to vehicle manufacturing.

Contrary to Japanese worries, it became clear that the American occupation forces were not going to ravage Japan and seek revenge for the war. As early as September 1945, Toyota officials were conducting talks with the General Headquarters of the Allied Forces (GHQ), America's organ for administering its occupation of Japan. GHQ permitted Toyota to resume production of trucks and buses for domestic use, but cars were still forbidden. Kiichiro's alternate schemes for the company's survival were shelved and all efforts were once again turned to vehicle manufacturing. Though the depressed economy meant that sales were painfully slow, it was a relief to know that Toyota might still remain in business.

As part of its effort to reshape Japan in America's image, GHQ ordered that trade unions be allowed to operate in Japan for the first time without government interference. Like their counterparts the world over, Toyota executives were leery about a unionized work force. Neither Toyota nor the affiliated Toyoda firms had experience with unions before, so company officials were unsure how one might affect its operations. Nevertheless, seeing that one was inevitable, in 1946 Toyota helped found the company's first union, The Toyota Motor Koromo Labor Union. Unlike in the United States, the union represented both white and blue-collar workers, in the hope that company viewpoints and concerns would be aired at meetings. Though this in-house union was to prove cooperative in the future, the poor economy at the time meant that Toyota had to cope with an increasingly dissatisfied and radical union leadership.

In addition to legalizing unions, GHQ also sought to restructure broad segments of the Japanese economy. Chief among its concerns was the degree to which capital and power was concentrated in relatively few hands. Since the Meiji Restoration in the 1860s, Japanese business and industry was largely controlled by large family-based enterprises known as *zaibatsu*. Most famous among the *zaibatsu* were firms such as Mitsui, Mitsubishi, and Sumitomo. Under the Enterprise Reconstruction and Reorganization Plan passed by the Japanese Diet in 1947 with pressure from GHQ, *zaibatsu* were compelled to decentralize and split off divisions as separate entities. Though the Toyoda Group was not officially considered a *zaibatsu*, it nevertheless was categorized as a "restricted concern", meaning that it was subject to some decentralization. As a result, it had to spin off Toyoda Spinning & Weaving. Moreover, Toyota Motors had to shed its electrical parts division, which later came to be known as Nippondenso, Japan's largest producer of automotive electrical components.

Despite GHQ's efforts at reshaping Japan, its economy remained dismal. Severe inflation gripped the country as goods and services were still in short supply. In an effort to curb spiraling prices, the GHQ adopted what was known as the "Dodge Line", named for the Detroit banker whose plan it was. Among its provisions, the "Dodge Line" called on the Japanese government to embark on a program of fiscal austerity. It further restricted union activities that threatened to disrupt the fragile economy, meaning that strikes were essentially outlawed for the time being. Though the plan indeed halted inflation and stabilized the yen at 360 to the dollar, its chilling effects further depressed what little life there had been in the economy.[17]

By 1950, Toyota was on the brink of bankruptcy. Though by then it was authorized to build cars in addition to trucks and buses, materials remained scarce and sales were insufficient to support the firm. Debt had climbed to the point where Toyota risked defaulting on its obligations. Toyoda Kiichiro was by then despondent, suffering from depression and alcoholism. Events spiraled beyond his control and, despite his valiant efforts, it seemed certain that the company would fold in a matter of months.

What eventually saved Toyota from bankruptcy was intervention from its bankers. In 1950 Takanashi Takeo, head of the Bank of Japan's Nagoya district office, called together representatives of the country's largest banks in order to rescue the company. It was decided that Mitsui Bank, Toyota's largest creditor, would take the lead in restructuring its debts. Mitsui was a natural ally of Toyota's, having had a relationship with the company since the time of Toyoda Sakichi. This did not mean, however, that Mitsui would allow Toyota a free reign with its money. In order to protect the bank's interests, Nakagawa Fukio of Mitsui became Toyota's senior managing director charged with overseeing the financial reorganization of the company. In the decade to follow, Nakagawa rose to become Toyota's president, securing that post in 1961.[18]

Mitsui's plan for Toyota restructured the entire company. As a first step, Toyota had to eliminate 2,146 jobs, approximately a third of its work force. Secondly, a parallel branch of Toyota was formed, the Toyota Motor Sales Company. Although the Toyota Motor Corporation initially was allowed to make staff appointments at Toyota Motor Sales (TMS), it could not own any stock in the new venture. It was a distinct entity whose function was to be Toyota Motor Corporation's sole customer. As such, TMS was responsible for ordering all the vehicles that the manufacturing arm of the company produced. TMS dictated the number of models to be produced, what options those vehicles might contain, what colors they would come in, and other details affecting the product mix. TMS based its decisions on consumer surveys and feedback from its retail dealers. Though TMS complicated Toyota's corporate structure, it was an attempt to ensure that the company responded to consumer demands effectively. It instilled a marketing discipline where one had not previously existed, eventually giving Toyota an edge on its competitors.[19]

Toyota's reorganization, and especially the dismissal of so many of its workers, was too much for Kiichiro to bear. He resigned from the company he founded, and died two years later in 1952 at the age of 58. Ishida Taizo, formerly the head of Toyoda Automatic Loom, succeeded him as president. Though Ishida initially took the appointment on a temporary basis, he remained Toyota's president until 1961, and its chairman until 1971. During his tenure as president, Ishida oversaw Toyota's evolution from near bankruptcy to becoming Japan's leading automaker. As had happened earlier in the company's history, however, outside events played the key role in shaping Toyota's fortunes.

Just as military orders had helped to launch Toyota in the 1930s, they once again came to the firm's rescue in the early 1950s. This time, however, the customer was not the Japanese military, but rather the United States. The unexpected outbreak of hostilities in Korea left American and United Nations forces in desperate need of trucks to transport soldiers and equipment. In addition to ordering vehicles from American manufacturers, the U.S. Army also purchased over $23 million worth of trucks from Toyota, Nissan, and Isuzu during the course of the war.[20] From the Army's viewpoint, buying from the Japanese made sense because it saved on shipping expenses and dramatically shortened delivery times. What mattered to Toyota was that cash was flowing once again into its coffers.

The combined effects of greater efficiency and U.S. military orders returned Toyota to profitability. Furthermore, it provided the capital necessary for the development of an affordable and economical passenger car. Though in theory Toyota was producing an automobile by the early 1950s, it was really a car body attached to the frame of a truck. Popularly known as the "Toyopet", the Toyota SA had been designed in 1947, when GHQ partially lifted its restrictions and permitted 300 passenger cars to be produced annually.[21] Shortly thereafter, restrictions were lifted entirely, enabling Toyota to broaden its market. Once it did go on sale to the general public, the Toyota SA was the vehicle of choice for Tokyo taxicab drivers.

In 1954, Toyota replaced the aging SA with an entirely new model, the Crown RS, and a slightly less expensive version of it known as the Master. The Crown marked a watershed in Toyota history, since it was entirely purpose-built as an automobile. Furthermore, its body was built by Toyota itself, another first for the company. Though sales to the public were slow, it immediately became the new favorite of taxicab drivers, a considerable feat since they made up 90 percent of Japanese car demand in the early 1950s.[22] The tide had clearly turned for Toyota.

Although sales of the Toyota Crown helped the company gain market share from its biggest rival Nissan, it was not until the Corona model was introduced in 1957 that Toyota secured its place as Japan's leading auto manufacturer.[23] Like the Crown before it, the Corona was popular among taxi drivers for its efficiency and, by Japanese standards, its large size. Under the leadership of Kamiya Shotaro, however, Toyota Motor Sales wanted to go beyond the taxi market and penetrate the Japanese public. Though a seemingly obvious goal, selling automobiles in a country where few people had a driver's license was no small task. Not easily discouraged, TMS president Kamiya arrived at a solution to the problem.

> Toyota realized fully that in order to promote the spread of motorization it was first necessary to increase the number of people having driver's licenses. In 1957, therefore, Toyota Motor Sales opened the Chubu Nippon Driving School, the largest of its kind in Asia. The fact that a company capitalized at ¥1 billion would invest ¥400 million in a driving school was called 'reckless' by some people. But this school contributed greatly to the spread of motorization in Japan by being a first-step in the long-term development of automobile demand.[24]

As might be expected, all the cars used at the training school were Toyota products. Upon successful completion of their lessons, Toyota salesmen, who also were ready to arrange financing for the graduates to purchase new vehicles, warmly congratulated students at Chubu. Kamiya had gambled that the new drivers would want to buy cars with which they were familiar and comfortable, and his instincts proved to be correct. So successful was the Chubu venture that TMS went on to organize driving schools throughout the country, often in conjunction with local dealers. Through their schools, TMS accomplished what all marketing organizations strive for: they created the market for their product.[25]

Though pleased with their accomplishments at home, TMS was already going ahead with plans to export Toyota cars abroad. In October 1957, only months after the Chubu school had been opened, the company established its marketing arm in the U.S., Toyota Motor Sales, U.S.A. What prompted Toyota to export to the U.S. was not so much supreme confidence in their cars as it was a defensive maneuver. Accustomed to Japanese protectionism, Toyota executives assumed that the American government would behave similarly. As Toyoda Eiji recalled,

> European cars had been making inroads in the U.S. market since about 1955, and the best-selling foreign car was Volkswagen of West Germany. At one time European cars had close to a 10 percent share of the American car market. We

saw all too well that at this rate America would eventually rise up in anger against foreign 'intrusion' in its markets.

Watching all this from Japan, Kamiya Shotaro, then president of Toyota Motor Sales, mused: 'If the U.S. goes ahead and restricts imports, Toyota will be cut out of the American market for good. We've got to get in there now or never.' That was the situation as we saw it, so we loaded a couple of Crowns on a ship and sent them over.

Although the Crown was doing well in Japan, we didn't have the slightest idea how it would fare over in the States. All we knew for certain was that once import restrictions were erected, any hope we had of exporting to the U.S. would vanish, regardless of how good our product was. There were no two ways about it; we had to get a foot in the door.[26]

As events would have it, the Crown had a miserable reception in the U.S. To begin, the car's engine was severely underpowered for American conditions. It could not maintain appropriate speed on highways, nor could it keep from seizing when motorists drove it for extended periods of time. Secondly, the Crown's small size, while an attractive feature in Japan, was unacceptable to most American car buyers at the time. Those consumers who did seek a compact automobile would, as Toyoda Eiji noted, buy Volkswagen products, if for no other reason than at least they functioned properly.

Although Toyota's foray into the U.S. market was thus something of a disappointment, it nevertheless achieved its goal of getting "a foot in the door." In time, appropriate products were developed for export. The important achievement in the short run was that Toyota had a marketing arm in the U.S. that was able to provide valuable feedback to TMS in Japan. And although the U.S. did not erect the trade barriers he had feared, Kamiya Shotaro demonstrated his ability to look ahead and anticipate future conditions. The Mitsui bankers who had insisted upon the creation of a separate Toyota sales and marketing entity in 1950 apparently knew what they were doing. So too did the Toyoda family when they appointed Kamiya as the president of TMS. The 1950s were the critical years for Toyota, and at the decade's close, its financial crisis had passed.

In 1964, Japan staged a coming out party of sorts. As the site of the Olympic Games that year, Tokyo and the rest of Japan was on stage for the rest of the world to see. And the world liked what it saw. Japan had emerged from the devastation of World War II modern, industrial, and democratic. The Tokyo Olympics symbolized the country's reemergence into the community of nations, and the Japanese took pride in their accomplishments. For the first time since the War a sense of national self-confidence swept the country, and the Japanese were eager for even greater growth and prosperity.[27]

Like the nation as a whole, Toyota entered the 1960s with optimism. In 1959 it opened a second factory near its original plant in Toyota City. The new facility, known as the Motomachi plant, was entirely devoted to automobile assembly, unlike its older counterpart that produced trucks and busses in addition to passenger cars. Within eight months of its opening, Toyota expanded the Motomachi plant to include a second assembly line, as well as a larger machine tool shop. Despite its efforts to expand, however, Toyota still had to struggle to meet rising demand for its cars. From the early 1950s until 1970, Japan's Gross National Product averaged an 11 percent annual growth rate.[28] This sustained economic expansion resulted in rising living standards throughout the country. And for Toyota, it meant a steady stream of orders from people who had never before owned a car.

Though exports to the United States remained sluggish in the 1960s, it mattered little to Toyota since it was focused on meeting domestic demand. The Crown remained a popular model, and soon Toyota expanded its product mix to include both less expensive as well as more luxurious cars. The diminutive Publica model was especially popular with first-time buyers, and in 1966 Toyota rolled out its first Corolla. All the while Toyota was producing its cars in only two factories. Between 1960 and 1965, both plants were operating at 115 percent capacity listed for one shift, meaning that orders were met through a combination of overtime and annual increases in productivity.[29]

Industry analysts have dubbed the 1960s as the decade of motorization in Japan, and Toyota's sales figures support the claim. In 1960 the firm sold 42,000 cars, but by 1969 it was selling one million units annually. In 1963, Toyota overtook rival Nissan as Japan's largest auto manufacturer, a position from which it never retreated.[30] Production capacity soared as Toyota added new factories in 1965, '66, '68, and 1970, all of which are located in or around Toyota City in Aichi prefecture. Quite clearly, these were boom years for the automaker.

Just as the 1950s were critical to the firm's survival, the 1960s were the years in which Toyota became a world-class player in the auto industry. Domestic sales provided it with a profitable foundation from which it could turn its attention to the export market. What had once been a dream of Toyoda Sakichi's was now an empire. By 1970, Toyota employed over 24,000 assembly line workers, with thousands more in marketing, sales, design, and engineering.[31] Though the Toyoda family continued to have members among the company's management ranks, Toyota was no longer a family enterprise. Its stock was publicly traded on the Tokyo exchange, and it counted among its employees the best and the brightest Japan had to offer. Toyoda Sakichi would have been pleased.

THE MAN WHO WOULD BE KING

By 1922, two years after having graduated from Tokyo Imperial University with an engineering degree, Toyoda Kiichiro was working for his father, Toyoda Sakichi. His job was to perfect the motors that powered Toyoda looms, experience that would later prove useful at the Toyota Motor Corporation. Kiichiro represented a new generation of Japanese, one that was well educated in modern science and technology. As a member of leading manufacturing family, Kiichiro was an elite member of society. He was a fortunate young man, one whose future was filled with promise and opportunity.

That same year, at the age of sixteen, Honda Soichiro was graduated from the Futamato Senior Elementary School. Though in time Honda's life would also abound in opportunity and good fortune, in 1922 his future did not look nearly as bright as Kiichiro's. Born into modest circumstances, Honda Soichiro grew up in a village on the outskirts of Hamamatsu in Shizuoka prefecture. His father, Honda Gihei, was a blacksmith whose trade was steady, but not terribly lucrative. The Honda family had the necessities of life, but enjoyed few luxuries. Likewise, Honda Soichiro's education equipped him with the basics, but it certainly did not measure up to a degree from the country's most prestigious university.

Although financial limits prevented Honda from going beyond the elementary school level, he was not inclined to do so in any case. Later in life, Honda recalled his disdain for school.

> I was hopeless as far as examinations were concerned. I did not like reading and writing because I found writing things down very troublesome. I hated calligraphy and composition classes. I often skipped these classes, went up to a hill behind the school, and stretched out on my back and watched the sky. Its much the same with me even now; I can understand things much more efficiently through my ears and eyes . . . while what I read in books does not go down well with me.[32]

As Honda was to amply prove, however, disliking school did not mean he was disinterested in learning.

A few months before completing school, Honda set out to secure an apprenticeship, the traditional means by which a young man learned a trade. In most circumstances, it would have been customary for Honda to apprentice himself to a blacksmith in order that he could eventually assume his father's business. Though perhaps he would have preferred this arrangement, the elder Honda did not prevent his son from entering an apprenticeship of his own choosing. Finally, after weeks of searching, Soichiro came upon an advertisement that struck his fancy. Arto Shokai, the firm that sought a journeyman, was one of Tokyo's few automobile repair shops. He successfully applied for the position, and on the day following graduation, left for Tokyo to learn the auto repair business. Thus began Honda Soichiro's entrance into the world of automobiles.

Or so he thought. Though Arto Shokai was indeed a Tokyo auto repair shop, Honda's master was more interested in using the 16 year old for odd chores around his garage and home than in teaching him the repair trade. As the days turned into months, Honda found himself sweeping, cleaning, hauling, and even baby sitting the owner's child, but not fixing cars. He later claimed that he would have returned home had it not been for fear of losing face and being ashamed.[33] Finally, on September 01, 1923, Honda had a stroke of good fortune. The Great Kanto Earthquake occurred that day, killing an estimated 130,000 people, and literally flattened the buildings of Tokyo and Yokohama. Ironically, though, this was the break for which Honda had been waiting.[34]

The Great Kanto Earthquake was one of the 20th century's worst natural disasters. For those who survived the quake and the subsequent firestorms, the period that followed was fraught with difficulties and hardships. Daily survival was itself a struggle, to say nothing of having to rebuild both cities. A few structures remained standing, however, and Arto Shokai's garage was one of them. Business boomed for the shop as Tokyo's elite sought to have their earthquake-damaged vehicles repaired. The only problem was that most of the mechanics stopped coming to work since they were preoccupied with taking care of their families. Single and unattached, Honda remained at the shop, where his master promptly put him to work on cars. Though he had no idea what he was doing at first, Honda proved to be a quick study, and soon began to practice his trade.

In the years that followed at Arto Shokai, Soichiro evolved from an apprentice to a mechanic in his own right. He gained a reputation for himself, and soon became known in Tokyo for his prowess. At the end of his six-year obligation, Honda returned to his native region to establish his own repair shop in Hamamatsu. In 1928, with an initial investment made by his former mentor, he opened the Hamamatsu Branch of the Arto Shokai.[35]

Despite his success in Tokyo, Honda initially found it difficult to compete with Hamamatsu's three other repair shops. His biggest hurdle was his age; at 22 he was considered too young by many potential customers to do the work. Nevertheless, by the end of his first year, Honda attracted enough business to stay not only afloat, but to make a profit of 80 sen—a whopping two cents in U.S. currency at the 1928 exchange rate.[36]

In addition to repairing cars, Honda also launched a small enterprise to manufacture cast-metal spokes for use in automobile wheels. Up until then, wheels in Japan had wooden spokes, which were apt to break with continued use. Not only were Honda's spokes something of a novelty, but they also earned him his first patent. By the early 1930s, the young Honda, still only 25 years old, employed 50 men in both his manufacturing and repair businesses, and his wheels were being sold as far abroad as India.[37] Though his profits paled in comparison to the enormous sums earned by the Toyoda enterprises, Honda Soichiro was nevertheless quite a success in the eyes of his neighbors.

While they indeed recognized his achievements, Honda's neighbors also knew him as something of a rogue. He was known for his hard drinking and his fondness for geisha, neither of which he attempted to hide.[38] His taste for adventure led him to racing both cars and powerboats at a time before either sport enjoyed broad popularity. He was a spirited man, and it reflected in all that he did. While many might have been satisfied with his profitable businesses, Honda was impatient to launch into new ventures. Thus, in 1934 he founded the Tokai Seiki Company, a research firm that was later to produce piston rings.

From Honda's perspective, the manufacture of piston rings was a logical step for him to try. A nascent Japanese auto industry was budding that would need large quantities of the vital engine part. Moreover, piston rings were needed for the gasoline powered pumps, generators, and aircraft engines that were then coming into use. Seeing a ready market for his product, Honda expanded Tokai Seiki in 1936, buying the necessary machinery and hiring 50 workers. His business plan was flawed, however, in that neither he nor his employees knew the first thing about piston ring production.

For nearly a year Honda toiled day and night experimenting with the rings. He would stay up until the early morning hours casting and testing the engine parts. All the while he fell deeper into debt, and despite his best efforts, he had little success. As Honda later reflected upon that time in his life,

> I could hold out only because I knew that all of us would starve if I gave up. Nevertheless, we made little progress. Finally I was driven to the last extremity. I realized that nothing more or less than my lack of knowledge was at the root of the problem.
>
> So I went to Professor Fujita of the Hamamatsu School of Technology and asked for help. Professor Fujita introduced me to another professor at the school, Professor Tashiro. After examining some of the piston rings we had made, Professor Tashiro told me that silicon was missing from our products. Looking back, I am shamefaced to admit that we not only had no knowledge of the application of silicon, but we didn't even know we needed it![39]

Finally, on 20 November 1937, Honda produced the first piston ring that he characterized as "more or less acceptable." As he had hoped, orders began streaming in from Nissan and Toyota, and a whole host of small and mid-size companies.[40] Like most Japanese manufacturing firms, orders placed by the military at the time played an increasingly significant role in Tokai Seiki's business. With the onslaught of World War II, or the Pacific War as the Japanese refer to it, all of Honda's piston ring production was designated for military procurement.

Honda's operations fared no better or worse than other Japanese industries during the war. Securing necessary raw materials was a daily struggle, and as Toyota had found, even labor became a precious commodity as the hostilities dragged on. Unlike Toyota, however, Honda Soichiro lost all but one factory to American bombing raids. His one remaining plant in Hamamatsu was destroyed in an earthquake during the summer of 1945, and thus by the war's end Honda was effectively out of business.[41] The few remaining machines that survived the war years were sold, and Honda decided to abandon piston ring production altogether despite offers of future orders from Toyota.

> During the war, I did not pick a quarrel with our 'in-law', the Toyota people, because we were all fighting for the same cause. But now that the war was ended, I wanted to be free to display my own originality.[42]

And with that said, Honda forged ahead.

THE DREAM AND BEYOND

Like all Japanese, Honda Soichiro was rather unsure what to do with himself once the war concluded, but his uncertainty did not last long. Amid severe fuel shortages and the destruction of infrastructure, transportation was a critical problem in post-war Japan. Even an enterprising individual such as Soichiro could not find ample gasoline for his car, nor were most roads any longer suitable for large vehicles. To solve his own transportation needs, Honda struck upon an idea that proved to be ideal not only for him, but for his countrymen as well. He began producing motorbikes.

Honda's motorbikes were exactly that—engines retrofitted onto existing bicycles. Drawing upon his extensive experience, he fashioned small motors based upon a design first used by the military during the war to operate radios and other mobile equipment. To solve the difficulty posed by gasoline shortages, Honda created a fuel based on pine resin that he refined into a crude turpentine. Though far from ideal, the combustible liquid was good enough to run the small engines. With the ability to sell a mode of transportation and the fuel with which to power it, Honda could not produce either good quickly enough. The motorbikes ran harshly and emitted foul smelling exhausts, but the product was right for the time.

As prosperity crept back into Japanese life, Honda was ready to meet the slightly higher aspirations of his fellow citizens. In 1948, with a capitalization of a mere $3,300, he and his associate Fujisawa Takeo founded the Honda Motor Company, Ltd. to produce motorcycles. The next year the new venture introduced its first model, the Dream, powered by a two-stroke engine that Honda designed.[43] Though small by contemporary European and American standards, the Dream was nevertheless a vast improvement over the earlier motorbikes. Its purpose-built frame was more rigid, and the 50cc motor was more powerful and smoother running. The Dream was an instant success. It was inexpensive to own and operate, and demand far outstripped the 1,000 units a month Honda Motor could assemble. [44]

Based on the success of the Dream, events unfolded quickly. In 1951 a new Dream model was introduced, this time with a four-stroke engine displacing 146cc. It compared favorably with other motorcycles in its class, but sales were slower than expected. Honda attributed the problem to the cycle's relatively heavy weight and inefficient fuel consumption. Though popular with enthusiasts, it missed the more important target group of the average Japanese motorist. Not to be discouraged, Soichiro pressed ahead with a new design that came out in 1952 as the Cub model. More of a scooter than a motorcycle, the Cub recaptured consumer interest. By 1955, due to the Cub's popularity, Honda became Japan's largest volume motorcycle manufacturer.[45]

To meet rising demand, Honda Motor desperately needed to expand its production facilities. Obtaining the necessary financing, however, was no easy matter. Unlike the Toyoda family, Honda had no chummy relations with Japan's big bankers, a decided disadvantage in the capital scarce Japan of the mid-1950s. To further complicate matters, Honda Soichiro's personal appearance was not exactly that of a successful entrepreneur. He spurned the conventional dark suit and tie of the businessman in favor of overalls and a mechanics cap, both of which were usually covered with grease. He preferred the factory floor to the office suite, and made no pretensions to the contrary. Fortunately for the company, Fujisawa Takeo, the man charged with marketing and financial affairs, had more of an executive demeanor. Through a combination of charm and financial genius, Fujisawa was able to convince skeptical officers at the giant Mitsubishi Bank to extend the firm credit necessary for expansion.

In 1958, Honda introduced the Super Cub model to replace the Cub. Like its predecessor, the Super Cub sported a 50cc motor mounted on a sturdy frame. Design improvements made the new model even easier to operate, and within six months Honda was selling a then-record 3,000 Super Cubs a month.[46] They were soon exported to the neighboring countries of Korea, Taiwan, and Southeast Asia where demand was strong for inexpensive and reliable transportation. Given the steady flow of orders and the profits they generated, Honda Soichiro was able to devote some resources to building a racing program. The beloved sport of his youth, Soichiro thrilled at the prospect of designing and manufacturing racing motorcycles, though of course he was too old to race them himself. The program was a success, and by the mid-1960s Honda motorcycles were noteworthy for winning races in Europe and the Americas.

With the completion of the Suzuka factory on the outskirts of Tokyo in 1960, Honda boasted not only the world's largest motorcycle plant, but also the most automated one.[47] The product line grew to include a whole range of cycles aimed at various market niches, and sales boomed at both home and abroad. American Honda Motor Co., established in 1959, marketed the firm's goods in the U.S., and by 1964 had made Honda the best selling motorcycle in the country.[48] Hondas were particularly popular with America's youth, who flocked to buy them because of their price advantage over brands such as American-made Harley Davidsons or imported European motorcycles. In a remarkably short time Honda went from being the new brand in the industry to its trendsetter.

As profits mounted, Honda Motor was able to strike out in new directions. Based on their success in motorcycle racing, the firm decided to branch out into auto racing, undoubtedly at the behest of their founder. After years of research and development work, Honda entered into the rarefied world of Formula One. The most technically advanced form of auto racing, Formula One was dominated by the likes of Ferrari and Lotus. Though Honda never swept the series in the dramatic fashion that it had competitive motorcycling, it nevertheless made a respectable showing in the few years that it raced in Formula One. Honda proved itself a worthy adversary, and in the process learned a great deal about producing competitive cars. In time, those lessons proved invaluable.

Amid the hustle of manufacturing motorcycles and competing in two forms of racing, Honda quietly introduced its first automobile to the public. Known as the S360, it was a high performance sports car aimed at the enthusiast. What it lacked in luxury and refinement was compensated by speed and a racing-inspired suspension. The S360 won wide acclaim, but its sales were slow. The sports car market was extremely limited in Japan, and for those few who desired such a vehicle, the allure of the famous European marques was simply too great. Nevertheless, the S360 enabled Honda to demonstrate that it could build a good car which, if for nothing else, was a boost to morale. It seemed as if the company could succeed at anything it endeavored.

The real test for Honda lay ahead as it planned production of a passenger car. Competition in the 1960s was stiff, with Toyota and Nissan leading the industry. Smaller automakers such as Fuji (maker of the Subaru), Toyo Kogyo (Mazda), and Mitsubishi had a head start on Honda and dominated the market for mini cars. Despite the challenges, Honda pressed ahead with a car of its own, and in March 1967 introduced its N360 model. Small even by Japanese standards, the N360 was powered by an air-cooled two-cylinder engine. It was an instant success. In May, two months after having introduced the car, Honda had captured a 31 percent market share of the mini car class with its N360. Production soared to 20,000 units per month, and in the next year the company added a station wagon and a small van to the 360 line.[49]

The 1960s ended well for Honda. By 1968 it had produced over ten million motorcycles, one million of which had been sold in the U.S.[50] Its Suzuka factory, already the world's largest motorcycle plant, was expanded to accommodate automobile assembly, which increasingly became a top priority. With an eye toward the future, engineers at Honda redoubled their commitment to engine development, an area in which the company had always excelled. Their efforts resulted a four-cylinder motorcycle, the CB 750. Displacing 750cc, it seemed large for a motorcycle power plant, but in reality was quite compact given its four cylinder configuration. In short order it became the standard by which competitors were judged.

Of even greater long-term significance was the work in automobile engines. In 1969 Honda launched research into a fuel efficient motor that emitted few pollutants, which in time came to be known as the CVCC engine. An abbreviation for Compound Vortex Controlled Combustion, the CVCC engine did not require a catalytic converter to pass the then-new U.S. clean air statutes. Honda knew that it had a winner on its hands, although the firm had yet to develop a suitable car in which to use the engine. By the time the CVCC motor was perfected in the early 1970s, Honda's revolutionary technology was poised to pay handsome dividends.

From the vantage point of 1970, the Honda Motor Company had come a long way from the days of motor scooters. It had become the preeminent marque in motorcycles, and was on the verge of taking the auto world by storm. Honda embarked on the new decade by introducing its first car to the U.S., the N600 sedan. Company executives knew that the small car was unlikely to sell in great numbers, but they nevertheless wanted to start establishing a network of auto dealers to handle future products. Fujisawa Takeo, Honda Soichiro's long time partner, saw in America the potential for phenomenal sales growth. With attractive vehicles already on the horizon, Fujisawa wanted to be ready for widespread distribution in the U.S. Throughout

Honda's short history, the firm had had a remarkable sense of timing; Fujisawa's plans for America were to add yet another dimension to this brilliant legacy.

NOTES

1. *Honda in America: Years of Achievement* (Marysville, OH: Honda of America Manufacturing, Inc., 1992), 15.
2. *Ward's 1991 Automotive Yearbook* (Detroit, MI: Ward's Communications, Inc., 1991), 16.
3. *Ward's 1974 Automotive Yearbook* (Detroit, MI: Ward's Communications, Inc., 1974), 47.
4. *Ward's 1991 Automotive Yearbook*, 208.
5. *Ward's 1990 Automotive Yearbook* (Detroit, MI: Ward's Communications, Inc., 1990), 282.
6. Toyoda, Eiji, *Toyota: Fifty Years in Motion* (Tokyo: Kodansha International, 1987), 12–13.
7. Michael A. Cusumano, *The Japanese Automobile Industry: Technology & Management at Nissan & Toyota* (Cambridge, MA: The Council on East Asian Studies, Harvard University, 1991), 58.
8. Toyoda, *Toyota*, 13.
9. Cusumano, *The Japanese Automobile Industry*, 58.
10. Cusumano, *The Japanese Automobile Industry*, 59.
11. Cusumano, *The Japanese Automobile Industry*, 59.
12. Toyoda, *Toyota*, 49.
13. Toyoda, *Toyota*, 64.
14. Toyoda, *Toyota*, 71-72.
15. Sol Sanders, *Honda: The Man and His Machines* (Boston: Little, Brown and Company, 1975), 54.
16. Ienaga Saburo, *The Pcific War, 1931-1945* (New York: Pantheon Books, 1978), 150.
17. Edwin O. Reischauer, *Japan: The Story of a Nation* (New York: McGraw-Hill Publishing Company, 1990), 198.
18. Toyoda, *Toyota*, 103.
19. Cusumano, *The Japanese Automobile Industry*, 74.
20. Cusumano, *The Japanese Automobile Industry*, 19.
21. Kamiya Shotaro, *My Life with Toyota* (Toyota City: Toyota Motor Sales, Ltd., 1976), 61.
22. Cusumano, *The Japanese Automobile Industry*, 120.
23. Cusumano, *The Japanese Automobile Industry*, 98.
24. Kamiya, *My Life with Toyota*, 119.
25. Kamiya, *My Life with Toyota*, 59.

26. Toyoda, *Toyota*, 120–121.

27. Edwin O. Reischauer and Albert M. Craig, *Japan: Tradition & Transformation* (Boston: Houghton Mifflin Company, 1989), 306.

28. Reischauer and Criag, *Japan*, 288.

29. Cusumano, *The Japanese Automobile Industry*, 232.

30. Cusumano, *The Japanese Automobile Industry*, 98.

31. Cusumano, *The Japanese Automobile Industry*, 234.

32. Sanders, *Honda*, 18.

33. Sanders, *Honda*, 26.

34. Reischauer, *Japan: The Story of a Nation*, 144.

35. Sanders, *Honda*, 203.

36. Sanders, *Honda*, 34–35.

37. Sanders, *Honda*, 35.

38. Sanders, *Honda*, 35.

39. Sanders, *Honda*, 46.

40. Sanders, *Honda*, 47.

41. *Honda in America*, 9.

42. Sanders, *Honda*, 50.

43. *Honda in America*, 9.

44. Sanders, *Honda*, 204.

45. *Honda in America*, 9.

46. *Honda in America*, 9.

47. *Honda in America, 9.*

48. *Honda in America, 10.*

49. *Sanders, Honda, 121.*

50. *Sanders, Honda, 205; Honda in America, 10.*

Chapter Two

Leaps and Bounds

After years of steady growth, the Japanese automobile market began to reach a plateau in the 1970s. The market was by no means saturated; many Japanese did not yet own cars, and those that did rarely owned more than one. Nevertheless, the boom years of the previous decade were fading, especially during the 1973/1974 oil crisis that crippled Japan's economy. Automotive executives could no longer rely upon the double-digit growth rates of the previous twenty years.[1] To maintain their pace of expansion, Japanese auto manufacturers had to look abroad for export sales. And as the world's largest and wealthiest marketplace, the United States became the obvious focus of Japanese attention.

The 1970s provided the Japanese with the kind of growth in the United States that they had sought. In the first year of the decade, sales of Japanese cars in the U.S. nearly doubled, from 422,000 cars and trucks in 1970, to over 814,000 units in 1971. All six Japanese automakers exporting to America broke sales records nearly every year, and their nameplates came to dominate the import segment.[2] By 1975, Toyota sold more cars than Volkswagen, the leading import since 1959. At decade's end, annual sales of Japanese vehicles in the U.S. topped the two million mark, an explosion in sales that went beyond all expectations.[3]

As a result of booming American sales, both Honda and Toyota underwent substantive transformations. The transition was especially visible at Honda, where automobile manufacturing had been secondary to its motorcycle business throughout the 1960s. Since rivals Toyota and Nissan enjoyed strong brand recognition and legions of loyal customers in Japan, Honda's future as a major automobile manufacturer hinged on exports. Statistics from 1980 illustrate Honda's position. In that year, Honda produced over 845,000 passenger cars in Japan and exported 77 per cent of the total, a much larger percentage than any other Japanese auto firm.[4]

The company's foray into the American market came in 1970 with the introduction of its N600 model. The car was a small sedan designed for the Japanese market, and Honda had to scramble to sell nearly 4000 of the vehicles in the United States during its introductory year. Sales of the N600 in the U.S. more than doubled in each of the next two model years, providing Honda with a welcome sales growth, if a still insignificant market share. Perhaps more importantly, however, it marked the entry into what would become Honda's most critical market. Nobody at the time could have predicted that in less than twenty years the best selling car in America would be a Honda.

At Toyota, the early 1970s brought gains in vastly greater numbers. Between 1970 and 1973, Toyota's annual sales in America grew from approximately 200,000 to over 300,000 cars, closing the gap with import leader Volkswagen.[5] Toyota's larger volume reflected its established dealer network in America, as well as its varied product line that consisted of six automobiles, pickup trucks, and all-terrain vehicles. During the 1970s Toyota became a major automotive presence in the United States. While it had long enjoyed the distinction of being Japan's largest auto manufacturer, the 1970s ushered in its role as an international giant. The transition it experienced was subtler than Honda's, but by becoming the third largest auto manufacturer in the world behind General Motors and Ford, its horizons had been greatly expanded. Though its traditional rivalry with other Japanese car companies still existed, Toyota set its sights higher than ever before.

Nevertheless, as the decade opened, it was not entirely clear that either Honda or Toyota were destined to have such spectacular years ahead. The international economy faced many challenges in the early 1970s, among them an uncertain currency system and a global energy crisis. Although in retrospect these factors proved pivotal to their successes as both importers and later as manufacturers in the United States, at the time they caused grave concerns for Honda and Toyota executives.

THE BIG TESTS: MONEY AND OIL

The first challenge of the new decade was posed by a fundamental change in the international currency system. Since the end of World War II, the world's currency markets had functioned under the terms of the Bretton Woods agreement. Exchange rates between currencies were more or less fixed, providing stability to the exchange process. For businesses such as Honda and Toyota that relied heavily upon exports, a generally fixed exchange rate was very convenient. When the automakers set out to price their goods in American dollars, they knew exactly how many Japanese yen they would receive in return. It was a predictable system that not only benefited the two automakers, but all firms doing business in the international arena. In 1971, however, the United States abandoned its commitment to the Bretton Woods currency structure, effectively killing the system. In the absence of Bretton Woods, Honda and Toyota were in an unfamiliar, and potentially dangerous, situation.

BRETTON-WOODS

During the summer of 1944, the United States hosted a summit at the Bretton Woods resort in the White Mountains of New Hampshire. The purpose of the meeting was to culminate negotiations that had taken place between the world's preeminent economists over the course of several years. The two principal architects of the Bretton Woods agreement were British economist John Maynard Keynes and his American counterpart, Harry Dexter White. The two had been meeting intermittently since 1942 to arrive at new mechanisms that would foster global trade and economic stability. Though constructive, their encounters were frequently marked by heated arguments over complicated macroeconomic issues. The two men usually sat next to one another at the head of a long table, with their British and American underlings on either side. According to participants, Keynes would often open the meetings by saying, "Well, Harry, what shall it be today—passivity, exchange stability, or the role of gold?"[6] Eventually all of these topics, in addition to a whole host of others, received their scrutiny.

Although the world was consumed by war when Keynes and White initiated their discussions, the British and American governments were looking ahead to what lay in the future. Both nations implicitly believed that they would emerge the victors, an assumption that was far from certain in 1942, but appeared more likely by the time of the signing of the Bretton Woods agreement in 1944. The purpose of Bretton Woods was to impose an economic order on a world that would be desperately in need of stability. To achieve their goals, the British and American governments recognized that the new economic order would have to be stable yet flexible for future developments. The economic crises that gripped the inter-war world were sure to be revisited if a new system were not in place.

As the final agreement was reached, both short- and long-term goals were addressed. For the immediate future, the United States and Great Britain anticipated the need to rebuild the war-shattered economies of Europe. To that end, institutions such as the International Monetary Fund and the World Bank were established to provide loans and services to recovering governments. Given its vast capital and productive resources, the U.S. took the lead in financing the IMF and the World Bank in order to redistribute a portion of its wealth. After all, by the 1950s the United States manufactured roughly half of all goods made in the world, and thus a balanced world economy would help to ensure continued American prosperity. Both institutions proved successful and in time, contrary to their original mandate, expanded their role to provide assistance to developing nations elsewhere in the world.

The long range focus of the Bretton Woods agreement centered on currency exchange. Lasting peace and prosperity necessitated a vibrant international economy, and the convertibility of currencies figured prominently in that goal. Currencies needed to be easily exchanged so that international free market trade could be conducted. To bring order and consistency to the system, exchange rates were pegged between the U.S. dollar and most other world other currencies. For example, the U.S. dollar/British pound exchange was set at a par value of $2.80 U.S./£1 U.K., while the Japanese yen was fixed at $1 U.S./¥360 when the yen became convertible in 1949.[7] The exchange rates were to be linked to respective nations' gold supplies and the balance of payments between trading partners.

Throughout the 1950s and 1960s these rates remained largely unaltered, making it easy and convenient for international financiers and governments to make plans and projections. Since exchange rates were set artificially low between U.S. dollars and their foreign counterparts, the economies of the free world were able to grow in part because of favorable export conditions. The U.S. commitment to open markets and generous exchange rates was another component in the attempt to reinvigorate the war-torn economies of Europe and Japan, but in time it caused America problems of its own.

Though Keynes and White envisioned a system whereby exchange rates would be periodically adjusted, as it turned out exchange rates essentially became fixed during the 1950s and'60s. Countries were reluctant to revalue their currencies, and they did so only after other measures had been tried and had failed. Debtor nations were loathe to devalue their currencies for fear of domestic political ramifications. Surplus countries, by contrast, saw no benefit in appreciating their currencies, and they did so only by relatively small amounts, after great delays, when subjected to strong international pressures.[8]

As a result, the U.S. found itself with a balance of payments problem beginning in the early 1960s. In short, American dollars were leaving the United States faster than they were being replaced with foreign currencies. What had once been a useful system for spreading American capital abroad became a threat to the American economy itself. As the economies of Europe and Japan recovered and expanded, the rates set in the 1940s no longer reflected economic reality. Their currencies were undervalued, and if the situation was not addressed, the U.S. Treasury faced a possible solvency crisis.

In August of 1971, therefore, the Nixon administration decided to take bold steps to address the pending emergency. In its first move, the administration declared that U.S. dollars could no longer be exchanged for gold. The complete abandonment of the gold standard, which had been used in one form or another throughout the history of the Republic, sent shock waves through the international community. Could the U.S. be relied upon to honor its obligations, or would post-War stability as it had been known collapse entirely? Moreover, if the dollar could no longer be converted into gold, what was its worth in relation to the world's other currencies? By the end of that year, the Nixon administration supplied the answers.

On 20 December 1971, a meeting of economic ministers at Washington's Smithsonian Institute put the world on notice that the Bretton Woods system was all but dead. Although agencies such as the International Monetary Fund were to remain in existence, the fixed exchange rates of the past thirty years were to be abandoned. By the terms set in the Smithsonian Agreement of 1971, the economic ministers of the free world declared that their currencies would gradually be set free to "float." The fixed rates would be repealed so that the value of international currencies would better reflect the state of their respective countries' economies. For the newly emerged industrial economies of Germany and Japan, the new world order of currencies was particularly disturbing. The artificially low exchange rates that had helped their firms compete and grow were coming to an end. Beginning in 1972, market forces would determine the value of the mark and the yen, both of which were sure to appreciate.

At first, international currency exchange rates eased toward the free "floating" market by adjusting the rates on a regular basis. In the case of Japan, the yen immediately rose in value from the former rate of $1 U.S./¥360. In 1972, the currencies exchanged at $1/¥303, and by decade's end the yen had steadily climbed to a value of approximately $1/¥190.[9] Although the new system meant that currencies were more accurately valued, it also ushered in an era of uncertainty. Of immediate concern to Japanese businesses was pricing goods for export. Since free-floating currencies could change in value without warning, it became difficult to predict future values.

For executives at Honda and Toyota, the ramifications of the floating currency market were troubling. Whereas they had formerly been able to price their vehicles based upon a fixed value for the yen, after 1971 neither manufacturer could count upon a stable exchange rate. Since changes in the yen's value directly affected the firms' profit margins, as well as their competitive position relative to American and European automakers, an increasingly valuable yen posed problems beyond the control of management. Through the 1970s and 1980s, both Honda and Toyota hiked vehicle prices beyond the rate of inflation due to the steadily increasing value of the yen. Though in the early 1970s these price increases were not large enough to impede the growth in their respective market positions, executives at both Honda and Toyota recognized the potential for danger in the future.

OIL

If alterations in the international currency system introduced an element of uncertainty for the two automakers, other events of the early 1970s caused additional disquiet. Perhaps the most unsettling development was the oil embargo of 1973–1974. When the flow of oil from the Mideast was cut off from the United States due to its support of Israel in the Arab-Israeli conflict, oil prices skyrocketed. Though the deleterious impact of this price increase was felt in all industrialized countries, few were affected as drastically as Japan. Unlike the United States, Japan imported virtually all of its oil from abroad. Although Japan was still able to buy oil from the Mideast, restricted output resulted in significantly higher prices. Between October and December 1973, Japan saw the price of crude oil jump from $3.00 to as much as $17.34 per barrel.[10]

With access to foreign oil severely curtailed, the Japanese economy slumped into deep recession. Between 1950 and 1970, automobile sales had increased by at least 20 percent annually, despite periodic recessions in the broader economy.[11] The oil shock interrupted this steady growth, however, and in 1974 automobile sales plummeted in Japan by 22 percent.[12] With an uncertain outcome to the oil crisis, Japanese consumers curtailed discretionary spending, leaving the automotive industry to feel the pinch. In light of poor economic conditions, Toyota cut production in 1974 by approximately 150,000 units from year-earlier levels. Although Honda actually increased production by 59,000 cars in the same period, virtually all of its additional automobiles were exported.[13]

In the U.S., auto sales were also severely affected by the oil crisis. Crude oil prices more than doubled between 1973 and 1974, rising from $4.17 to $9.07 per barrel.[14] The impact of higher crude prices was felt at the gasoline pump, where regular gasoline jumped on average from $0.38 to $0.53 per gallon.[15] The higher energy costs triggered not only inflation, but recession as well. Sales of imported cars slipped by 19.6 percent in 1974 from previous annual sales, closely mirroring the 24 percent decline in domestic automobile sales.[16] Although Honda was able to eke out a slight increase in 1974 American sales volume to 41,719 cars compared to year earlier sales of 38,957 units, Toyota's U.S. sales declined by 8.2 percent to 269,376 cars and light trucks in the same period.[17]

Despite the setbacks experienced both at home and abroad, the oil crisis did have a silver lining for Honda and Toyota. When OPEC oil began to flow again in March 1974, American consumers remained wary. The country was slow to recover from recession, and inflation pressures lingered. Gasoline prices also remained relatively high, and motorists remembered all too well the long lines at filling stations during the winter of 1974. The combined result of these memories and the weak economy meant that consumers wanted more affordable and fuel efficient cars to drive. Both Honda and Toyota were ready and able to give Americans what they wanted.

Honda replaced the modest N600 sedan in the U.S. with its Civic model in 1974. The new model was produced in two configurations, as either a two-door coupe or a hatchback, both of which received a warm reception. Equipped with the company's new Compound Vortex Controlled Combustion engine (CVCC), the Civic was the first automobile to comply with the country's strict 1975 emissions laws without the aid of a catalytic converter. The car was an instant success. *Road Test Magazine* named the Honda Civic import car of the year in 1974, but more importantly, consumers flocked to dealer showrooms.[18]

HONDA ENTERS THE BIG LEAGUES

By the middle of the 1970s, Honda found itself in an unfamiliar situation. Long accustomed to being seen first as a motorcycle manufacturer, and only secondarily as an automaker, the company was growing into a new identity. By 1977 Honda was producing over 576,000 automobiles annually.[19] With 1977 U.S. sales topping 223,000 cars, or nearly 40 percent of its total output, Honda relied heavily upon the American market.[20] People who would not think about buying a motorcycle were comfortable buying the firm's automobiles. Consumers continued to favor its fuel-efficient cars and, with the introduction of its mid-sized Accord sedan in 1976, the appeal of Honda's products broadened.

Concern for the company's prosperity lingered, however, as upward pressure on the yen's value continued. Honda was forced to raise prices several times each model year in the late 1970s in order to keep pace with the stronger yen, but still the company had to absorb costs associated with the Japanese currency. In 1978, for example, Honda posted a 49 percent decline in profits, despite a 13 percent sales increase.[21] Company officials attributed the decline to the yen's steep rise against other currencies, particularly the U.S. dollar, which cut into profit margins.[22]

The end of the decade presented Honda with mixed blessings. The 1978 oil crisis, which particularly affected gasoline prices, led to a windfall in Honda's auto sales in the U.S. When the price of a gallon of regular unleaded gasoline leapt by 34.7 percent between 1978 and 1979, Honda sales increased by 28.5 percent to 353,291 units in the same period.[23] Even with an appreciating yen eroding profits, Honda was doing well. With the addition of the sporty Prelude coupe in 1979, Honda offered American consumers three distinct automobiles. The Civic continued in its role as an entry-level economy car, and the mid-sized Accord remained so popular that dealers regularly reported shortages.[24] Although Honda thus found favor among the motoring public, it and the other Japanese importers were also coming under increasing criticism. American auto manufacturers and their employees began calling for restrictions on imported vehicles, and their voices were heard on Capital Hill.

Worries about U.S. reaction regarding Japanese imports were not entirely new to Honda. Long before Japanese cars were seen as a significant threat to the U.S. auto industry, Honda had foreseen the day when it might come under fire. Just as Toyota Motor Sales president Kamiya Shotaro had worried about an American backlash to Japanese imports in the late 1950s, Honda saw in its current success a potential for future tariffs and barriers. Toyota's solution in the 1950s had been to establish a sales office in California before it was prevented from doing so. Honda's defense against possible trade barriers in the 1970s, however, was much bolder.

THE BEGINNINGS OF MANUFACTURING IN AMERICA

As early as 1974, Honda began searching for an appropriate site upon which to build a factory in the United States.[25] By shifting some of its production to the U.S., Honda hoped to appease its critics. Moreover, increasing demand for its vehicles necessitated greater production capacity, and Honda thought it worthy to consider the United States as a location for a new plant. Deciding to do what it knew best, Honda first conceived of the plant as a motorcycle factory. Although the firm had left open the possibility that one day the plant might produce cars, its publicly stated goal remained focused on motorcycle production. Motorcycles were simple to build, and capitalization for plant and equipment was far below that which would be required for an auto plant. As both its cars and motorcycles met with ever-increasing sales levels, the desire to push ahead with an American facility came to fruition.

In 1977, Honda announced that its search for an American manufacturing site had been completed. After reviewing several possible locations, Honda chose the rural community of Marysville, Ohio, 40 miles northwest of Columbus as the site of the new motorcycle plant.[26] The proposed 260,000 square foot plant was to be built at an initial cost of $35 million, but by the time the plant was completed in 1979, overall capitalization in plant and equipment neared $90 million.[27] According to James A. Duerk, Ohio's director of Economic and Community Development at the time the plant was built, Ohio provided Honda with $2.5 million in aid, as well as tax abatements on the plant's land, and agreed to make highway improvements in the area as incentives to locate in Marysville.[28] The plant was to produce motorcycles particularly popular with American consumers, such as the large touring cycles with engines displacing over 1000cc. Those particular models were very profitable for Honda, and since they were more popular in the United States than elsewhere, Honda thought that building them in America made sense. Moreover, with the competitive advantage of a weak yen fading quickly, exporting motorcycles from Japan did not provide the benefits that it once had. So long as quality standards were maintained, Honda believed that it could manufacture the products in the U.S. at a profit, while saving on the expenses of transporting them from Japan.

Once the Marysville motorcycle plant was operational in 1979, Honda executives stood back to see how it performed. If the plant proved to be a success, they promised that they would consider building cars in the U.S. But first the plant and its workers had to prove their worth. Was it possible, with American workers, to build motorcycles comparable to those being turned out by Honda's giant Suzuka facility in Japan? In a 1981 report, Japan's Nikko Research cast doubts on Honda's experiment when it concluded,

> In general, the quality of American (blue collar) workers is lower than that of Japanese workers in terms of education, ability, turnover and morale, and this is the biggest obstacle to the transfer of technology from Japan.[29]

The company also had its detractors among its loyal customers. With mounting bad publicity regarding the quality of American-made goods, consumers doubted that Americans could build as good a product as Japanese workers. And even if they could, would people actually be willing to risk their money in order to find out? This question was particularly vexing for Honda.

Despite repeated concerns voiced by dealers, Honda's Marysville plant rose to the challenge of producing world-class products. At first production was slow; managers wanted to ensure that only quality products rolled off the line, even if it took an entire day to build only a few good cycles. The initial goal was to make the motorcycles properly; in time, the production line could be brought up to speed. As events would have it, production goals were met faster than originally thought. The first motorcycle came off the plant's assembly line on 10 September 1979, and soon thereafter production reached the company's goal of 235 units per day.[30] And as customer feedback began to show, the products were as good as those fabricated in Japan. Speaking in early 1980, a Honda official admitted that,

> We had been most worried about labor quality, but it turned out okay through our local production of motorcycles. We have produced about 3,000 motorcycles since September 1979 and, in terms of quality, there aren't any problems.[31]

With success at hand, the green light was given to auto production.

THE TOYOTA PERSPECTIVE: STAYING THE COURSE

The 1970s had also been good years for Toyota. Although the company did not expand on a percentage basis as quickly as Honda, sales nevertheless grew at a steady rate. From Toyota's perspective, it was not in direct competition with Honda in the United States for most of the decade. At a time when Honda was selling 40,000 cars per year in the mid-1970s, Toyota was selling a quarter of a million units annually. Just like Honda, high gasoline prices and a weak economy made the company's efficient and inexpensive products quite attractive. Unlike Honda, though, Toyota had several vehicles to satisfy the needs of the American motoring public.

By 1975, Toyota had overtaken archrival Volkswagen as the leading vehicle importer into the U.S. With a steadily growing share of the automobile market, Toyota was beginning to become a formidable competitor to American domestic producers. With a reputation for building the highest quality automobiles in the world, Toyota had little difficulty convincing consumers that it had a good product.[32] Its early efforts at selling cars in the U.S. paid handsome dividends. Toyota knew the American marketplace and advertising techniques, and even more importantly, had a well-established network of dealers.

Not wanting to meddle with a successful formula, Toyota expressed little interest during the 1970s in building automobiles in the United States. Despite pressure from both the Japanese and American governments to locate factories in the U.S. as a means of reducing trade friction, Toyota remained leery of any such venture. As company president Toyoda Eiji insisted in a 1980 interview, "The economic impact [of building a plant in the United

States] has more importance than the political aspect."[33] Given that its sprawling industrial complex at Toyota City featured the most efficient automobile plants in the world, it seemed unlikely that a factory in America could ever be as productive or profitable.[34]

During the course of its growth and expansion, Toyota developed unique relationships in Japan with both its workers and its suppliers that would be difficult to replicate elsewhere. One feature that was central to Toyota's manufacturing formula was the *kanban*, or "just-in-time," delivery system for component parts. First conceptualized by Toyoda Kiichiro before the Second World War, the *kanban* system came into full practice by Toyota during the 1950s and 1960s under the direction of Ono Taiichi. The word *kanban* refers to a card upon which would be printed data regarding parts information. The data would specify the type and quantity of a given part or component needed by an assembly line worker. As an assembler exhausted his supply of a given part, he plucked out the *kanban* card and sent it down the line where it would be gathered by delivery men working for the supplier. The data would be relayed to the supplier's factory where a new batch of the part in question would be sent over to the Toyota plant just as the assembly line worker needed it.

The *kanban* system was a model of efficiency. By having parts delivered when a worker required them, Toyota eliminated the need for inventory storage. Compare, for example, the inventory practices of General Motors to those of Toyota. Whereas a GM factory stored an average of two weeks' worth of parts, Toyota typically had a two-hour inventory of parts.[35] By keeping inventories at lean levels, Toyota eliminated the need for storage space and the associated costs of overhead. Although it took Toyota several decades to perfect just-in-time manufacturing, the effort yielded favorable results.

An obvious key to just-in-time delivery of parts and components was the close proximity of Toyota suppliers. If parts were to arrive as they were needed, the suppliers had a minimal lead time in which they could ship their goods. To make a foreign factory operate as smoothly as the ones at Toyota City, therefore, Toyota not only had to build its own plant, but needed its suppliers to build near its site as well. Herein lay a problem of locating a factory in the U.S. Kanban simply could not be replicated if parts had to be shipped from Japan, a process that would take weeks, not hours. Without the ability of implementing a *kanban* type system in America, Toyota rightly feared that it would lose its competitive edge.

A less obvious, though no less important, feature of the *kanban* system was the links that Toyota had with its suppliers. In the United States, parts suppliers were either wholly owned subsidiaries of automobile manufacturers, such as General Motors' AC Delco division, or were independent firms doing business with perhaps several different auto manufacturers at the same time. Toyota, on the other hand, developed much closer and exclusive links with their Japanese suppliers. Known as the *keiretsu* system, Toyota and its major suppliers were tightly linked to one another in terms of both finance and manufacturing. Though theoretically independent of one another, Toyota and its suppliers formed an umbrella group that shared many responsibilities of design, manufacturing, and in some cases, personnel. Their relationship was thus somewhere inbetween the traditional American models. Toyota did not produce its own parts, nor did it conduct business with firms that were wholly independent.

Toyota's parts suppliers were divided into two broad categories, or tiers. The first-tier suppliers had the closest ties to Toyota itself and were responsible for delivering entire component structures. Nippondenso, for example, was Toyota's supplier of electrical components, and as such was considered a first-tier supplier. It would be responsible for manufacturing such devices as alternators, heating and air conditioning equipment, and fuel injectors.[36] These components would reach the Toyota plants fully assembled and ready to be installed in cars on the production line. Second-tier suppliers, on the other hand, were those firms that provided parts to first-tier suppliers in manufacturing their components. Though they did not deal with Toyota directly, second-tier suppliers were fundamental to Toyota's quality control since their parts formed the base upon which all components relied.

By buying most components fully assembled, Toyota saved the investment in plant and equipment that was necessary for manufacturing those items. Moreover, Toyota did not have to devote resources in personnel, especially engineers and managers, that were needed to develop components; that responsibility remained with the supplier itself. Nevertheless, Toyota did have an interest in its suppliers' well-being. On the most basic level, Toyota's commitment to its suppliers owed to equity positions that the auto firm had in them. Typically, Toyota owned at least some stock in its suppliers, and often made capital investments in their buildings or machinery as well. In turn, the first-tier suppliers often held an equity stake in the second-tier companies. The interlocking ownership of these firms meant that their destinies were tied to one another. At each step in the manufacturing process, all concerns were committed to seeing that Toyota products were successful, for if they were not, all would suffer.

The links between Toyota and its suppliers went beyond stock ownership. As the automaker planned new vehicles, engineers from the various firms would work together in product development. By so doing, each firm could contribute its individual expertise and experience for the collective benefit. Since every participant could bring to bear its specialty, Toyota was not responsible for having to do everything in bringing a new product to market.

This arrangement enabled Toyota to concentrate on perfecting automobile assembly, while not being distracted by research and development at more basic levels. Supply firms, on the other hand, could undertake research responsibilities secure in the knowledge that their relationship with Toyota was for the long term.

Decentralized management was a key feature of the *keiretsu* arrangement. The members in the Toyota keiretsu were responsible for their own affairs, yet they coordinated their efforts to a degree unknown in American automotive circles. If there was a drawback to keiretsu, it was that the system was difficult to export. Since Toyota relied upon its suppliers for a large degree of both design and manufacturing work, it was difficult for the company to envision finding new suppliers abroad. As for having the entire keiretsu relocate to a foreign locale, the sheer cost and complexity of doing so appeared formidable. Having spent so much time, energy, and money to develop their keiretsu, Toyota was loathe to abandon it in order to satisfy pressure from within the United States.

In addition to *kanban* and *keiretsu*, Toyota credited its efficiency to its labor system that, like its other operating procedures, would be difficult to replicate in the U.S. In his book *Japan in the Passing Lane: An Insider's Account of Life in a Japanese Auto Factory*, Kamata Satoshi related his experience as a temporary seasonal worker in Toyota's main factory in Toyota City in the early 1970s.[37] Aside from workers employed by food concerns such as canneries, seasonal work is rarely associated with industrial employment in the United States. As Kamata explained, however, seasonal employment was frequently used in Japan when business warranted it. Since Toyota extended lifetime employment to its permanent work force, it maintained very lean personnel rosters. By so doing, Toyota could avoid ever having to layoff its regular workers, and when production needed to expand, it took on only temporary employees. When the business cycle contracted, it merely needed to adjust its number of seasonal workers, leaving the regular employees secure with their jobs. It was an innovative system that contrasted starkly with the bloated payrolls plaguing U.S. auto firms.

What was also remarkable about life at Toyota in the 1970s, however, was the pace of work. Kamata recounts grim working conditions under which workers toiled for twelve hours, six days a week. Productivity gains owed to steady increases in the line speed. According to Kamata,

When I left Toyota in February 1973, assembly time at the Main Plant for transmissions was one minute and fourteen seconds. This had been shortened by six seconds in the six months since I had begun, while production had been increased by 100 to 415 units. Now, seven years later, the assembly time is forty-five seconds and the production is 690 units. This increase was achieved solely through accelerating the work pace. Knockdown part packing at the Takaoka plant needed sixty minutes for a Set (which included 20 cars) three years ago. Today it takes twelve minutes, and still the manpower has been reduced from 50 to 40. Before, workers stood in front of conveyors; now they rush around from one part to another, pushing mobile work desks with wheels.[38]

In addition to maintaining a brisk work pace on the factory floor, Toyota also exercised control over many of its employees outside of the plant. Unmarried personnel, including both permanent and temporary workers, were housed at company dormitories. Like their counterparts on American universities, Toyota dormitories offered rather small and sparse living quarters. All of the day's meals were eaten in company cafeterias, which were once again notable for their institutional efficiency. As described by essayist Kusayanagi Daizo, life at Toyota sounded benign.

> The rice is cooked instantly in a vacuum cooker. After eating this rice, the-workers go to work in the plant. And when they have finished work, they go back to their dormitories, which are well equipped with modern facilities and have cost the company $200 million. . . . Toyota Motor Company is trying to create human beings, too. I was fascinated and much impressed by this "Great Country Town" after the complete tour of the company.[39]

From Kamata's perspective as an employee, however, a very different picture emerged.

> The rice here is bad for the digestion because it's cooked too fast. The workers eat the rice in a hurry, go to the plant in a hurry, and work in a hurry in order to keep up with the "famous" assembly line. After they are finally released, they have no choice other than to go back to the dormitories, which have facilities that are advertised by the Public Relations Department to have cost the company $200 million. There, former Self-Defense Forces men now working for Toyota keep a close eye on everyone's private lives.[40]

Regardless of which depiction of Toyota is more accurate, it was clear that the company's employment practices differed from those of its American counterparts. Though supervised dormitories may have fit into the general scheme that the Lowell, Massachusetts manufacturing plants advocated for their employees in the early nineteenth century, the American working landscape no longer found such notions acceptable. And although Toyota's labor force had been unionized since the late 1940s, the union was far more conciliatory than the United Automobile Workers union in the United States. Kamata recounted with disappointment that the union rarely, if ever, protested the regular increases in production quotas. Upon reading the Asahi Shimbum (newspaper) one day, Kamata and his fellow assembly line workers were surprised to learn that auto plants in the U.S. operated under a different set of expectations from its personnel.

> The Lordstown (Ohio) General Motors plant has been the site of a number of acts of sabotage in the last few months. Angered by the inhumane working conditions, workers have simply walked out of their workshops, leaving the moving line behind. Engine parts arrived unassembled at the end of the line. Windows of finished cars were broken, seats were slashed with knives, dashboards were smashed with hammers. Every time one of these "accidents" happened, the line was stopped and the defective cars were sent to the repair section. Operation efficiency dropped by half.

> The workers were rebelling. But the most amazing part of the article is that the correspondent reported that he saw workers smoking and chatting while they worked on the line. Those with free time gathered at a table in the corner and played cards. Dissatisfaction among workers grew very strong when the production schedule was raised from 60 to 100 cars per hour, and the workers reacted with sabotage. How could they smoke and play cards when the speed of the line was increased to raise productivity? The article says that the time allowed for one operation was reduced to thirty-six seconds, but that only ten seconds were actually needed. GM workers are well treated as compared with Toyota workers. It's hard to believe.[41]

If Kamata and his fellow workers were surprised by what the article revealed, it undoubtedly left an impression upon Toyota managers as well.

Articles such as the one that appeared in the Asahi Shimbum showed an American labor force far different from Japan's. While Toyota's employees were resigned to increases in the line speed, General Motors' workers rebelled when they perceived ill treatment at the hands of management. Given the choice between obedient workers and those who aired grievances by the means of sabotage, Toyota understandably preferred the former. Combined with the anticipated difficulties of implementing their parts sourcing arrangements in the United States, Toyota saw little reason to commit to auto production in America.

NOTHING VENTURED, NOTHING GAINED

That Honda and Toyota viewed manufacturing in the United States differently was a reflection of the companies themselves. To an extent, both had similar experiences during the 1970s in America. Both firms had seen their sales soar and, with the energy markets mired in crisis once again in 1978, the immediate future promised to yield strong results as well. And yet, just as it had at the beginning of the decade, a gulf continued to separate Honda and Toyota. Honda was still the newcomer, the risk taker, the brand name that not everyone associated with automobiles. By experimenting with motorcycle production in America, Honda was treading where no Japanese vehicle manufacturer had ventured before. It was the company that could least afford the $90 million investment in Marysville, but it also had the most to gain from a factory in the U.S.

Motorcycle production afforded Honda a unique opportunity to test the American waters. If the quality of the product was inferior to models made in Japan, at least Honda did not have to invest in an entire auto plant to discover the discrepancy. If events warranted, Honda could have closed the Marysville motorcycle plant, absorbed the losses to the best of its ability, and continued to export quality cars and motorcycles from Japan. Since Honda targeted different consumers for motorcycles and automobiles, damage to one's reputation would not necessarily affect sales of the other. Moreover, Honda's initial commitment had only been to produce a few motorcycle models, not its entire product line. It was an ideal opportunity that Toyota did not have.

Scenarios of failure aside, Honda had a greater incentive to move toward auto production in America than did Toyota at the time. Since the U.S. was Honda's largest single market, it could least afford sanctions against imported automobiles that were already being threatened in the late 1970s. Of more immediate concern, however, was its exposure to an increasingly valuable yen. It was more vulnerable to the yen's appreciation than Toyota. Honda could not shift currency costs on to other products or other markets as easily as could Toyota. The degree to which it could become an American manufacturer, of either motorcycles or automobiles, had a direct impact on its ability to be insulated from currency fluctuations. And although there was no guarantee that the yen would continue its ascent, indications to the contrary were few and far between.

Lastly, Honda did not have the deep-rooted relationship with its suppliers that Toyota did. As far as motorcycles were concerned, Honda always had produced the majority of its own parts. If the Marysville venture proved to be viable, it could increasingly manufacture parts in the U.S. as easily as in Japan. As for automobile parts, Honda had not established its own keiretsu. Though it was unusual in the Japanese setting, Honda either manufactured what it needed or purchased its parts and components from wholly independent firms. That it did so was not a matter of preference so much as a matter of necessity. Since it had only been in the auto business for a short period, it had neither the time nor the resources to enter into equity arrangements with supplier firms. Quite simply, it required less capital to buy parts from outside vendors. Although this hampered Honda's efficiency in Japan when compared to Toyota, it also meant that Honda had greater freedom to find alternative parts sources in the U.S.

In 1980, Honda and Toyota took their positions. A couple of months after Honda announced it would be expanding its Marysville plant to accommodate automobile production, Toyota's chairman was digging in his heels and resisting pressure to invest substantially in the U.S.[42] Though it was a stand from which Toyota would later retreat, Honda had once again established its reputation as a risk taker. And as a result of its plunge into America, a new phrase entered into the automotive lexicon: the Japanese transplant manufacturer.

NOTES

1. *World Motor Vehicle Data, 1981 Edition* (Detroit: Motor Vehicle Manufacturers Association of the United States, 1981), 88.

2. The six Japanese automobile manufacturers importing cars to the United States during the 1970s were Toyota, Nissan (which were marketed at the time under the Datsun brand name,) Honda, Subaru, Mazda, and Mitsubishi. Mitsubishi vehicles were sold under the Chrysler brand name until 1982, at which time Mitsubishi established an independent distribution arm.

3. Michael J. Smitka, *Competitive Ties: Subcontracting in the Japanese Automotive Industry* (New York: Columbia University Press, 1991), 79.

4. *World Motor Vehicle Data, 1981 Edition*, 83.

5. *Ward's 1974 Automotive Yearbook* (Detroit: Ward's Communications, Inc., 1974), 34.

6. David Rees, *Harry Dexter White: A Study in Paradox* (New York: Coward, McCann & Geoghegan, 1973), 230.

7. *International Financial Statistics* (Washington: The International Monetary Fund, 1961), 264; and, *International Financial Statistics*, 1953, 192.

8. Anne O. Krueger, *Exchange Rate Determination* (Cambridge: Cambridge University Press, 1983), 4.

9. *International Financial Statistics* (Washington: International Monetary Fund, 1979), 210–211.

10. "More Countries Set to Cash in on Oil Shortage, " *The Wall Street Journal* December 17, 1973, 2.

11. Smitka, *Competitive Ties*, 66.

12. *World Automotive Data, 1981 Edition*, 88.

13. *World Automotive Data, 1977 Edition* (Detroit: Motor Vehicle Manufacturers Association, 1977), 35.

14. *1982 Annual Energy Review* (Washington: Energy Information Administration, 1983), 91.

15. *1987 Annual Energy Review* (Washington: Energy Information Administration, 1988), 145.

16. *Ward's 1975 Automotive Yearbook* (Detroit: Ward's Communications, Inc., 1975), 23, 11.

17. *Ward's 1975 Automotive Yearbook*, 34.

18. *Honda in America: Years of Achievement* (Marysville, OH: American Honda Motor Company, Inc., 1992), 10.

19. *World Automotive Data, 1981 Edition*, 71.

20. *Ward's 1979 Automotive Yearbook* (Detroit: Ward's Communications, Inc., 1979), 52.

21. *World Automotive Data, 1981 Edition*, 71.

22. "Honda Motor Posts 49% Decline in Net for the Feb. 28 Year," *The Wall Street Journal*, May 29, 1979, 6.

23. *1987 Annual Energy Review*, 145; *Ward's 1985 Automotive Yearbook* (Detroit: Ward's Communications, Inc., 1985), 168.

24. *Ward's 1979 Automotive Yearbook*, 31.

25. *Honda in America*, 10.

26. The Honda motorcycle plant is technically located in Allen Township, Ohio, but is usually said to be in Marysville, Ohio, the county seat of Union County. Honda literature and public relations officials usually refer to the site as the Marysville factory, as do journalists and most scholars. The reason for this inaccuracy is unclear, but it may have to do with Allen Township's small size. It is little more than a cross-roads, and has no public buildings, churches, or small businesses, nor does it provide any municipal services. All available services in Allen Township, including road and sewer maintenance, schools, and emergency are provided either by Union County or the town of Marysville. In keeping with convention, therefore, the Honda motorcycle plant and the adjacent auto plant in Allen Township will hereafter be referred to as the Marysville plant in this and subsequent chapters, unless otherwise noted.

27. *Marysville Motorcycle Plant* (Marysville, OH: Honda of America Manufacturing, Inc., 1991), 1.

28. Mike Tharp and Robert Simison, "Honda's Move to Build $200 million Plant in Ohio Could Spur Other Japanese Firms," *The Wall Street Journal*, January 14, 1980, 2.

29. Masayoshi Kanabayashi, "Honda's Accord: How a Japanese Firm Is Faring on its Dealings with Workers in the U.S.," *The Wall Street Journal*, October 02, 1981, 1.

30. Andi Gates, "Trees Grown in Marysville Symbol of Honda's Success," *The Columbus Dispatch*, December 20, 1980, 1G.

31. Mike Tharp and Robert Simison, "Honda's Move to Build $200 million Plant in Ohio Could Spur Other Japanese Firms," *The Wall Street Journal*, January 14, 1980, 2.

32. James P. Womack, Daniel T. Jones, and Daniel Roos, *The Machine that Changed the World* (New York: Charles Scribner's and Sons, 1990), 80.

33. Mile Tharp, "Toyota and Nissan Say They Will Resist Pressures to Build Auto Plants in the U.S.," *The Wall Street Journal*, April 10, 1980, A6.

34. James P. Womack et al., *The Machine that Changed the World*, 49.

35. James P. Womack et al., *The Machine that Changed the World*, 81.

36. Michael A. Cusumano, *The Japanese Automobile Industry* (Cambridge, MA: The Harvard University Press, 1991), 251.

37. Kamata Satoshi, *Japan in the Passing Lane: An Insiders Account of Life in a Japanese Auto Factory* (New York: Pantheon Books, 1982).

38. Kamata, *Japan in the Passing Lane*, 206.

39. Kusayanagi Daizo, *The Enterprise as Kingdom* (Tokyo: Bungei-Shunju Co., 1969), 174.

40. Kamata, *Japan in the Passing Lane*, 32.

41. Kamata, *Japan in the Passing Lane*, 63–64.

42. Mike Tharp and Robert Simison, "Honda's Move to Build $200 million Plant in Ohio Could Spur Other Japanese Firms," *The Wall Street Journal*, January 14, 1980, 2; Mile Tharp, "Toyota and Nissan Say They Will Resist Pressures to Build Auto Plants in the U.S.," *The Wall Street Journal*, April 10, 1980, A6.

Chapter Three

What Power the Dollar?

When officials from the State of Ohio and the Honda Motor Company Ltd. called a press conference on 10 October 1977, the deal they announced was not entirely a surprise. It had been known for some time that Honda was in the process of selecting a site for a motorcycle factory on American soil, and that Ohio was among the top contenders for the future plant. Two weeks earlier, on 26 September, the Japan Broadcasting Corporation (NHK) and the financial newspaper *Nihon Keizai* ran a story suggesting that Honda had chosen a site in Ohio, but details were sketchy.[1] Thus, when Ohio Governor James A. Rhodes and Honda executive vice president Kawashima Kihachiro officially announced that Honda would start construction on the anticipated plant, the rumors were confirmed. The press room at the Governor's office buzzed with excitement, and nobody appeared happier than the Governor himself.[2]

Honda's selection of Ohio as the site for its new motorcycle plant was more than a matter of good luck for the state. Despite the state motto, "With God All Things Are Possible," it was clear that human efforts brought Honda and Ohio together. The state had long been interested in developing economic ties abroad, and it was among the first to open a trade office in Japan. Initially, the purpose of the office was to promote goods manufactured in Ohio for export. With economic stagnation during the 1970s, however, the Tokyo trade office began to take on an expanded role. Although it continued to promote Ohio-made products, the office also acted as a solicitor for Japanese investment. To underscore the trade office's enlarged mission, Governor Rhodes and State Development Director James A. Duerk visited Tokyo in April 1976. It was on this occasion that Rhodes and Duerk met with Honda's Kawashima for the first time.[3] They knew that Honda was looking for a factory site in the United

States; a personal visit from the governor certainly would not hurt Ohio's chances.

Speaking to journalists at the 11 October news conference, Kawashima gave a brief account of how Honda had come to choose Ohio for its motorcycle factory. He noted that, "Our initial studies indicated that Ohio would be an excellent place for our first U.S. manufacturing facility because of its market location, outstanding transportation system, its supply of good labor, supply of parts, and good industrial environment."[4] If these features brought Ohio to Honda's attention, it was the intense effort put forth by state leaders that furthered the firm's interest. "In addition," Kawashima continued, "we received the most efficient and enthusiastic assistance and support from the Governor, legislative leaders, the State Development Department, other State agencies, Union County officials, and Marysville City officials."[5]

To take Kawashima at his word, Honda was initially attracted to Ohio because of its market location, transportation system, supply of labor and parts, etc. Indeed, the attributes Kawashima ascribed to Ohio did exist. It is located near the major hubs of both the Northeast and the industrial Midwest. As for good transportation, rail links, major highways, and freighters navigating Lake Erie served Ohio. Lastly, Ohio had a supply of workers and an industrial infrastructure compatible with manufacturing. As useful as these qualities were, however, they were hardly unique to Ohio; undoubtedly they could be found in any one of a half dozen other states. Something had to distinguish Ohio from other contending states.

As Kawashima noted at the press conference, Honda had received *the most efficient and enthusiastic assistance and support* from Ohio's leaders and officials. Here too there was no reason to doubt him, but it was not entirely clear what he meant. Efficiency and enthusiasm are somewhat difficult to measure. Did he mean that state workers responded to Honda's inquiries quickly and with good cheer? Perhaps, but he did not elaborate, and there are no records or transcripts to shed light on the matter. What does exist, however, is evidence that relates to the assistance and support Kawashima mentioned. State officials wanted the Honda facility, and were willing to invest in its future. The subject merits scrutiny in so far as it reveals not only Ohio's role in wooing Honda, but how the firm came to choose its precise location within the state as well.

THE SITE

With an area of over 41,000 square miles, Ohio ranks as the 35th largest state in the Union.[6] Its many industrial cities such as Akron, Cincinnati, Cleveland,

Columbus, and Dayton produced automobiles, steel, and rubber products to name but a few. By 1977, when Honda announced its intention to locate a motorcycle plant in Ohio, many of these traditional manufacturing cities were heading into trouble. Although the severe recession and high unemployment that would befall Ohio in the late 1970s and early 1980s were a couple of years away, signs of decline were beginning to appear. According to state development officials, one out of every ten manufacturing jobs in Ohio had disappeared since the end of 1970.[7] Moreover, in 1978, Cleveland declared insolvency and failed to repay $15.5 million in loan obligations, further evidence that the state's economy was in peril. As the state's largest city, as well as its most industrial, Cleveland took on the appearance of a bad omen. Along with other former steel-producing states such as Pennsylvania, New York, Indiana, and Michigan, Ohio was now described as part of the nation's "rust belt," an area that was in industrial decline. The term seemed appropriate.

In light of its growing problems, Ohio sought to attract new manufacturing investment. As unemployment inched higher in its industrial cities, state officials emphasized the need for job creation. As Ohio's Tokyo trade office demonstrated, state officials looked around the world to promote economic development, but the challenge was tough. The state's main agency for coordinating corporate incentive programs was the Business Development Division of the Ohio Department of Development. Hundreds of businesses, including both industrial and service oriented firms, had worked with the division before first locating in Ohio. Once there, firms also often found assistance in expanding their businesses through a wide variety of state programs.[8] Like others before it, Honda received pertinent data and information on prospective sites through the Business Development Division before it made any commitments.

The Business Development Division also oversaw financial assistance programs of the Ohio Development Financing Commission. Beginning in 1965, the Ohio Development Financing Commission (ODFC) provided subsidized financing to companies locating or expanding existing facilities within the state. The ODFC oversaw several incentive programs, including direct loans, loan guarantees through private banks, minority business loans, and industrial revenue bonds.[9] Through 1978, the ODFC directly loaned $11 million to private industry, and had backed over $100 million in industrial revenue bonds.[10] According to state estimates, projects in which the ODFC was involved had a total value of $200 million, and created 6 million new jobs by 1979.[11]

Honda's needs, however, were different from those of many other firms. Subsidized financing was not a priority; Honda Motor Company Ltd. of Japan provided the capital. Moreover, it did not want to reoccupy one of the surplus factories that dotted the state, even though it probably could have received state aid for doing so. It sought a new facility that it could build to suit its own needs. Although Honda did not commit to launching additional factories in the United States, it wanted a site where there was sufficient room for expansion should that become desirable. A traditional urban industrial setting was thus inappropriate. On the other hand, an area too remote was not feasible either. Honda still needed access to major transportation routes in order to ship its products as well as to receive supplies. It required substantial sewer, water, and electrical services for its operation, as well as a labor pool that could be drawn from a reasonable distance. And as with any firm, Honda wanted to meet its criteria at an appropriate cost.

The site that Honda eventually chose suited its needs. The Allen Township location in Union County was 40 miles northwest of Columbus, the state's capital, and near major rail and highway links. Union County had a rural cast, but it was not a strictly agricultural area. Indeed, in recent years, the number farms in the county had dropped by over 20 percent. On the other hand, the majority of manufacturers there employed fewer than 100 employees.[12] The vast majority of the county's 29,500 residents were trades people, service-sector employees, or farmers. Heavy manufacturing was conducted elsewhere in Ohio, not in Union County. The county seat, Marysville, was a town of 7,400 residents, and the majority of its businesses served the surrounding community.[13] On its wide Main Street stood stores, a pharmacy, an insurance agent, a photography studio, the offices of the local daily newspaper, and the police station. In the adjoining streets off Main Street were restaurants, banks, churches, schools, the county courthouse, and municipal buildings. Marysville appeared prosperous and solid, the quintessential American town.

The land Honda desired, a 210-acre parcel owned by Cincinnati industrialist Ralph J. Stolle, was offered to the company at $500 per acre, the price Stolle paid for it when he purchased it in 1969 as a member of an earlier Rhodes administration.[14] This alone was a significant enticement for Honda since, according to an employee in the Union County Auditor's Office, "There's nothing in that area selling for less than $1,000 an acre today (1977), and a lot of it's going for more than that."[15] There had been a brief flurry of controversy in the press when it was learned that Stolle would be selling the property to Honda; many speculated that as the Governor's friend, Stolle would reap a windfall from the sale. When the actual selling price became known, however, the story dropped from the headlines, and the sale went through without incident.

Although Honda did not avail itself of ODFC financing, it did take advantage of some other state incentives. The General Assembly granted Honda an option to purchase an additional 260 acres of land bordering on the real estate it bought from Stolle in the hope of future expansion. The state owned the land as part of the Ohio Transportation Research Center, a state-owned 8,300-acre motor vehicle testing complex that adjoined the Honda site. The option specified that Honda had 48 months in which to buy the land at a sum of "not less than $750 per acre."[16] The Rhodes administration furthermore offered to upgrade local utilities to suit Honda's needs. Specifically, it offered to construct the necessary electric and sewer lines that Honda would need for its operation. To improve transportation, it also offered to redirect a rail spur to the Honda plant. In order to facilitate the rail project, the Ohio Rail Transportation Authority purchased an abandoned Erie-Lackawanna Railroad line as well as the property on which the new rail spur was constructed.[17]

The initial incentives Ohio offered to Honda were not out of the ordinary. The state Controlling Board authorized the release of $2.5 million in emergency funds to help finance the construction of public water, sewer, and rail facilities to serve the plant. Moreover, the Ohio General Assembly authorized an $860,000 loan to Marysville in order to help upgrade a sewer line to accommodate waste water from the plant.[18] Since Honda projected its new factory would cost over $35 million to construct, and would bring several hundred jobs once completed, Ohio made a prudent investment in the guise of incentives. Given the assistance that the state had provided businesses over the years, Honda's utility and site preparation package was seemingly modest. Interestingly, the most generous incentives came not from the state, but rather from Union County itself, which offered Honda tax abatements that would extend into the future years.

It was within the quiet offices of the County Building in Marysville that local officials worked out the details providing Honda with considerable tax relief. The notion of granting Honda tax incentives to locate in Union County, however, did not originate there, but rather from the governor's office. The county commissioners charged with implementing the tax scheme, Ernest Bumgarner, Glenn Irwin, and Max Robinson, were handed the tax package as a *fait accompli*. They were told by state officials that tax abatements had been part of the package negotiated with Honda, and that they had to go about implementing them if the deal was to go through. Not surprisingly, this irritated some local residents. An editorial in *The Marysville Journal-Tribune* summed up local frustration when it said:

"Honda Talks Should Have Included Commissioners"

The Union County Commissioners made probably their most difficult decision this week when they passed a resolution granting a real estate tax abatement for an area in Allen Township.

The main thrust of the abatement was for the Honda company . . .

We heartily thank Gov. James Rhodes and James Duerk, director of the Ohio Dept. of Economic and Community Development, for their efforts in persuading Honda to locate here.

However, the exact details of the county tax abatement were negotiated without including any of the commissioners in the talks and this we feel was unfair.

Maybe this is what it took to persuade Honda to build in Union County and in the end, the same decision may have been made had the commissioners been present at the bargaining table. The citizens of Union County certainly want to do their part, knowing the good that will come with Honda's locating here.

But we feel strongly that our elected officials, who, after all was said and done, were charged with the responsibility of passing the resolution granting the abatement, should have been asked to participate in the negotiations.[19]

Editorial opinion aside, the three commissioners unanimously approved a tax abatement for the new motorcycle plant. From the perspective of Commissioner Glenn Irwin, the decision was not difficult whatsoever.

Well, I think the paper just wanted to get its two cents worth in. I certainly wasn't mad at what the governor had done, nor did I feel left out. He and I were in the same [political] party (Republican), and I saw it as a pretty straightforward deal. I thought that if we could do something reasonable to bring Honda here, it would benefit both the county and the state. I still think that it was a good decision.[20]

Although they could grant tax relief, the Union County commissioners could not pass a resolution on Honda's behalf alone. The State Code did not empower counties to provide broad corporate tax exemptions. However, the commissioners were able to establish a "Community Reinvestment Area" the purpose of which was to spur investment and development in areas that were economically troubled. Tax abatements were extended to the value of any improvements that were made to properties, whether commercial or residential. Indeed, the commissioner's resolution of 30 January 1978 did not specifically address Honda at all.

WHEREAS, the Board of County Commissioners desires to pursue all reasonable and legitimate incentive measures to assist in encouraging housing maintenance and economic and community development in areas that have not enjoyed reinvestment by remodeling or new construction; and

WHEREAS, the Board has been briefed on new state enabling legislation that allows for financial incentives to be offered in certain areas; and

WHEREAS, within Allen Township existing housing facilities were found to exist with little evidence of new housing construction and repair of existing facilities or structures; and

NOW, THEREFORE, BE IT RESOLVED, that for purposes of fulfilling the requirements set forth under Sections 3735.655 to 3735.70, inclusive, of the Ohio Revised Code, the Board establishes "Community Reinvestment Area #1" within Allen Township, to be effective on the date of adoption of this resolution, within the following described boundaries: An area designated by the Zoning Commission of Allen Township, Union County, Ohio, as being in a Heavy Manufacturing District, and a 260.00 acre area contiguous to the Heavy Manufacturing District . . .

BE IT FURTHER RESOLVED, that this Board finds that the area included in the foregoing description of Community Reinvestment Area #1 is one in which housing facilities or structures of historical significance are located and new housing construction and repair of existing facilities or structures are discouraged.

BE IT FURTHER RESOLVED, that the tax exemption provided for in Revised Code Section 3735.67 shall be granted in Community Reinvestment Area #1 for the following periods: 10 years for the remodeling of a dwelling containing more than two family units upon which the cost of remodeling is at least two thousand five hundred dollars and described in Division A in Section 3735.67; 12 years for remodeling of a dwelling containing more than two units, and commercial or industrial properties, described in Division B of Section 3735.67, and fifteen years for construction of a new dwelling, or commercial or industrial structure, as described in Division C of Section 3735.67 [emphasis added].[21]

Allen Township fit the criteria of a community in need of investment and improvements in housing. According to Commissioner Glenn Irwin,

That part of the county was pretty poor. We had folks living up there with substandard, or in some cases, nonexistent, plumbing. Although Honda was certainly the target of the tax abatement, we all felt that our resolution could do some good for the residents as well.[22]

Be that as it may, the 30 January 1978 Union County resolution was squarely aimed at providing Honda with tax relief. The land designated as "Community Reinvestment Area #1" contained only twenty houses, half of which were said to be in good condition in a survey authorized by the county commission. The remaining ten that were reported to be "deteriorating housing" were likely to be those that Commissioner Irwin said would benefit from the tax abatement.[23] However, the resolution stated that the abatement was in direct proportion to the amount of money spent in renovation or construction.

Residents of deteriorating dwellings who could not spend more than $2,500 to improve their homes were ineligible to receive tax abatements. Only upon spending more than $2,500 to repair or renovate a dwelling could the owner be eligible for a tax abatement for 10 years. If one spent more than $5,000, the abatement would be extended to 12 years.

In 1978, the $2,500 threshold was a considerable amount of money for somebody to invest in a substandard home. The poorest residents were unlikely to take advantage of the county's tax relief if for no other reason than they could not afford the minimum investment. The sliding scale that rewarded greater investment was not realistic either. Had owners of decayed housing held back on expensive improvements in the past for fear of greater tax liability? It would seem unlikely. To qualify for the maximum 15-year exemption, the resolution stated that a completely new structure, either residential or commercial, had to be built. Once again, residents and/or landlords who owned Allen Township's humblest homes were unlikely candidates to build new dwellings. Moreover, since the resolution noted that most of the Community Reinvestment Area had been zoned as a "Heavy Manufacturing District," it was obvious that housing developers were not going to flock to Allen Township.

Providing Honda with incentives, however, did not mean that Union County was denied revenue from the company's presence. Specifically, Honda was exempted from paying taxes on any improvements made to its real estate for a period of 15 years. According to Ohio law,

> If the construction of the structure qualifies for an exemption . . . the structure shall not be considered an improvement on the land on which it is located for the purpose of real estate property taxation.[24]

Therefore, the company still had to pay the county taxes on the real estate that it owned, but not on buildings situated on that property. Union County received more property taxes than it formerly had since Honda's property was assessed at a higher value than when the land was unimproved. Moreover, the county also could collect taxes on tangible personal property, which included such items as inventory and equipment. At the time of the abatement resolution, Commissioner Ernest Bumgarner estimated that the tangible personal property taxes alone would net the county an additional $227,000 in annual revenue.[25]

As events would have it, however, Bumgarner's estimate proved to be too high. Although Union County benefited from higher property taxes on the Honda land, as well as enhanced revenue from a portion of the firm's tangible personal property liability, the county could not collect taxes on all of

Honda's personal property. Bumgarner's revenue estimate assumed that Honda had to pay taxes on its inventory, but he failed to anticipate that the Honda factory would be granted status as a foreign trade subzone by the United States Commerce Department, a development that exempted Honda from paying taxes on inventory. According to the Ohio Revised Code Title Section 5709.44, tangible personal property was exempted from taxation within a foreign trade zone. According to the Section,

> Tangible personal property means the . . . average value of all articles purchased, received, or otherwise held by a manufacturer for the purpose of being used in manufacturing, combining, rectifying, or refining, and the average value of all articles that were at any time manufactured or changed in any way by the tax-payer, either by combining, rectifying, or refining, or adding thereto.[26]

Bumgarner's overestimation of Honda's taxes to the county was under-standable in so far as the county itself had not granted the company the ex-emption. The tax relief was provided by a state provision that in turn relied upon the federal government granting Honda the special trade zone status. His error was in not foreseeing how Honda might avail itself of federal statutes. Title 19, Section 81 (O) of the United Sates Code provided that, "Tangible personal property imported from outside the United States and held in a [foreign trade] zone . . . shall be exempt from State and local ad valorem taxation."[27]

Still, the county did receive far greater revenue from Honda than it had be-fore the company located its motorcycle plant there. According to Honda vice president Yoshida Shige, "Before we moved to Marysville, Union County was receiving $1,127 a year in property taxes from the land [that Honda owned]." By contrast, in 1980 Honda paid the county more than $208,000 in combined real estate and personal property taxes.[28]

FOREIGN TRADE ZONE STATUS

In December of 1979, Honda secured from the Commerce Department a for-eign trade subzone for its Marysville facility.[29] By so doing, Honda was ex-empted from much more than taxes on its inventory from the State of Ohio. Foreign trade zones are areas that are physically located within the United States, but are legally outside of U.S. Customs territory. Consequently, any products imported into a foreign trade zone are not subject to customs duty. The zones are designated in one of two different ways. A general foreign trade zone is one that is used mostly for warehousing and repacking of imported goods. This type of trade zone is established near ports, and is utilized simultaneously by various importers. Within the jurisdiction of a Foreign Trade Zone can exist subzones operated by one company or industry. In Honda's case, its facility was a subzone of the Greater Cincinnati Foreign Trade Zone. Subzones such as Honda's are discrete entities often used by firms that import goods used in the manufacture or assembly of finished products.[30] The subzone enabled Honda to import components and parts for its motorcycles, and later automobiles, duty free.

The State of Ohio long recognized the value that the Subzone would have to Honda, and worked to make this part of an incentive plan to the firm. As early as August 31, 1977, six weeks before Honda officially announced that it was locating in Ohio, state officials were already lobbying on its behalf to include the new plant in the Greater Cincinnati Foreign Trade Zone. James Duerk, the Director of the state's Department of Economic and Community Development, pressed Honda's case in a letter to the Economic Development Department for the Cincinnati Chamber of Commerce in the following way:

> Please accept this letter as a request to include a major industrial prospect of the state of Ohio within the jurisdiction of the The Greater Cincinnati Foreign Trade Zone.

> The prospect, which must remain unnamed at this time, wishes to locate at a site in Union County; and, wishes that site be designated a "Foreign Trade Subzone." The prospect wishes that all its plant facilities and grounds be included with the "Subzone."

> Under policies formulated by the Foreign Trade Zone Board, U.S. Department of Commerce, Union County is an acceptable location for a "Foreign Trade Subzone" in that Union County is contiguous with Franklin County. Franklin County is one of eleven designated "customs areas" (port of entry) existent in Ohio. Further, it is my understanding that the jurisdiction of the proposed Greater Cincinnati Foreign Trade Zone is not limited to any specific geographic boundaries.

> The prospect will be a major employer and will create tremendous public benefits for the entire State of Ohio. Further, because of the nature of the prospect's business, a foreign trade zone status is of utmost importance. For these reasons the prospect should meet all conditions required by the Foreign Zone Board, U.S. Department of Commerce.

> Within a few weeks of the writing of this letter, the prospect will most likely allow its identity to be revealed and be willing to work directly with anyone concerned with the establishment of a "Foreign Trade Subzone."[31]

If state development officials were initiating the subzone application process at a time before Honda was even willing to be named, clearly the subzone designation was of critical importance to the firm.

When first passed in 1934, the Foreign Trade Zone Act forbade manufacturers from attaining zone status. Trade zones were limited to the general variety used by shippers to store or repack merchandise. However, in 1950 the Act was amended to enable manufacturers to apply for zone status of their own. According to the Act,

> Foreign and domestic merchandise of every description, except such as prohibited by law, may, without being subject to the customs laws of the United States, . . . be brought into a zone and may be stored, sold, exhibited, broken up, repacked, assembled, distributed, sorted, graded, cleaned, mixed with foreign or domestic merchandise, or otherwise manipulated, or be manufactured except as otherwise provided in this chapter, and be exported, destroyed, or sent into customs territory of the United States therefrom, in the original package or otherwise; but when foreign merchandise is so sent from a zone into customs territory of the United States it shall be subject to the laws and regulations of the United States affecting imported merchandise.[32]

Honda's interest in attaining subzone status stemmed from the U.S. Customs Service tariff schedule. According to Customs regulations, duty must be paid on goods imported into the United States from abroad. As the Foreign Trade Zone Act provides, items may be imported into the zone duty-free, but once shipped from the zone into U.S. Customs territory, duty must be assessed and paid. The significance of this for Honda was that motorcycle and automobile component parts were subject to higher import tariffs than were finished cars and cycles; parts were subject to duty fees that ranged from 4–8 percent, whereas completed vehicles were taxed at a 2.5 percent rate.[33]

Of course, when Honda applied for a foreign trade subzone, it put a slightly different spin on the matter. At the public hearing regarding its application, Honda emphasized how it planned to export approximately 25 percent of its American-made motorcycles, further justifying the need for a special trade zone.[34] Lest the point be missed, Honda explained that its new motorcycle plant would have national ramifications in that,

> Another important economic benefit will be derived from the fact that motorcycles produced in the Ohio plant will not be assembled and produced in Japan. Thus, the Ohio production will not only reduce current imports, but will also replace production of the models previously described for markets outside the U.S. presently supplied by Japan. The estimated value of exports from the Ohio plant will be in the range of 30 to 35 million dollars annually, further improving the U.S. trade balance.[35]

In time, Honda pressed similar claims when it came to automobile production, further casting a foreign trade subzone a matter of national economic interest.

Foreign subzone status played a crucial role in Honda's early years in the U.S. as a motorcycle and automobile manufacturer. According to Title 15, Section 2003 (E) of the United States Code, vehicles were considered imported if less than 75 percent of the vehicle's cost was not attributable to value added in the United States or Canada. In other words, the finished vehicle was subject to import tariff if many of its parts and components were foreign, regardless of where it was finally assembled. Since Honda imported the vast majority of parts from Japan in the early years of its U.S. operation, its vehicles were treated as imports even though they were assembled in Ohio. Therefore, one way or another Honda had to pay import duty; since its factory was a foreign trade subzone, it qualified for the lower rate assessed on finished vehicles. Had it been unable to attain subzone status, it would have been at a competitive disadvantage with other importers and domestic manufacturers.

TO BIGGER AND BETTER THINGS

When Honda announced in December 1979 that it would build an automobile factory adjoining its motorcycle facility, Ohio officials were delighted. Although they had been pleased when Honda committed to the motorcycle plant, an auto factory was even more significant. The company initially estimated construction of the plant to cost $200 million. When it was up and running, the facility was projected to employ 2,000 people assembling 10,000 cars per month.[36] It was a landmark announcement for all parties concerned. For Honda, it was an unprecedented decision on two counts. The announced plant would be Honda's first automobile factory outside Japan, in addition to being the first auto plant in the United States operated by a Japanese manufacturer. And it was all going to happen in the same rural community in Ohio where Honda assembled its motorcycles.

Within weeks of its announcement, Honda set out to secure the necessary land for its auto plant. It already had an option on 260 acres negotiated earlier with Ohio in 1977. At the time, Honda was able to attain a price of about $750 per acre, roughly what the state had paid when it acquired the land for use on the Ohio Transportation Research Center. By late spring, the company sought an additional 400 acres on which to build a distribution center for both its motorcycle and automotive products. In this endeavor, however, Honda did not find any bargains. Although Governor Rhodes lobbied on behalf of Honda in order that it could secure the land at cost to the state, many Democratic legislators were vocally unwilling to go along. The state had to honor the option price on the 260 acres, but the additional 400 would not be so cheaply had.

By June 1980, debate between the Rhodes administration and state law-makers became public. After a closed-door meeting in the Governor's office, Senate President Oliver Ocasek told reporters,

> If they [Honda] want to develop a facility, that's fine. If they want to buy some land, that's fine. But if they want favors or some special price, no. I'm not in-tending to pass any bill for any benefits for Honda at this point. I've been in the position of having to cut [the state budget].[37]

With both chambers of the state legislature controlled by the Democratic Party, the Republican administration appeared to have a battle on its hands. In 1977 the governor smiled broadly when he stood with Honda executives at the news conference regarding the pending motorcycle factory. He could take credit for helping to secure the Honda deal, and there was little role left for the Democrats to play. Their task was to legislate the promises Rhodes had made. Had they not done so, the Democrats would have been accused of try-ing to stop one of the few major investments coming into Ohio at the time. Essentially they had to let Rhodes have his victory. This time around, how-ever, the legislative majority could take a more active role. As Ocasek stated, the state could come to some sort of an agreement with Honda, but it didn't have to sell land at an unrealistic price.

The environment had changed for Honda as well. When it secured the op-tion on the 260 acres at the Transportation Center, Honda pointed to the $500 per acre that it paid Ralph Stolle for the motorcycle plant's land. If a private investor sold land for one price, the state could not justify selling adjacent property for a significantly higher one. But the additional 400 acres Honda now desired was another matter. Honda already had one factory in operation and another under construction; it no longer had to be wooed to the site. It made sense to locate its distribution center near its plants, not at some remote locale. The state had the stronger bargaining position in regard to its land.

There was also a growing sense that perhaps Ohio had done enough on be-half of Honda. Earlier in June, the United States General Accounting Office issued a report to the Commerce Department in which it advised that "the costs and effects of incentives" offered to foreign direct investors should be studied.[38] Although the report did not conclude that Ohio had been overly generous, it did raise concerns in Columbus. Honda sales in the United States were at then-record levels, with no sign of slowing in the near future. Honda could afford to pay market value for its land.

Before the debate heated up to a frenzy, James Duerk, the state's director of Economic and Community Development, notified state Senators that Honda did not seek any special treatment in regard to buying the land. Honda wanted it known that the $750 per acre price for the 400 acres had been the administration's idea; it was not going to press the issue. Honda was willing to pay fair market value for the 400 acres, which ultimately came to $2,125 per acre, and wanted to complete the sale as soon as possible.[39] It did not take long. On 25 June 1980, Senate Bill 427 was read in the Senate Finance Committee, and it was approved by the legislature two days later on 27 June. The Act stated that,

> The transportation research board of Ohio shall cause the land and real estate to be appraised at its current fair market value by two independent appraisers and, on the basis of these appraisals, shall determine the consideration to be paid for the sale and conveyance of the real estate.[40]

Under the Ohio Constitution, bills enacted by the General Assembly cannot take effect for 90 days unless an emergency clause is added. To help speed the process along, the General Assembly added the clause, and with that Honda was cleared to buy its land. It opted to exercise its option on the 260 acres for the auto plant at the same time, bringing the firm's total purchase to 660 acres.

Given the consternation surrounding the land sale, it might have seemed doubtful that Honda could gain any incentives to build its auto plant. To the contrary, however, it received similar benefits that it had for the earlier plant, except on a larger scale. Once again the state offered to help prepare the site for the construction, at an estimated cost of $2.5 million. The rail line was extended to the auto plant, and state authorities performed various sewer and utility work.[41] In late May 1981, Union County officials approved the issuance of a $1 million industrial revenue bond to help fund new equipment for the factory.[42] The county made a token gesture given the costs that Honda incurred outfitting its new facility, but the bond nevertheless demonstrated its goodwill. And although it had yet to file an application, Honda also felt assured that it would once again receive tax abatements on its structures.

There was one promise made by lawmakers in 1977 that Honda still awaited. The weakest feature of the Union County site was the road that led to the factories, Route 33. Although Honda was pleased with the highway system near the plant site, the access road itself was only a two-lane affair. As part of the deal between the administration, Honda, and state lawmakers, U.S. Route 33 was to be improved by widening the highway to four lanes between Marysville and the plant, in addition to adding turning lanes and traffic control devices to improve traffic flow.[43] Nevertheless, by 1980 the work still had not been done. The road was barely adequate to handle the traffic generated by the employees and shippers at the motorcycle facility. Once the auto plant expansion was completed, the potential for crippling traffic problems was very real.

On 16 November 1981, Honda filed its application with Union County for tax exemption on the auto plant. The application estimated that the facility would be 50 percent completed in January 1982, and that it would be finished by August.[44] Accordingly, Honda applied for the factory to have a two-tier exemption schedule, 50 percent beginning in 1982, and the remaining half to begin in 1983. The resolution establishing the Community Reinvestment Area in January 1978 was valid until 31 December 1981.[45] Since Honda filed for exemption on the auto factory one month before the deadline, the Commissioners were not required to vote on the package. With the 15-year exemption provided under the Community Reinvestment Act, half of the factory would become taxable in 1997, and the other half in 1998.

Honda's push to assemble autos in the U.S. came at a good time. Japanese-made cars enjoyed a growing share of the U.S. auto market, leading some in industry and labor to call for import restrictions. To head off sanctions, the Government of Japan ordered its Ministry of International Trade and Industry (MITI) to voluntarily restrain the flow of cars into the U.S. Effective 01 April 1981, Japan restricted the export of cars to the United States to 1.68 million units, a reduction of 7.7 percent from 1980's 1.82 million. Japan pledged to hold its exports to 1.68 million units until March 1984, in the expectation that "the U.S. auto industry and the auto workers union will jointly make every effort to renovate the U.S. auto industry."[46] Despite MITI's haughty tone, it still had the desired effect of curbing potentially more protectionist measures generated from within the U.S.

Honda's share of the cutbacks was targeted at 31,500 autos.[47] Due to the Ohio assembly plant, however, Honda had a loophole through which it could more than compensate for import reductions. The voluntary export restrictions applied only to finished motor vehicles; the export of parts and components were not addressed by MITI. Even though U.S. Customs assessed import tariffs on the Ohio Hondas due to their content, they were not assembled in Japan, and thus were not subject to the voluntary restraints as defined by MITI. Since the U.S. was the passive recipient of Japan's largesse, it had no redress in the matter. With an approximate annual output of 120,000 units in Ohio, Honda was the only Japanese auto manufacturer to show an increase in American sales during the restraint period. Timing could not have been better.

On 01 November 1982, the first American-built Honda Accord sedan rolled off the assembly line. Like motorcycle production before it, auto assembly proceeded slowly until the company was satisfied with quality standards. Indeed, in November 1982, Honda employed only 350 people at the auto plant, compared to 2,000 when production was up to capacity in 1984. The official dedication of the auto plant came on 26 April 1983 amid great fanfare. Even though the factory was shy of full production output, company officials heralded the day as a milestone. Former Governor Rhodes and his successor Richard F. Celeste were on hand to join in the celebration, as were officials from Honda's headquarters in Tokyo. To further underscore the significance of the event, Japan's ambassador to the United States, Okawara Yoshio, took part in the ceremony.[48]

Over time, output at the Marysville plant steadily increased. In 1983, Honda assembled 32,398 Accords in Ohio, or roughly 8.4 percent of the 385,000 cars that it sold in the U.S. that year. By 1984, the plant churned out over 117,000 Accords, nearly 25 percent of its total 483,200 unit sales.[49] Pleased with these results, Honda announced that it would construct yet another assembly line in Union County to manufacture its compact Civic model as well. With the expansion estimated to cost approximately $250 million, Honda's investment in the county was becoming significant indeed.[50] For their part, the county commissioners extended the tax benefits to which Honda had grown accustomed. In order to do so, the county created a new Community Reinvestment Area to replace the expired one established for the earlier factories.

The Resolution enacted on 31 December 1984 was similar to the one adopted in 1978 that covered both the motorcycle and the first auto plant. It spelled out precisely what the boundaries of the area were, and laid out the qualifications necessary to receive tax relief on property improvements. Like its predecessor, the 1984 Resolution rewarded larger investments with lengthier abatements, ranging up to 15 years. There were, however, differences between the 1978 and 1984 versions that signaled a limit to Union County's generosity.

The most significant difference between the two resolutions was the time frame in which the tax abatements were scheduled. The 1978 package specified that with an investment of more than $2500, the real property improvements would be abated from taxation for 10 years; in excess of $5,000, for a period of 12 years; and improvements costing more than $10,000 would be abated for 15 years. The provisions of the resolution were to remain in effect until the end of 1981.[51] The 1984 version offered the same abatements if the investment was made in the calendar years 1985 or 1986. Investments made subsequent to 1986, however, would not receive as lengthy of an abatement. The provision that affected Honda read as follows:

Section 4. Within said Community Reinvestment Area exemptions from real property taxes for improvements to real property . . . shall be granted for the following periods:

(C) For the construction of any dwelling, commercial structure or industrial structure as described in Division (C) of said Section 3725.67 . . . applications so certified in the calendar year 1985, through the thirty-first day of December, 2000, and as to applications so certified in the calendar year 1986 or any subsequent calendar year, through the thirty-first day of December, 2001.[52]

In other words, investments made after 1986 would be subject to taxation beginning in 2002. Taking the limitations on tax abatements one step further, Section 7 of the 1984 resolution stated,

The Board reserves the right to re-evaluate the designation of the Community Reinvestment Area from time to time after 01 July 1989, at which time the Board may direct the Housing Officer not to accept any new applications for exemptions in any or all categories as described in Section 3735.67, Ohio Revised Code.[53]

By adopting changes to the tax abatement program, Union County Commissioners exerted a measure of independence not apparent in the 1978 resolution. They offered Honda the same terms, but placed a firmer limit upon them. Furthermore, the 1984 resolution sent the message that after 1989, additional applications for abatements might not be accepted. The commissioners were not exactly threatening Honda, but made clear their right to end the program at a later date if they saw fit. Another pointed sentence found in the new resolution noted that, "No application for exemption . . . shall be made until such construction or remodeling has been completed."[54] One senses displeasure with Honda for splitting its abatement on the original auto plant in 1982 and 1983. The commissioners remained hospitable, but they were certain to tighten the language of the resolution.

Like the state legislators, perhaps the County Commissioners no longer felt the need to accommodate Honda with quite so generous terms. If the state was not going to sell land at subsidized prices in 1980, perhaps the county no longer had to provide tax abatements indefinitely. There was no rancor or long debate regarding the 1984 resolution. The same three commissioners that had drawn up the first one, Ernest Bumgarner, Glenn Irwin, and Max Robinson, unanimously passed the second resolution. But conditions had changed in the intervening years. By the mid-1980s Honda had committed over $500 million to facility construction. Union County had a motorcycle plant, an auto plant, a Bellemar Parts Industries facility that supplied Honda, and a huge addition to the auto plant on the way. The firm had set down deep roots in the county; gone was the urgency to attract it there. Moreover, the commissioners were now in firmer control, whereas in the case of the motorcycle plant, and by extension the first auto plant, the county was fulfilling the governor's promises.

It was not the first time that the commissioners displayed their independence, however mildly. On 27 July 1981, the commissioners stepped into the debate concerning the widening of Route 33 where the Honda plants were located. Despite Governor Rhodes' pledge to widen the two-lane road, nothing to date had been done with it, and the issue was becoming increasingly contentious. Not to be left unheard, the Union County Commissioners unanimously approved the following:

> WHEREAS Ohio Department of Transportation (ODOT) has announced plans to widen US 33 from a point west of the Marysville By-Pass westward to a point where widening adjacent to the Honda Motorcycle Plant has been completed, and
>
> WHEREAS, at a public hearing held on 27 May 1981 at Marysville High School, public sentiment was expressed concerning the hazards to the traveling public and to abutting landowners and residents, the Union County Commissioners concurring with said sentiments, and
>
> WHEREAS, following public hearing, David Weir, Director of ODOT, has announced that this project to widen US 33 will go forward as planned;
>
> THEREFORE BE IT RESOLVED that the Union County Commissioners do hereby urge the said Director of ODOT, David Weir, and the Governor of the State of Ohio, the Honorable James A. Rhodes, to reconsider the decision to widen this section of US 33, either in favor of a relocated route or maintaining the status quo until funding for relocating can be obtained.[55]

More than any other incentive offered by Rhodes to Honda, the issue of U.S. Route 33 proved to be the most divisive.

Though incentives such as tax abatements, utility preparation, inexpensive land, and bond issues for equipment procurement had both supporters and detractors, it was hard to find anybody who liked the idea of widening Route 33. Rhodes found trouble even getting support from his fellow Republican lawmakers. In March 1982, GOP State Representative Charles R. Saxbe introduced House Bill 889 that delayed the road's widening for one year. The 12 month wait was adequate to essentially halt any work on Route 33 since Rhodes had announced that he would not seek reelection, and would therefore leave the governorship in the following January. In arguing on behalf of his Bill, Saxbe cited the Union County Commissioner's resolution of the previous summer.

At the core of the debate was the issue of safety. Local residents formed a group known as CARE (Citizens Against Route 33 Expansion) to voice their concerns. They argued that a widened Route 33 would be dangerous since it would come within 20 feet of existing homes.[56] Honda meanwhile offered no public comment on the matter. It was interested in getting a superior road into its plants; it was not particularly concerned whether that meant improving the existing Route 33 or building an alternative highway. The debate itself was not over Honda's needs, but rather focused on what plans would yield the best results. When Richard F. Celeste became the governor in 1983, Honda anticipated that the long-awaited road would continue to be postponed. As Honda's public relations representative Bonnie Shiffler observed, "Obviously, when you have a new administration, things will change. That's something you deal with."[57]

In the end, the Celeste administration abandoned Rhodes's plan and opted to build an altogether new Route 33. Ground was broken in July 1986 for the new 17-mile four-lane highway that was finished in September 1988. The new road skirted around the old Route 33, but had designated exits near Honda's growing complex and the Transportation Research Center. It fulfilled the biggest pledge made to Honda in the late 1970s, specifically providing easy access to its facilities. Though it was not precisely what Governor Rhodes had promised, the final result was essentially the same for Honda. The cause of the long delay, however, was somewhat obscured. Beginning with the county commissioner's resolution in 1981 opposing Rhodes' plan, the most frequent complaint against widening the old Route 33 was safety. Lurking in the background, however, was the issue of money.

Regardless of which plan was adopted, Route 33 was going to be expensive. The question, however, was who would bear the expense. Due to arcane federal highway regulations, constructing a new Route 33 was a less expensive option for the state since it would qualify for substantial federal aid. Widening the existing road would bring in some federal assistance, but the state would bear most of the funding burden. Obviously it was in the state's best interest to have the federal government pay as much of the bill as possible, and in the end this was a decisive factor in favor of the new Route 33. When the final tally was calculated, the federal government paid roughly 75 percent of the $35 million project.[58] In the end, the cost of Route 33 made the U.S. government the biggest single contributor to Honda's incentives to locate in Ohio at the time.

If state and county officials saved their constituents money by building a new road, at least one lawmaker also profited from it. The new highway required purchases of considerable acreage for its construction, most of which was farmland owned by local residents. One Union County resident who sold property for the new Route 33 was Commissioner Glenn Irwin, the sponsor of the 1981 resolution against widening the existing road. Although Irwin claimed not to have known that the new route would pass through his cornfields at the time of the 1981 hearings, it must have been rewarding to capture some of the fallout from a Honda incentive after having worked on the firm's behalf.[59]

In the midst of the Route 33 flap, Honda continued to conduct its business and expand its Ohio operations. A significant development in the Honda odyssey was the construction of an engine plant in Anna, Ohio in 1985. Following its earlier pattern, Honda first manufactured motorcycle engines before later producing automobile engines for use in its Accord and Civic models. The Anna engine plant built the powerplants in their entirety, from casting, to machining, to final assembly. It was a significant step in Honda's evolution from a vehicle assembler to a manufacturer in the U.S. When production reached capacity, the Anna facility turned out 500,000 motorcycles and automobile engines annually, in addition to transmissions, crankshafts, drive shafts, brake, and suspension parts for Honda's various models. With its addition, Honda no longer had to import the costly components from Japan.

Unlike the Marysville complex, Honda did not pursue many financial incentives to build the Anna plant. Located in Shelby County, Ohio, Anna is approximately 45 miles from the auto and motorcycle factories. The contrast in the prosperity of the two counties, however, was very broad. In 1985, for example, Union County's unemployment rate was at 8.2 percent, whereas Shelby's was over 11 percent.[60] If Honda had made financial concessions a condition for bringing the plant to Anna, it might well have been turned down. As it happened, however, Honda asked nothing of Shelby County. For its part, the state offered to prepare the site for utilities, much as it had done previously in Marysville. Fortunately, the Anna location did not require extensive roadwork; its access road, Route 119, had a direct exit off of Interstate 75.

In the autumn of 1987 Honda announced that, in addition to the expansions at Anna and Marysville, it would build yet another automobile plant in Ohio. As its site, the company chose to purchase the Ohio Transportation Research Center in its entirety. The massive 7,500-acre property that extended through both Logan and Union counties abutted the company's existing auto and motorcycle assembly sites. Honda paid $31 million for both the center and its land in terms approved by the state legislature in January 1988. As part of the agreement, the state offered $11 million for utility improvements such as sewer, water, and power lines, as well as $2.1 million for training the plant's future workers.[61]

Honda's purchase of the Transportation Research Center was a good bargain. Considering that the state provided $13.1 million in assistance money to close the $31 million sale, Honda's net cost was $17.9 million. Working with that figure, Honda paid $2,387 for each of the center's 7,500 acres, nearly what it paid the state in 1980 for 400 acres of the center's land. Moreover,

Honda bought the research center itself, a complex that cost the state $30 million to construct in the early 1970s.[62] The center had a 7.5-mile test track, a crash simulator, and other facilities contracted for use by a variety of auto-related companies. It was a useful asset for Honda to add to its American operations, especially for future product development.

The construction of the new auto factory itself began in the spring of 1988. Located in East Liberty, Ohio, the 1.4 million square foot plant started production of Accord and Civic four-door sedans in December 1989. As in the case of the Union County factories, Logan County Commissioners granted Honda tax relief for 15 years on the new facility, but still collected real estate and certain personal property taxes. With 1,800 new jobs brought to the county, the abatement was a reasonable investment. Although the Union County Commissioners agreed that the abatements provided a fair return, they learned over the years that it was an on going process. At both the Marysville motorcycle and auto plants, Honda regularly made improvements and expansions for which it sought, and was granted, tax relief. For example, in 1987 and 1988 Honda applied for tax abatements on new construction that totaled over $25.2 million, and on remodeling projects that cost $1.3 million.[63] Individually, none of these projects sounded impressive. They were structures such as "auto weld mezzanines for robot control equipment" and "restrooms and locker rooms," but together they were expensive. Due to the time restrictions that the county enacted in the 1984 Resolution, all projects became taxable in 2002.

Despite the 1984 Resolution's clause that stated the commissioners might no longer grant abatements on projects after 1989, Union County indeed continued to do so. Honda's 1990 application specified $2.2 million in new construction and remodeling, and its 1991 filing noted $4.4 million in building expenses.[64] By this time, however, construction at Honda in Marysville had become so routine that even the local daily newspaper no longer carried articles about the activities. The firm's novelty had worn off, and it had become part of the landscape.

In explaining the state's participation in Honda's acquisition of the Research Center, state Development Director David J. Baker said, "It goes way beyond inducements and enticements and goes into what's becoming a well-used word here of partnerships."[65] Although he was quibbling over semantics, Baker perhaps had a point that applied generally to the interaction between the state and the automaker. Ten years after building its initial motorcycle plant, Honda operated four manufacturing sites in Ohio. According to company filings, by 1990 it had committed over $2.5 billion for capital investment in its Ohio facilities. Its factories employed over 9500 people, and its 1991 payroll taxes totaled $134.9 million.[66] In a relatively short period of time, Honda had indeed made a significant impact in central Ohio.

On its side of the ledger, the State of Ohio had directly spent over $25 million on Honda-related projects such as road and utility work by 1990. The figure does not include soft expenses such as subsidized land, site studies conducted for Honda's benefit, travel expenses for state officials to meet with company executives, etc. that are nearly impossible to calculate. Considering Honda's investments over the years, however, state incentives anywhere near the $25 million range were modest. As Union County Commissioner Irwin noted,

> The benefits of having Honda here far outweigh the expenses. It has provided high paying jobs in our community that simply would not exist otherwise. Young people have been able to buy homes and remain close to their roots. Twenty years ago they would have to have moved away to enjoy such a lifestyle.[67]

Honda's commitment to manufacturing in Ohio increased further over time. By 2003, 25 years after opening the Marysville motorcycle facility, the firm had invested over $5.3 billion in five manufacturing facilities, and an additional $758 million in research, development, engineering, parts distribution, and export facilities.[68] As a result, Honda directly employed over 16,000 people at its manufacturing and support facilities in Ohio by the early 21st Century, giving it a significant presence in Ohio's economic landscape. In 2003 alone, for example, the firm paid $1.129 billion in wages and salaries in the state, providing not only a living to its employees, but also an important source of tax revenue to the state as well. Without question, the return on Ohio's investment to lure Honda was superb.

It is inconceivable that Honda located in Ohio strictly on the basis of limited state incentives and partial county tax abatements. The dollars were too few to justify spending billions of its own capital. By the same token, however, it is unlikely that Honda would have invested there in the absence of any assistance whatsoever. Ohio had to compete with neighboring states to secure the firm's presence, and self-promotion alone might have been insufficient to the task. The state made a calculated risk in offering the aid that it did, and events proved its gamble worthwhile. But as the case of Toyota will demonstrate, others were willing to spend a great deal more.

NOTES

1. Honda to Build Plant in Area?," *Columbus Citizen-Journal*, September 27, 1977, 1A.

2. "Honda to Build Near Marysville," *Marysville Journal-Tribune*, October 11, 1977, 1A.

3. Honda to Build Near Marysville," *Marysville Journal-Tribune*, October 11, 1977, 1A.

4. Official Press Release, Office of the Governor and Honda Motor Company, LTD, October 11, 1977, p.4. This press release is filed at the Ohio State Archives, Columbus, Ohio, Box 3788, File 1857/30/16.

5. Official Press Release, Office of the Governor and Honda Motor Company, LTD, October 11, 1977, p.4.

6. U.S. Department of Commerce, *1980 Census of the Population, Characteristics of the Population, Ohio* (Washington: Bureau of the Census, 1982), 8.

7. Press Release, State of Ohio, Department of Economic and Community Development, July 9, 1977, p.1. This release is on file at the Ohio State Archives, Columbus Ohio, Box 3788, File 1857/30/3.

8. Ohio Department of Development, *Ohio's Economic Development Incentives*, March, 1984, 1. This document is located in the State Library of Ohio, Depository D, Columbus, Ohio.

9. Ohio Development Financing Commission, *1982 Annual Report*, 4. This document is located in the State Library of Ohio, Depository D, Columbus, Ohio.

10. ODFC, *1982 Annual Report*, 11, 20.

11. ODFC, *1982 Annual Report*, 7, 6.

12. Ohio Department of Development, *1977 Statistical Guide*, 376, 372. This document is located in the State Library of Ohio, Depository D, Columbus, Ohio.

13. *1980 Census of the Population: Volume 1, Ohio*, 22.

14. Gonwer News Service, Ohio Report, Volume 54, Report 193, October 11, 1977, p1. This report is on file at the Ohio State Archives, Columbus Ohio, Box 3788, File 1857/30/3.

15. "Land for Honda Offered at Cost," *Columbus Citizen-Journal*, September 29, 1977, 1A.

16. Act of the 112th General Assembly of the State of Ohio, Regular Session, 1977–1979. Act noted as House Bill Number 941 in the State of Ohio Legislative Journal.

17. Letter from James A. Duerk, Director of the Ohio Department of Economic and Community Development to Charles F. Kurfess, Minority Leader, Ohio House of Representatives, October 14, 1977, p1. The letter is on file at the Ohio State Archives, Columbus, Ohio, Box 3787.

18. Gonwer News Service, Ohio Report, Volume 54, Report 193, October 11, 1977, p2. This report is on file at the Ohio State Archives, Columbus Ohio, Box 3788, File 1857/30/3.

19. "Honda Talks Should Have Included Commissioners," *The Marysville Journal-Tribune*, February 03, 1978, 4A.

20. Union County Commissioner Glenn W. Irwin, interview with author, June 17, 1994.

21. Union County, Ohio, "Resolution Establishing and Describing the Boundaries of a Community Reinvestment Area," January 30, 1978, *Commissioners Journal*, v. 32, 575.

22. Union County Commissioner Glenn W. Irwin, interview with author, June 17, 1994.

23. Union County, Ohio, *Commissioners Journal*, January 30, 1978, v.32, 576.

24. State of Ohio Revised Code, Title 37, Section 3735.67.

25. "Commissioners Grant Honda Tax Abatement," *The Marysville Journal-Tribune*, February 01, 1978, 1A.

26. State of Ohio Revised Code, Title 57, Section 5709.44, subsection (A) (1).

27. United States Code, Title 19, Section 81o (e).

28. Robin Yocum, "Honda Tax Revenue Aids School Budget," *The Columbus Dispatch*, February 15, 1980, 6B.

29. Gwenell L. Bass and Lenore Sek, "Foreign Trade Zones and the U.S. Automobile Industry," *Congressional Research Service Report for the United States Congress*, October 14, 1988, 11.

30. Bass and Sek, "Foreign Trade Zones and the U.S. Automobile Industry", 1.

31. James A. Duerk to Charles E. Webb, August 31, 1977. This letter is on file at the Ohio State Archives, Columbus, Ohio, Box 3788, File 1857/30/15.

32. United States Code, Title 19, Section 81c (a).

33. Bass and Sek, "Foreign Trade Zones and the U.S. Automobile Industry", 1; *Tariff Schedules of the United States Annotated (1984),* Schedule 6, Part 6, Item 692.10.

34. "Request for a Foreign Trade Zone at the Honda of America Manufacturing Facility, Marysville, Ohio," p. 5. Public Hearing, October 19, 1978, Greater Cincinnati Chamber of Commerce, Cincinnati, Ohio. This report is on file at the Ohio State Archives, Columbus Ohio, Box 3788, File 1857/30/16.

35. "Request for a Foreign Trade Zone at the Honda of America Manufacturing Facility, Marysville, Ohio," p. 7. Public Hearing, October 19, 1978, Greater Cincinnati Chamber of Commerce, Cincinnati, Ohio. This report is on file at the Ohio State Archives, Columbus Ohio, Box 3788, File 1857/30/16.

36. "State Draws Japanese Car, Food Companies," *The Columbus Dispatch*, February 10, 1980, 13C.

37. Lee Leonard, "Land Deal for Honda Is Attacked," *The Columbus Citizen-Journal*, June 20, 1980, 1A.

38. Gerald D. Peterson, "Cost Analysis of State Incentive Programs for Industrial Development," *General Accounting Office Report to the United States Department of Commerce*, June 09, 1980, 2.

39. Dick Kimmins, "New Honda Auto Plant Will Mean $800,000 More to School District," *The Columbus Citizen-Journal*, July 11, 1980, 11A.

40. Ohio Senate Bill 427, Section 2, Adopted as a Legislative Act by the 113th General Assembly, Regular Session, 1979–1980.

41. Peterson, "Cost Analysis of State Incentive Programs for Industrial Development," 17.

42. Union County, Ohio, "Resolution Authorizing County to Enter into an Agreement with Honda of America Mfg., Inc.," May 26, 1981, *Commissioners Journal*, v.34, 254.

43. Gonwer News Service, Ohio Report, Volume 54, Report 193, October 11, 1977, p2. This report is on file at the Ohio State Archives, Columbus Ohio, Box 3788, File 1857/30/3.

44. "Community Reinvestment Area Tax Exemption Program Application by Honda of America Manufacturing, Inc.," November 16, 1981, Union County Auditors Office, Marysville, Ohio.

45. Union County, Ohio, "Resolution Establishing and Describing the Boundaries of a Community Reinvestment Area," January 30, 1978, *Commissioners Journal*, v.32, 576.

46. Japan Ministry of International Trade and Industry, "Measures Concerning the Export of Passenger Cars to the United States, May 01, 1981," submitted as part of the record of *The Hearings Before the Subcommittee on Economic Goals and Inter-governmental Policy of the Joint Economic Committee*, Ninety-Eighth Congress of the United States, October 25, 1983, 40.

47. "Honda's Ohio Auto Plant May Open Early," *The Columbus Dispatch*, July 06, 1981, 1A.

48. Peter D. Frankling, "Honda Dedicates Its $250 Million Investment in Ohio," *The Columbus Dispatch*, April 26, 1983, 6A.

49. *Ward's 1985 Automotive Yearbook* (Detroit: Ward's Communications, Inc., 1985,) 215.

50. *The Columbus Dispatch*, January 17, 1984, 6A.

51. Union County, Ohio, "Resolution Establishing and Describing the Boundaries of a Community Reinvestment Area," January 30, 1978, *Commissioners Journal*, v.32, 575.

52. Union County, Ohio, "Resolution Establishing and Describing the Boundaries of a Community Reinvestment Area—Honda," December 31, 1984, *Commissioners Journal*, v.36, 119.

53. Union County, Ohio, "Resolution Establishing and Describing the Boundaries of a Community Reinvestment Area—Honda," December 31, 1984, *Commissioners Journal*, v.36, 120.

54. Union County, Ohio, "Resolution Establishing and Describing the Boundaries of a Community Reinvestment Area—Honda," December 31, 1984, *Commissioners Journal*, v.36, 120.

55. Union County, Ohio, "Resolution Regarding the Widening of U.S. 33," July 27, 1981, *Commissioners Journal*, v.34, 299.

56. Union County Commissioner Glenn W. Irwin, interview with author, June 17, 1994.

57. James Bradshaw, :Honda Plans No Immediate Push for Rt. 33 Changes," *The Columbus Dispatch*, February 06, 1983, 1C.

58. *The Columbus Dispatch*, July 01, 1986, 4D; Robert W. Reiss, "He Fought for Slice of Nature," *The Columbus Dispatch*, September 02, 1988, 6F.

59. Union County Commissioner Glenn W. Irwin, interview with author, June 17, 1994.

60. Ohio Bureau of Employment Services, *Ohio Labor Market Information, County Profiles, Shelby and Union County*, 1989 Edition, 2. This document is located in the State Library of Ohio, Depository D, Columbus, Ohio.

61. Act of the 11th General Assembly of the State of Ohio, Regular Session, 1986–1988. Act noted as Senate Bill 321 in the State of Ohio Legislative Journal.

62. Duane St. Clair, "Auto Center Sale OK'd in Assembly," *The Columbus Dispatch*, January 21, 1988, 7D.

63. "Community Reinvestment Area Tax Exemption Program Application by Honda of America Manufacturing, Inc.," December 14, 1988, Union County Auditors Office, Marysville, Ohio.

64. "Community Reinvestment Area Tax Exemption Program Application by Honda of America Manufacturing, Inc.," December 18, 1990 and December 16, 1991, Union County Auditors Office, Marysville, Ohio.

65. "Community Reinvestment Area Tax Exemption Program Application by Honda of America Manufacturing, Inc.," December 18, 1990 and December 16, 1991, Union County Auditors Office, Marysville, Ohio.

66. Honda of America Manufacturing, Inc., 1992 statistical data submission, "Guide to Ohio Manufacturers," State of Ohio Archives, Columbus, Ohio.

67. Union County Commissioner Glenn W. Irwin, interview with author, June 17, 1994.

68. http://www.ohio.honda.com/ohio/direct.cfm *Honda's Economic on Ohio*, 9.

Chapter Four

My New Kentucky Home

If Ohio officials could be described as excited about securing investment from Honda, their counterparts in Kentucky should be portrayed as ecstatic with Toyota's decision to build its automobile complex there. The Bluegrass state, known for its coal, tobacco, whiskey, and horses, had never been notable for its heavy industry. Though Toyota alone would not dramatically change the state's image, it clearly was going to have an impact. The event was considered so newsworthy that Kentucky's top politicians scrambled to be the first to disclose the information. The winner of that race was United States Senator Mitch McConnell, then the state's freshman Republican lawmaker, who held a press conference from his office in Washington on 10 December 1985. Democratic Governor Martha Layne Collins, in addition to many of her supporters, viewed McConnell's announcement as an unfair attempt to reap political profit from negotiations in which he had no role.[1] Nevertheless, in the months and years to follow, Collins had ample time to bask in the media spotlights alongside Toyota executives.

That the mere announcement of Toyota's arrival in the state could unleash political grandstanding underscored the significance of the company's decision. Toyota's commitment to construct a 3.7 million square foot factory in Georgetown, Kentucky, at a cost of $800 million, was of great importance to the state.[2] The firm estimated that it would employ 3,000 people to produce 200,000 automobiles annually.[3] Beyond the economic implications for Kentucky, however, Toyota's announced plans had symbolic significance as well. It was a vote of confidence in the state and its people. The American auto producers were on the run, and now Toyota was going to challenge them on American soil. It was going to do so, however, not in the traditional places, but rather in the Bluegrass. It was the home of Colonel Sanders, not General Motors, and it suited Toyota just fine.

Interestingly, the greater Lexington, Kentucky area where Toyota located its plant is somewhat similar to the company's base in Japan. It is, first and foremost, a rural, hilly area similar to the region around Toyota City. Though Lexington itself offers urban amenities, the surrounding communities quickly take on a bucolic cast. Furthermore, the population in both locales had been largely employed in agriculture or small business before the arrival of the motor company. The result in both Japan and the United States was that the local population didn't have much previous experience with manufacturing, enabling Toyota to start with a "clean slate" of workers. Characterized as "a countrified, conservative producer" by American auto analyst David Cole, Toyota found Kentucky's atmosphere suitable.[4] According to Toyota general manager Hoshinoya Masaru, the state and his homeland shared another similarity as well. "Kentucky is popular among the Japanese. Almost all of the Japanese people know about Kentucky Fried Chicken. It's all over Japan."[5]

Though the anecdote about Kentucky Fried Chicken went over well in the local press, Toyota in fact had chosen the state based on more weighty criteria. The company did not become one of the world's largest auto manufacturers by whimsically constructing $800 million factories. Like Honda before it, Toyota experimented with American manufacturing before committing to a full-fledged venture of its own. Toyota's first foray into auto production in the U.S. was in partnership with General Motors. The resulting company, New United Motor Manufacturing, Inc. (NUMMI), produced sub-compact cars in an idle G.M. plant in Freemont, California. The vehicles were marketed as the Chevrolet Nova and the Toyota Corolla. By terms of their agreement, Toyota supplied the engineering and management expertise to produce a sub-compact car, while G.M. provided the factory and machinery. Since Toyota and General Motors shared financial responsibility for NUMMI, Japanese executives believed it would provide a relatively inexpensive way to experiment as a transplant.

Though the NUMMI experiment was just under way, Toyota's management decided to forge ahead with a plant of its own. Even with the site selection process complete, it would still take Toyota a couple of years to build and equip a new factory, providing plenty of time to learn from the NUMMI venture. Concerns over an appreciating yen, combined with mounting protectionist sentiments in the U.S., made its decision all the more urgent. When Toyota president Toyoda Eiji declared in 1980 that his firm must put economic considerations ahead of all others when deciding to build new auto plants, he was arguing that the firm could not justify building an American facility at the time.[6] But conditions had changed significantly in just a few short years. Indeed, mounting financial burdens made a U.S. plant urgent. Of course, concerns over parts procurement and the quality of American labor lingered, but they were problems that could be addressed in time. The immediate concern was to find a suitable location for a factory.

Interest in the Toyota project was so great that the firm received proposals from 30 states regarding potential factory sites. Corporate executives eventually visited 21 states before narrowing Toyota's possible sites down to locations in Kentucky, Indiana, Kansas, and Missouri.[7] According to Governor Martha Layne Collins, Kentucky was determined from the beginning to secure the Toyota project. When her administration learned that the company was seriously looking for manufacturing sites in the United States, the Governor herself became the state's leading promoter. In March 1985, she flew to Japan to meet with Toyota executives, and returned once again in October to press Kentucky's case. From that point on, state and company officials were in daily contact.[8] The state had considerable incentives to offer Toyota, and there were many details to discuss.

The location that the state promoted, and the one that Toyota eventually chose, was located in Georgetown, Kentucky. The seat of Scott County, Georgetown is located 15 miles north of Lexington, 69 miles east of Louisville, and 69 miles south of Cincinnati, Ohio. The small city straddles Interstate Highways 75 and 64, and is served by the Southern Railway Company, thereby affording it easy access to transportation links. In 1986, shortly after Toyota made its intentions known, Georgetown had a population of 12,360, while Scott County's residents numbered over 22,000.[9] Greater Georgetown appeared to be a farming community but, like most of rural America, the majority of its residents supplemented their income through other forms of employment.

One feature that made Georgetown particularly attractive to Toyota was the price of land. Though Honda had the good fortune to secure land in Ohio at favorable prices, Toyota was able to do better yet. As part of its incentive package to lure the automaker, the Commonwealth of Kentucky agreed to provide Toyota with free acreage. The company asked for a 1,600 acre parcel for its proposed facility, and the state readily agreed. It was a significant commitment on the part of Kentucky in so far as it did not own the land promised to Toyota. It had to approach local residents and purchase the land parcel by parcel until accumulating the necessary property for the firm. It was a slow and expensive process that at times appeared threatened by some of the landowners. Once word leaked that the property was being bought on behalf of Toyota, land prices escalated quickly as individuals jockeyed for the best deal.

Toyota waited to announce its decision to locate in Georgetown until the state had in fact secured the necessary land options. By the first week of December, 1985, only a few parcels remained to be bought, but they were perhaps the most important given their proximity to rail lines. One critical parcel, 136 acres owned by farmer Billy Singer, ran along both the railroad tracks and Interstate 75; his was the last to be signed under option. By stalling agents of the state, Singer profited handsomely. He had first been offered $2,250 per acre, but by December the offer had risen to $6,000 per acre.[10] Despite the lucrative offer, however, Singer's wife Marilyn was reluctant to let the sale go through. After negotiating one evening with top Commerce Cabinet officials, as well as receiving pleas from people such as Louisville Mayor Harvey Sloane, Marilyn Singer told newspaper reporters, "They say it's now or never. Maybe it's never. I'm not doing anything tonight."[11]

The next day, however, the impasse had apparently been resolved, and the option was signed. Attorneys for the state determined that Mrs. Singer's signature was not needed on the document so long as Mr. Singer signed. He was apparently persuaded to do so, and in exchange for his signature and 136.6 acres, the Singer's received $819,600. Speaking to reporters from his front porch, Billy Singer reasoned, "Why should I stand in the way of something that will be worth a billion dollars to the state of Kentucky."[12] And with that, the land issue was settled and a couple of days later Toyota made its intentions official.

On 17 December 1985, Governor Collins held a press conference in which she outlined some of the incentives the state had offered to Toyota. While the drama over land acquisition had received coverage for a couple of weeks in the local media, little was disclosed about the broader incentive package. Given the size of the package she was about to announce, Collins began her presentation by couching the incentives as an investment in Kentucky's future. Said Collins,

We're here this afternoon to discuss the incentive package my administration put together to bring Toyota to Kentucky and to move this state into a new economic era. The package is an investment in our future . . . Kentucky's future. It is an investment in the future of every community—of every man, woman and child in the Commonwealth. With our success . . . we vastly improve the prospects for the people of Kentucky to have a greater share of the new and better jobs being created in America's economy. We've demonstrated to the world that Kentucky can compete with any state on a project of this scale . . . or, for that matter, any project.

To put the package together, we started with our own ideas of the value to Toyota of Kentucky's central location . . . our fair tax system . . . the productivity of our people. Then we added incentives in these areas: Purchase of the land . . .

site preparation . . . training of employees . . . roads . . . and education. We calculated these incentives just as a business would, that is, based on the return we could expect from each dollar invested.[13]

Collins then went on to speculate that Kentucky would recover its entire investment in Toyota in five years. Her calculations took into account revenue projections from payroll taxes, road use taxes, and taxes from the factory itself. Still, she had not yet disclosed what the state's commitment was. The governor finally addressed the issue at hand a little more than half way into her speech.

As to our investment . . . we made it in this fashion: $10 million for buying the land. Up to $25 million for preparing the site. $33 million for initial training of employees. I should note that there is the possibility we will be able to add $22 million in federal funds to this figure.

$10 million for a specialized educational facility to keep them current with changing technology. $47 million for road improvements.

An option that is available to Toyota . . . but which has not been decided upon . . . is the possible use of taxable revenue bonds that could provide Toyota with savings of $43.3 million in state taxes over the 15-year life of the bonds. If Toyota uses this option . . . the company will pay $395,000 annually in lieu of school taxes to the Scott County School District . . . a total of $5.9 million over the 15 years.[14]

To help fund these incentives, the governor announced that she would be asking the legislature for additional bonding authority. She anticipated that "the annualized cost of these economic development bonds will be from $12 to $15 million."[15]

The package that the governor outlined was a generous one. According to Collins, the projected cost to the state would be $125 million. However, this estimate neglected to take into account interest payments on economic development bonds and revenue losses if Toyota took advantage of offered bond programs. If those figures were included in the calculation, the cost to Kentucky ballooned to somewhere between $348.3 million and $468.3 million over 15 years, depending upon the bonds' interest rates. Toyota itself would not directly benefit from the bond expense in the package since that was strictly part of the state's cost to pay for the incentives. Regardless of how the figures were calculated, however, it was going to be a costly investment for Kentucky.

Before the euphoria surrounding the Toyota announcement faded, the Collins administration sought quick legislative approval for the promised incentives. As it did so, however, it became clear that the package was not quite as simple as the governor had outlined on 17 December. Consider, for example, the issue of providing land for the factory. Although it was accurate to say that the acreage would cost the state $10 million, Kentucky offered Toyota three different alternatives regarding its occupation of the land. In testimony before Kentucky's House Appropriations and Revenue Committee, Gordon Duke, the state Secretary of Finance and Administration, explained the three options that had been presented to Toyota officials. They were:

(1) The immediate conveyance of land to Toyota. The State Property and Buildings Commission would enter into a biennial lease with the Commerce Cabinet, with the annual lease payments from the Commerce Cabinet being used to retire the debt incurred to purchase the land. (2) Nominal, long term lease to Toyota. The Property and Buildings Commission would enter into a lease with Toyota for the same period. The annual lease payment would be a nominal amount. The property, at the end of the lease period, would remain with the state. (3) Lease-purchase agreement with credit. The state, through the Property and Buildings Commission would enter into a sublease with Toyota for the period of time that it would take to retire the bonds. At the termination of the lease, the Toyota Motor Corporation would have the option to purchase the land and improvements at a cost equal to the state's investment in the project. Toyota would receive credit against the eventual purchase price an amount equal to all taxes paid to the state.[16]

At the time of the hearing, Toyota had yet to notify state officials its intentions. In the end, the firm elected to choose the first option, and Kentucky gave it the land outright.

Secretary Duke's testimony to Kentucky lawmakers underscored how little most legislators knew about the incentives offered to Toyota. Although the governor claimed to have kept in touch with House and Senate leaders concerning the Toyota talks, she was apparently not forthcoming with details. At the public hearing noted above, some representatives questioned the legality of deeding state-owned property to Toyota without compensation. Members of the governor's administration were uncertain about the constitutionality of the issue as well, but expressed their desire to hold off discussion of potential problems until Toyota exercised one of three acquisition options.

Despite constitutional questions surrounding the land issue, in addition to dissent over the generosity of the package, the Kentucky General Assembly approved the incentives early in the 1986 legislative session. Passage of the measure, known as Senate Joint Resolution 7, came first in the Senate on 24 January 1986 with a vote of 31-2 in favor of funding the incentives.[17] Eighteen days later, on 12 February, the House gave its approval with a 91-4 vote, making the deal official, with overwhelming support form state lawmakers.[18]

Following a lengthy preamble that addressed Toyota's commitment to construct an auto assembly plant in Scott County, the Joint Resolution read as follows:

Be it resolved by the General Assembly of the Commonwealth of Kentucky:

Section 1. That as soon as practicable after the enactment of this resolution, the General Assembly during the 1986 Session shall appropriate and authorize the expenditure during the 1986–1988 Biennium, all funds necessary to develop, staff, fund, support and maintain the programs and incentives pledged to the Toyota Motor Corporation including, but not limited to, those generally set forth below with the corresponding funds in return for Toyota's commitment to the economic development of the Commonwealth:

(1) Acquisition of real estate in Scott County, Kentucky which shall serve as the site for the Toyota Automotive Manufacturing Facility at an approximate cost of $10,000,000 to $15,000,000.

(2) Certain Toyota Automotive Manufacturing Facility site improvement expenses at an estimated cost of $20,000,000.

(3) Highway improvement and construction program in the vicinity of the Georgetown, Kentucky site to serve the transportation needs of the Toyota Automotive Manufacturing Facility, its employees and the community, estimated to cost $47,000,000.

(4) Development of an employee recruitment and skills training program for persons to be employed at the Toyota Automotive Manufacturing Facility at an estimated cost of $65,000,000.

(5) Develop and fund an educational curriculum to serve the needs of Japanese families brought to the Scott County Community.

(6) Develop and fund college level research and development in technical fields relating to automotive manufacturing, initial funding to be a minimum of $10,000,000.[19]

And with that, the Commonwealth's incentive program to lure Toyota was codified into law.

Senate Joint Resolution 7 was a notable document. First and foremost, it was unusual to legally obligate the state to honor promises made to a private firm. Customarily, incentive programs were administered through state development agencies not subject to legislative approval. The General Assembly normally appropriated an annual budget for the agencies, and it was left to the governor's staff to decide how to spend the funds on individual projects. Clearly it was the unprecedented size and scope of the Toyota project that moved Governor Collins to seek approval in the Assembly. But the Resolution was remarkable for more than its mere existence. It was striking both for what it said as well as for what it omitted.

Section 1 of the joint resolution committed the state to appropriate "all funds necessary to develop, staff, fund, support and maintain the programs and incentives pledged . . . including, *but not limited to*, those set forth below . . ." In other words, it enabled the governor to carry out incentives that may have been unknown to legislators at the time at which they voted for the resolution. It also did not forbid the governor from offering additional incentives or adjustments to incentives at a future date. Assumably there were limits to changes the General Assembly would tolerate. Nevertheless, Governor Collins had been given considerable freedom of action by terms of the resolution.

There was some discrepancy between the six points specified in Senate Joint Resolution 7 and the program outlined by the governor. The first glaring difference appeared in point four of the resolution. The General Assembly approved employee recruitment and training at an estimated cost of $65 million, whereas the governor specifically said in December that the training would cost approximately $33 million.[20] She had noted that the state might qualify for some additional federal funds for the project, but never mentioned a $65 million figure in any context. The $32 million discrepancy between the $33 and the $65 million amounts was due to the recruitment costs that the legislators alluded to in the resolution. Though the governor never mentioned it in her press conference, Kentucky had agreed to absorb the expenses of recruiting Toyota's work force. That the state was willing to pay $32 million for this process indicated that Toyota had some elaborate hiring plans. Although the company's intentions were not specified in the resolution, it was clear that the General Assembly was aware that recruiting the work force was not going to be a simple matter.

Likewise, in her 17 December announcement Governor Collins did not mention the incentives raised in point five. The idea of creating an educational outreach program for the families of Toyota's Japanese executives was understandable, especially in light of then plant's Georgetown setting. Unlike an urban environment that might have cultural and language programs in place, Scott County, Kentucky lacked such resources. Legislators were vague about important details, however, and thus failed to estimate the cost of the program in point five. It also made no mention of building a structure for the outreach program; presumably the activities were to be conducted in an extant facility such as a school or other public building.

Lastly, point six of the resolution called for the development of academic research programs related to automotive manufacturing. The entry was short and to the point, providing no details about the initiative other than to estimate that it would cost approximately $10 million to pursue. Interestingly, Governor Collins had also raised the issue of a university/auto industry link at her December announcement, but she specifically denied a connection between such a program and the Toyota venture. Said Collins,

> Now . . . you will note that I have not included any money for the much discussed robotics institute at the University of Kentucky. There is good reason. Toyota did not ask for such technological assistance from the university. We did offer it to them because I have plans for a robotics institute as part of the higher education package I will present to the General Assembly. I'll probably be asking for $10 million for the robotics institute . . . not the $23 million as has been reported. For now . . . I want to make clear that my administration has been planning for this institute for some time.[21]

And yet point six, in direct contradiction to her statement, made the program part of the Toyota package.

That the university issue was raised in Senate Joint Resolution 7 was noteworthy not so much for what it said, but rather because it drew attention to the governor's strong denial in December. After listing programs that were going to cost Kentucky well over $100 million, she went out of her way to disavow any connection between the robotics program and Toyota. Collins stated that the program was not considered an incentive since Toyota did not ask for it. Nevertheless, she then stated that it was offered to the company anyway, as if to suggest that her administration viewed the institute as an incentive regardless of Toyota's opinion. The governor attempted to show that her administration had been thinking about matters other than Toyota, but raising the issue in the manner she did was awkward. To have the funding for the project in the joint resolution only made the episode appear more peculiar.

Regardless of appearances, the entire package passed both chambers of the legislature and was signed into law. But by no means was the debate finished in the public arena. The legislators had committed the state to an enormous and costly venture, and public emotions simply had not been fully aired by the time of the resolution was adopted. Public debate centered on a wide array of issues, ranging from general matters of principle to very specific points. One of the biggest concerns was raised by veterans' groups whose members had fought in the Pacific during World War II. Their argument was simple: why should the taxpayers of Kentucky, among them World War II veterans and families of those killed in action, help finance a large, successful, and wealthy Japanese company in the United States? It was a question that many people might have posed, but it took on special poignancy coming from veterans who had fought the Japanese forty years earlier.

There were other groups opposed to the Toyota venture as well. One coalition organized against the package was the Concerned Citizens and Businessmen of Central Kentucky. During legislative hearings on Senate Joint Resolution 7, this group, represented by Don Wiggins, testified before the Senate Appropriations and Revenue Committee. Wiggins argued that the state should aid Kentucky firms before doling out large outlays to foreign businesses.[22] Wiggins' organization continued its line of argument after the legislature approved the incentive package, but to no avail. On 01 March 1986, Governor Collins signed the final accord with Toyota regarding incentives, and soon thereafter construction of the plant began.

In late March, Toyota submitted its site plan to the Scott County Joint Planning Commission for approval. The plan called for buildings totaling over 3.3 million square feet, including a 2.6 million-square-foot main plant housing distinct areas for stamping, welding, painting, and final assembly. The proposal also detailed a 300,000 square-foot plastics plant, a 97,000 square-foot administration building, and several smaller structures such as a test laboratory and utility buildings.[23] On 10 April, the commission approved the site plan, clearing the way for construction to commence.[24] Less than a month later, amid much fanfare, ground was broken for the Toyota factory.

The timing of the ground-breaking ceremony coincided with the running of the Kentucky Derby, the state's grandest annual event. Governor Collins hosted top company officials for the Derby, including Toyota president Dr. Toyoda Shoichiro. That the ground breaking and the Derby happened within days of each other symbolized both the tradition of the Commonwealth and, in the words of Collins, "a new economic era in Kentucky." During the course of the ceremony, Governor Collins praised Toyota, specifically directing her comments to Dr. Toyoda. She again noted that the automaker would have an annual payroll of $80 million, and that the firm's presence would create other new jobs elsewhere in the state. To commemorate the occasion, Collins presented Toyoda with a painting of the mansion that inspired Stephen Foster to write "My Old Kentucky Home," a song that Toyoda had told the governor he found moving.[25] Soon thereafter the ceremony concluded, enabling Toyota's general contractor, Ohbayashi-GUMI Ltd. of Japan, to begin its work.

With the state unemployment rate hovering above eight percent, many people were eager for the Toyota project to get under way.[26] In addition to the plant providing an estimated 3,000 jobs, there was considerable employment opportunity in the factory's construction. Building a three million square-foot facility required specialists from all of the building trades, in addition to many non-specialists to perform more mundane tasks. According to Ohbayashi estimates, thousands of construction workers eventually would be required for the project. Not all of those workers, however, would be needed immediately.

By its nature, construction work progresses through various stages, and thus creates demand for various numbers of workers with differing skills. In the initial phase of laying the foundation, for example, Ohbayashi estimated that it would require some 500 individuals. As the project developed, additional craftsmen would be needed for structural work, and eventually still others would be needed for electrical and mechanical projects. At the peak of demand, Ohbayashi predicted the need for over 3,500 construction personnel.[27] Projects requiring so many construction workers were rare, and many looked forward to gaining the positions.

Despite the demand for thousands of construction workers, the supply of such personnel was greater still, ultimately leaving many individuals disappointed. One group of people particularly dismayed at the prospect for work on the project was unionized construction workers. Ohbayashi, as Toyota's general contractor, subcontracted the work to many different firms. Since Ohbayashi tended to award contracts to the lowest bidder, the subcontractors usually employed non-union craftsmen. Though Ohbayashi did not cast its hiring policies on the basis of union versus non-union workers, the result was that unionized craftsmen were often excluded. Ohbayashi maintained its right to hire subcontractors that set independent wage and work rules, a policy that was anathema to the AFL-CIO's Kentucky State Building and Construction Trades Council. As the umbrella organization for several small trade unions, the Council championed the standardized wages that unions set for members. Construction at the Georgetown site had barely begun when the unions filed grievances against Ohbayashi for its hiring practices. Although Toyota was not directly involved in the dispute, it could not escape the fallout.

An example of union sentiment was apparent in a letter sent to members of the International Association of Bridge, Structural, and Ornamental Iron Workers, Local Union Number 70. In it, the union's leadership did not once mention Ohbayashi, but rather complained about the Japanese in general and Toyota in particular. The 10 July 1986 letter signed by John L. Bruce, the local's business manager, began,

Dear Brothers and Sisters:

I am sure you are as concerned as I am over what is happening at the Toyota Auto Assembly Plant in Georgetown, Kentucky. As you are aware, I have let it be known to all parties involved that the membership of this Local Union wanted to work on this project.

However, it was our understanding that the issue was wording in the so called "Peace and Harmony Agreement" that was detrimental to the Labor Movement. But when I was finally educated to the facts of Boycotting the project, then I realized that more than one issue was involved.

I will try to explain to you the real issues that affects [*sic*] not only the Labor Movement but all taxpayers and citizens of the State of Kentucky and the United States.[28]

Bruce's complaints against Toyota related to the incentive package it received to locate in the Commonwealth. Some of his points, such as the overall cost of the incentive package, were accurate and perhaps warranted. Other arguments he made about Toyota, however, distorted reality. For example, Bruce noted that,

Millions of Tax Dollars are going to the University of Kentucky to teach Japanese families Japanese culture and heritage so that they don't become Americanized.[29]

He then continued,

When the project was first given public notice, it was estimated by the Japanese that 3000 production workers would be employed. Now it is 2000 and possibly 600 of them Japanese technicians.[30]

Bruce's remark about the program to ease Japanese families into their new surroundings was obviously inflammatory. Nobody had ever suggested that the children of Toyota executives should be kept away from American culture. Furthermore, the site for the educational program had yet to be selected in early 1986, and thus was not the University of Kentucky as he suggested. His second claim, that Toyota reduced its employee estimate from 3000 to 2000, was a fabrication. Toyota never lowered its payroll estimates, nor had it disclosed the number of Japanese executives it intended to bring. It was striking that Bruce did not refer to Toyota as such, but rather as "the Japanese," appealing to xenophobic fears. Though his assertions might have stirred the membership, the statements were heavy-handed and crude.

Iron Workers Local Number 70 was not the only union involved in the controversy surrounding the Toyota project. Front and center in the matter was the Kentucky State Building and Construction Trades Council itself. Executive secretary Jerry Hammond was determined to force Ohbayashi to hire union tradespeople. Although he too wrote to union members, Hammond went further and challenged Ohbayashi by more vigorous means. On 10 July 1986, the same day that John Bruce wrote to members of local number 70, Toyota representatives, Ohbayashi officials, and leaders from the Kentucky Trades Council met in Washington, D.C. to discuss their differences.

The union's demands were straightforward. It wanted all workers on the project to be union members, earning union scale wages. As a gesture of compromise, Lucky McClintock, president of the Central Kentucky State Building and Construction Trades Council and business manager of the Plumbers, Pipe Fitters and Steam Fitters Local 452 in Lexington, offered to allow non-union personnel to work at the site provided that the supply of local union construction workers had been exhausted. He furthermore proposed that both union and non-union workers be referred for jobs through local union offices, although the non-union members would not be compelled to join.[31] It was an unacceptable proposal to Toyota and Ohbayashi, both of which maintained the right to construct the factory as they wished. As a result of the discussions, McClintock threatened to carry out a national publicity campaign protesting what he called the unfair trade practices of Japanese manufacturers in the United States.[32]

Speaking to a newspaper reporter in Lexington, Kentucky, Jerry Hammond noted that the union's proposal to Toyota was similar to the one accepted by General Motors when it built its Saturn plant in Tennessee. He claimed that by not hiring unionized workers at the construction site, many of the jobs would be given to people outside of Kentucky since there were not sufficient numbers of non-union personnel in the state to fulfill Ohbayashi's needs, though he was unable to provide statistics supporting his assertion. Hammond concluded his remarks by saying that, "it would be a betrayal of union principles" for a union worker to take a job at the Georgetown site if Toyota did not accept the proposal.[33]

Since neither Toyota nor Ohbayashi showed any sign of accepting the union's offer, Hammond and his cohorts resorted to alternative means to press their case. A few weeks later in July 1986, Hammond filed a suit in Scott County Circuit Court that in effect would have halted construction at Toyota. Hammond and fellow plaintiff Charles Hoffmaster, a unionized sprinkler fitter, filed the suit against Kentucky's Natural Resources and Environmental Cabinet arguing that the agency acted improperly in issuing a permit for the company's air pollution-control facility at the Scott County site on 19 June 1986. According to Hammond, the state should have held an exhaustive public hearing before issuing the permit. Although state officials in fact had held a public review of Toyota's application on 12 June, Hammond maintained in his suit that the process was incomplete and rife with flawed data, and that therefore a new hearing was in order. He wanted the court to order a new hearing, an action that presumably would have invalidated the permit at least for the time being.[34]

A little more than a week later, on 28 July, Scott Circuit Court Judge David L. Knox dismissed Hammond and Hoffmaster's suit against the state. Knox ruled that Hammond had not exhausted his administrative remedies with state agencies, and that therefore the court would not intervene in the matter.

This court notes that only one day lapsed from the time of the plaintiff's demand for a hearing to the time he filed this action. The Cabinet in question has 21 days to grant a hearing, and that as of today only 10 of those days have elapsed. It therefore appears to this court the plaintiff still has adequate remedies within the administrative process.[35]

Undeterred by Knox's opinion, Hammond's attorney Kyle T. Hubbard of Louisville vowed to appeal the decision to a higher court. According to Hubbard, Hammond considered seeking a court injunction halting construction while the appeal was under way.[36]

As Hammond's appeal wended its way through the State Supreme Court, and later still through the federal courts, construction of the Toyota plant continued to progress since no court would issue an injunction. Though Hammond and other union leaders tried to derail the Toyota project, or at the very least dampen public enthusiasm for it, events unfolded undeterred. In the summer of 1986, Governor Collins journeyed to Japan to meet with Toyota officials, a trip that combined business with pleasure. During the course of her visit, she was entertained by Dr. and Mrs. Toyoda in a reciprocal gesture of hospitality. In a handwritten letter composed on the day of her return to Kentucky, Collins thanked the Toyodas for a gift of an ornate mirror crafted by Mrs. Toyoda.[37] Though Hammond was disenchanted with the auto maker, Collins was still clearly pleased with the relationship between her state and the company.

By the end of the year, however, Hammond and the construction unions had reason to celebrate. On 25 November, the AFL-CIO and Ohbayashi reached an agreement in Washington that cleared the way for unionized workers to take part in building the Toyota factory. Just as the Kentucky construction unions had hoped, the agreement was patterned after one used in the construction of General Motors' Saturn plant in Tennessee. The agreement called for both union and non-union workers to be referred to Ohbayashi through the local union hall, regardless of an individual's standing as a union member. Nevertheless, given the union hall's role, it was difficult to imagine that non-union workers would be referred before their unionized counterparts. Though the accord called for protection of workers already hired on the project, non-union subcontractors were clearly disappointed that the union had prevailed in its year-long dispute with Ohbayashi. Neither AFL-CIO nor Ohbayashi spokespersons commented on how the agreement came to pass other than to say its purpose was to, "enhance the employment opportunities and other benefits for the people of Kentucky by assuring success of this project and those which follow its lead."[38]

Analysts observed that the settlement may have been reached due to pressure from Toyota. Ronald L. Filippeli, chair of the Labor Studies and Industrial Relations Department at Pennsylvania State University, said,

> My guess is that the companies [Ohbayashi and Toyota] may have won in the long-run, but they figured that the cost in terms of public relations was too great a cost to pay.[39]

Jerry Hammond, however, did not savor his apparent victory over Ohbayashi. "This represents a beginning in our dealing with a Japanese industry," he said, adding that the one agreement "doesn't get to the heart of the problem of foreign investments."[40] Regardless of that sentiment, the construction unions clearly had scored a victory for their members.

Though the construction controversy had been resolved, the Toyota project remained a matter of contention. Environmental groups, for example, fretted over the plant's emissions and the resulting impact on air and water quality. Residents near the site threatened to sue local, state, and federal authorities if they were not provided with safe drinking water.[41] The fear behind such threats appeared groundless. As part of the site preparation package, the state had guaranteed that a proper water treatment plant would be built. That it had not been constructed by October, 1986, when the residents threatened their suit, should not have been cause for alarm; the factory itself would not be operational until 1988. What appeared to motivate local concern was anxiety over change. Though the new factory would bring jobs and other benefits, residents began to appreciate that it would alter life as they had known it. Fear of negative consequences, such as polluted drinking water, prompted people to try to postpone change by pursuing whatever remedies might be available.

Compounding residents' concerns was a report commissioned by the state entitled *Impacts of the Toyota Plant on Scott County, Kentucky*. Written by five professors from University of Louisville's College of Urban and Public Affairs and the School of Business, the 1987 report projected the effects Toyota would have upon the county. One part of the report outlined the demands that would be placed upon Scott County as a result of newly settled Toyota employees. According to the authors,

> Over the next ten years, the population of Scott County will grow significantly. Toyota workers will be relocating to the area. Expanding opportunity in the service sector or potential satellite development will attract even more migrants. In addition, the population will grow through natural increase . . . Many of the newcomers, particularly the unskilled Toyota plant workers, will be young and will be having additional children in the near future.[42]

The researchers estimated that population growth in the county would exceed 27 percent in the period 1985–1995, with growth in the county's incorporated towns greater yet. In the same 1985–1995 time frame, Georgetown's population was projected to expand by 38.1 percent, and the county's towns of Sadieville and Stamping Ground were estimated to grow by 32.8 percent and 29.6 percent respectively.[43]

As far as county government was concerned, the financial burden of the growth would be most acutely felt in school construction and increased need for public services. At the time the report was written in 1987, the Superintendent of Scott County Public Schools reported that the current enrollments in the county schools had already reached capacity levels, forcing the local high school to add portable classrooms to meet demand. With the school age population between 5 and 18 years old expected to jump by 15.1 percent between 1985 and 1990 alone, classroom space had to be added immediately.[44] Though eventually the additional county residents would help fund building expenses through their property taxes, there was a time gap between the increased revenue stream and the need for immediate construction. Initially, current residents would have to shoulder the burden. Combined with the need to more than double expenditures on police and fire protection between 1986 and 1990, the county faced a considerable short-term investment.[45]

Despite concerns raised in the impact study, the report also contained considerable data demonstrating benefits that would accrue to the county and its residents. First among these were job opportunities at the Toyota plant and in the service sector. As the report noted,

Sustained impacts will be generated by employment at the Toyota plant. During Toyota's first few years of operation, Scott County will experience substantial growth in employment and population. Growth in manufacturing employment attracts population which, in turn, increases demand for service sector employment. Scott County employment will increase from direct employment at the Toyota plant, complementary development in service jobs, and potential satellite and other economic development. Total employment in the county could increase by as much as 80 percent above the current base of 6,300 non-farm jobs within the next five years. There would appear to be some potential for short-term labor shortages in Scott County and the region between 1988 and 1990.

As more Toyota employees are hired, the secondary impacts are naturally increased. By 1991, approximately 1,281 new jobs will have been created. . . . The bulk of these secondary impact jobs will be in services (343 jobs,) trade (262 jobs,) and government (217 jobs.)[46]

With the Georgetown branch of the state unemployment bureau reporting an unemployment rate of 8.7 percent, totaling 2,827 people, the notion of short-term labor shortages was welcome indeed.[47]

Reaction to the Toyota project thus appeared to be mixed. In certain quarters, most notably among labor groups, environmentalists, veterans organizations, and those questioning the cost of incentives to the state or the expenses thrust upon the county, negative sentiments were expressed. On the other hand, however, there remained thousands throughout the state who looked forward to Toyota's arrival. Governor Collins' office, for example, was flooded with letters praising her efforts to secure the Toyota deal. Some of the letters were from people seeking employment at the new facility. One correspondent was a woman named Martha Kimbell, who wrote,

> My husband has been out for work for nearly a year. His name is John. He is a hard worker. We hope that you can help him get work at Toyota.[48]

Though most job-seekers did not write to the governor, Martha Kimbell and her family were only one of many that sought employment at Toyota. The automaker had no trouble finding applicants for the estimated 3,000 employees that it would need. The Kentucky Department of Employment Services, the initial clearinghouse for Toyota applicants, received over 40,000 preliminary applications for work at Toyota by early 1987.[49] According to Toyota, by 1990, when the first phase of hiring had been completed, the state received a total of 200,000 applications, of which over 70,000 were referred to the company.[50] Most of these individuals never received coverage in the press, unlike those who protested Toyota's arrival or its incentive package. But the numbers bear witness to their existence, and to their desire to see Toyota begin production.

In June, 1987, Toyota announced that it had hired its first employees for the Scott County facility. The 22 individuals were to be supervisors or, in Toyota parlance, group and team leaders. Though widespread hiring did not occur until 1988, it was a symbolic beginning. After a two-week orientation session, the group departed to Japan for a month of training at Toyota's Tsutsumi factory near Nagoya. According to company personnel manager Dewy Crawford, the Kentucky contingent would learn how their Japanese counterparts assembled the Toyota Camry, the same model that would be produced at the Georgetown factory.[51] A few weeks later, Governor Collins also journeyed to Japan for her own tour of the plant.

Collins interrupted her trip, however, to return to Washington, D.C., where hearings were being held on Toyota's application for a foreign trade subzone, similar to the one secured by Honda for its facilities in Ohio. As in Honda's case, Toyota sought subzone status in order to import automotive parts duty free with which to assemble cars that would then be assessed a tariff at a lower rate. Though Collins rushed back to the United States for the 12 August 1987 hearing, its opening had been long awaited. On 16 June 1986 Collins had written to Commerce Secretary Malcolm Baldridge inquiring about Toyota's application for subzone status that had been filed on 04 June. He responded that the matter would undergo the standard review process; apparently it took more than a year to reach the public hearing phase.[52]

That the governor interrupted her scheduled trip to Japan underscored the importance of the foreign trade subzone issue. By some estimates, a subzone would save Toyota $30 to $40 per car in duties. With production targeted at some 200,000 units, the figure would total upward of $8 million annually.[53] Moreover, approval of Toyota's application was far from assured, thereby requiring extraordinary efforts on Collins's part. American auto parts producers were voicing concerns that foreign trade subzones worked against industry interests by encouraging car manufacturers to import components instead of finding domestic suppliers. With broader trade friction mounting between the U.S. and Japan over the issue of auto parts, Toyota's application for a foreign trade subzone became controversial. On 30 March 1987, several months before Collins' testimony, hearings were held in the U.S. Senate regarding the parts issue. Entitled "Examining the Market-Oriented, Sector Specific (MOSS) Talks between the United States and Japan and their Effect on U.S. Employment in the Auto Parts Industry," the hearing was conducted before the Subcommittee on Employment and Productivity of the Committee on Labor and Human Resources of the United States Senate.

The hearing was presided over by Senator Paul Simon, Democrat of Illinois, and attended by, among others, then-Senator J. Danforth Quayle, Republican of Indiana. The Senators heard from several witnesses, including representatives from three American auto parts firms (Stant, Inc., FEL-PRO Inc., and the Gates Rubber Company,) Congressional Representatives Marcy Kaptur of Ohio and Sander Levin of Michigan, and Alex M. Warren, Jr., a vice president of Toyota Motor Manufacturing U.S.A., Inc. The testimony of the assembled witnesses was decidedly one-sided, with only Toyota's Warren having anything positive to say about the relationship between Japanese auto firms and the American parts industry. Apparently Senator Simon also had invited Kuroda Makoto, the Vice Minister of Japan's Ministry of International Trade and Industry, and Japan's representative to the MOSS talks, to attend, but he declined, saying that his presence might "cause some confusion."[54]

The most scathing testimony of the day was delivered by Representative Kaptur of Ohio. Kaptur said that her interest in auto parts, foreign trade, and foreign trade zones was attributable to the massive layoffs people in her district had experienced in recent years. Though she did not directly blame Japanese firms for the plight of her constituents, her testimony suggested as much. She was in favor of protectionist measures that would hinder not only importing Japanese vehicles, but their manufacture on American soil as well. She singled out Kentucky for its incentive program that lured Toyota, and questioned if it hurt national interests. Addressing Senator Simon, Kaptur said,

> In fact, the Kentucky Legislative Research Commission recently analyzed that incentives offered to Toyota cost that State $125 million over 20 years, or $42,000 per job. I would suggest to you, Mr. Chairman, that you look seriously at this haphazard struggle for foreign direct investment by various localities to see if we really are better off nationwide because of it, or have experienced a net displacement and a loss of jobs and ultimate control due to foreign company business structures where decisions and high-value-added production take place in the home country, not in the U.S.[55]

Continuing her theme of national versus local interests, Kaptur turned to the issue of foreign trade subzones.

> While one effect of existing zone practice is to provide economic benefits to zone manufacturers and the local area, the net effect of such practices is a loss of tariff protection to domestic suppliers. Through the misuse of the trade zone principles, the various tariff acts of Congress are effectively repealed. . . . We do not even know the exact dollar value of imported goods flowing from the current zones into domestic commerce, though I can assure you it is staggering. However, the number of approvals and applications pending warrant an updated look at this program. . . . I suggest a moratorium on all new foreign trade zone approvals, certainly in the auto industry, until we have a better grasp on the workings of these zones, and whether or not their function supports our national interest over the long term.[56]

Unlike Honda, which was granted a foreign trade subzone without much fanfare, Toyota clearly faced obstacles.

Nevertheless, Toyota's Alex Warren was prepared to respond to Kaptur's concerns. In explaining Toyota's position, he said,

> First, we want to combine the best of Toyota with the best of America in establishing a new business operation firmly based in the United States. We hope to contribute to the quality of life in the United States by providing Americans with the highest quality cars at reasonable prices.
>
> Second, we want to contribute to the development of the Commonwealth of Kentucky and to the United States economy in general by providing capital re-

sources, procuring parts and materials, transferring the very latest technology, expanding employment opportunities and increasing the tax revenues.

Third, and most pertinent to your inquiry today, Toyota is firmly committed to maximizing U.S. content at the start-up of production and to increasing that content in the future. This will be done without compromising our product quality standards. U.S. procurement has distinct economic advantages in terms of lower transportation costs and more effective communications with suppliers. Local sourcing also is necessary for Toyota's well-known just-in-time production supply system.[57]

Warren then explained Toyota's efforts to secure parts from American suppliers.

The parts supply selection process began many months ago. Toyota produced more than 1,000 drawings, a 1,500 page compilation of specifications in English, and provided several hundred thousand dollars worth of sample parts for local suppliers to analyze. We conducted a preliminary survey of about 1,200 North American parts and materials suppliers, including all suppliers who had indicated a desire to do business with us. We then formed a study team of purchasing, engineering and production specialists, which visited 180 of these companies.[58]

Given the mood of the March hearing, it was understandable that Governor Collins flew back from Japan in August to testify before the Department of Commerce's Foreign Trade Zone Board. She opened her remarks by noting how important Toyota was to Kentucky. She cited a study conducted by the University of Kentucky that estimated Toyota's presence would generate as many as 35,000 jobs throughout the state. She then told the assembled panel that,

Toyota has awarded 13 contracts to parts suppliers in Kentucky totaling more than $50 million. In addition, 21 new auto-related plants have either begun construction or announced their decision to locate in Kentucky. These plants mean an additional investment of nearly $450 million, and will put 3,500 more Kentuckians to work. We expect additional investment in parts facilities, distribution centers, and transportation and other services. I want to emphasize, however, that this project does not mean jobs for Kentucky alone. Toyota has awarded contracts of more than $600 million to firms in 13 other states.[59]

Collins' testimony was directed at Kaptur's remarks in March. Although Collins could be expected to discuss Toyota's impact on Kentucky, her figures showing that Toyota was awarding contracts in additional states were squarely aimed at the issue of national interest. Toyota was not only good for

Kentucky, but it was also generating considerable business in 13 other states. Impressive as her figures were, however, they were not necessarily germane to a subzone application. Because a firm generates employment or revenue for other companies does not necessarily entitle it to preferential Customs treatment. Collins therefore argued that what was at stake was a matter of fairness to Toyota. Said the governor,

> This request for a foreign trade subzone is one of equity in the marketplace. In our discussions with Toyota, the question of a subzone was raised. We pointed out that an existing subzone is located only about half a mile from the Toyota site, at what was formerly the Clark Equipment Company. In addition, Ford Motor Company has a subzone at their plant in Louisville, Kentucky. We were also aware that foreign auto manufacturing plants in states to our north and south have subzone status as do most domestic auto makers in the U.S.
>
> All this evidence suggested that Toyota would not be discriminated against. Hence, we assured Toyota that we knew of no reason that a subzone would not be approved for the Scott County location. And we pledged to do everything we could to ensure that Toyota received subzone status. We wanted to make sure that Toyota was treated fairly like other automobile manufacturers who have foreign trade zone benefits.[60]

Collins stood on firm ground. The precedents had been clearly set. For the Department of Commerce to deny Toyota's application would have singled it out for unique, and arguably unfair, treatment. Finally, on 18 December 1987, the Department of Commerce's Foreign Trade Zones Board granted Toyota a foreign trade subzone for its new factory in Scott County.[61]

As 1987 drew to a close, Toyota's factory was nearly complete. Employees were being hired and trained for their future positions in the plant. As the hiring process continued, and construction activities were winding down, Toyota announced a $300 million expansion to the plant in order to manufacture power train assemblies. It was an important addition for Toyota Motor Manufacturing, U.S.A. since it would enable the firm to make four cylinder engines, axles, and steering components in Kentucky instead of importing them from Japan. These are some the most expensive components in an automobile, and the ability to manufacture them domestically was an important step toward making the Kentucky venture independent. By making the power train on site, Toyota would be considerably closer to achieving its goal of a just-in-time delivery schedule. Moreover, since engines were costly, making them in the U.S. would further shield Toyota from the steadily increasing value of the Japanese yen. So long as the components were made in Japan, the company was exposed to the value of the yen in its Kentucky cars. The November announcement, therefore, was further evidence that Toyota was committed to domestic supply sources. And unlike the original factory, Toyota did not request, nor did it receive, any financial incentives from the state for the expansion.

In May 1988, the long-awaited event came to pass; the first Toyota Camry rolled off the assembly line in Georgetown, Kentucky. Though volume production would not begin at the plant until July, corporate, state, and local officials were on hand to herald the beginning of a new era. Exactly one year later in 1989, the first shift had achieved full production, and by that autumn, two shifts were producing at capacity.[62] It had been a remarkable few years. By December 1989, four years after Toyota and Kentucky announced that the firm would be establishing a factory in Georgetown, over 3,500 people were employed at Toyota's automobile and power train facilities, and over 100,000 Camrys had been produced.[63]

SETTLING IN

During an interview in the autumn of 1986, Toyota's Alex Warren reflected on the controversy surrounding Kentucky's incentives for the auto maker.

> I feel it's unfortunate that the project is facing temporary concerns over individual issues. But in three to five years, the question of whether this was right will never be asked again.[64]

Though he may have sounded a bit optimistic at the time, Warren's words proved to be prophetic. In time, the complaints and the criticism faded, and indeed, few seemed to ask if the incentives were worthwhile. When Governor Collins first presented the incentives Kentucky used to woo Toyota, she said that her administration "calculated these incentives just as a business would, that is, based on the return we could expect from each dollar invested."[65] If that was indeed the case, Kentucky's politicians undoubtedly concluded that they had made a wise investment.

In November 1990, five years after making the original decision to build in Kentucky, Toyota announced that it was going to spend $800 million to double the size of the Georgetown facility. An additional $90 million also was going to be invested in an expansion of the power train plant to meet the increased production of the auto plant. When the expansions were fully implemented, Toyota estimated that it could produce 400,000 Camrys annually, along with 500,000 four- and six-cylinder engines. The company would need to hire additional employees and, once again, it would create jobs in construction and in other areas of the economy as well. As could be expected, the announcement was met with praise. Since Toyota did not request further incentives from the state, Kentucky's "investment" in the automaker yielded a greater return than first anticipated.

The final cost of the state's incentive package totaled $147 million, $22 million more than the governor had originally announced. Including interest on bonds, the cost to Kentucky would total $327 million over a 20 year period from 1986–2005. However, according to a University of Kentucky study, over the course of the same 20 years, state tax revenue would be $993.4 million greater than it otherwise would be because of Toyota's presence.[66] Thus, from the perspective of revenue alone, Kentucky made a good investment, reaping approximately three times what it spent.

In addition to its tax contributions and the $2 billion spent on plant and equipment at the Scott County complex, Toyota showed itself to be a good corporate citizen. It donated $2 million to the University of Kentucky to expand its library, $1 million to construct a new Georgetown community center, $500,000 for Lexington's Thoroughbred Park, and $50,000 to Georgetown College, a small liberal arts college in Georgetown, Kentucky.[67] It even donated 12 Camrys to Scott County for use as official vehicles and police cars.[68] The county's highest-ranking officeholder, Judge Executive George Lubby, was so effusive in his praise of Toyota that the firm's own public relations department could not have done better.

> Our experience with Toyota has been super. Financially we have done well because we attach a one percent payroll tax and a one percent net profits tax on Toyota and its work force. Since the time of their arrival, the county budget has soared from approximately $2.5 million to over $9 million in six years. Now, we could have been in a lot of trouble if all of their people moved here. Our expenses would have been out of sight. But, at least as it stands now, 80 percent of the Toyota work force commutes here from other counties around the state. We've never seen the influx of people that were at one time projected to come here.

> Since Scott County underwrote Toyota's 20 year industrial revenue bond, they are exempt from paying property taxes until the bond matures. They volunteered, however, to pay an alternative school tax. Just last year (1993), they wrote us a check to cover that tax for the next 15 years so that we could build a new school. That's unprecedented. I know of no other company that pays its taxes 15 years in advance. They could go out of business tomorrow, and we would still have that money. It was incredibly helpful to us, I can tell you that.[69]

Lubby was understandably impressed with Toyota's advance payment of taxes and its contribution of automobiles to the county. Moreover, many of the negative consequences that had been predicted regarding Toyota's arrival to Scott County had not occurred. Although the population had in fact increased, it had done so much more moderately than the University of Louisville impact study had forecasted.

What at first had appeared to be an unlikely partnership was developing into a good arrangement. Incentives, of course, played only a partial role in bringing Toyota to Kentucky. The company took many factors into consideration when it searched for the site of its first independent factory in the United States. It looked at geographical location, transportation access for shipping and receiving and, as will be seen, labor pool characteristics. Nevertheless, the state's incentives served an important purpose. They helped to attract Toyota to the Commonwealth, and from there the relationship grew. It was an unprecedented undertaking for Kentucky to invest over $300 million for an industrial development project. Likewise, Toyota had never spent $2 billion on a venture outside of Japan. Both parties had taken considerable risks, but each anticipated long-term rewards.

In addition to the reaction of people such as George Lubby, it was even more striking that the company could elicit acclaim from its earlier critics. Speaking about the expansion of the facility in the early 1990s, Jerry Hammond, president of the Central Kentucky Building and Construction Trades Council, said,

> We have developed an extraordinary labor/management relationship. They have treated us decently, they've dealt with us fairly, and they break bread with us regularly.[70]

To have assuaged Jerry Hammond, the company's most vocal critic during the first phase of construction, was a real accomplishment. Alex Warren knew of what he spoke; even the firm's most passionate opponents could be brought around. Toyota indeed had found a home in the Bluegrass.

NOTES

1. Governor Martha Layne Collins received hundreds of letters from outraged constituents regarding Senator McConnell's press conference of December 10, 1985. Though she still received credit in the media for her central role in the Toyota negotiations, Governor Collins was nevertheless denied the opportunity of breaking the story to the media and the citizens of Kentucky. The letters are part of the Governor's Correspondence File, 1983–1987, Box 64, Series 00240, Kentucky State Archives, Public Records Division, Frankfort, Kentucky.

2. Toyota Motor Manufacturing, U.S.A., *Facts and Figures 1993*, 1. This fact sheet is part of the Toyota collection housed in the Kentucky Special Collections Room at the Lexington Public Library, Lexington, Kentucky.

3. *Lexington Herald-Leader*, December 07, 1986, A18.

4. Cheryl Truman and Andy Mead, "Analyst Says State Attractive for Toyota," *Lexington Herald-Leader*, November 28, 1985, A24.

5. Alecia Swasy, "Toyota Executive Seeking Harmony in the Bluegrass," *Lexington Herald-Leader*, August 25, 1986, D3.

6. See Chapter 2.

7. Cheryl Truman and Kit Wager, "Land Options Sought in Scott for Possible Toyota Site," *Lexington Herald-Leader*, November 26, 1985, A1.

8. Speech of Governor Martha Layne Collins announcing Toyota's arrival in Kentucky, December 11, 1985, Georgetown, Kentucky. The speech is filed in the Governor's Economic Development File, 1983–1987, Box 10, Series 00240, Kentucky State Archives, Public Records Division, Frankfort, Kentucky.

9. The Kentucky Cabinet for Economic Development, Division of Research and Planning, *Resources for Economic Development, Georgetown, Kentucky*, 1989, 1.

10. Andy Mead, Cheryl Truman, and Art Jester, "Snags Hit in Completing Land Package for Toyota Plant," *Lexington Herald-Leader*, December 05, 1985, A1.

11. Cheryl Truman, Roger Nesbitt, and Michael York, "Toyota Land Package Nearly Complete," *Lexington Herald-Leader*, December 06, 1985, A1.

12. Roger Nesbitt, Andy Mead, and Art Jester, "Way Appears Clear for Deal on Plant Land," *Lexington Herald-Leader*, December 07, 1985, A14, A1.

13. Governor Martha Layne Collins, *Toyota Incentive Plan Announcement*, December 17, 1985. The speech is filed in the Governor's Economic Development File, 1983–1987, Box 10, Series 00240, Kentucky State Archives, Public Records Division, Frankfort, Kentucky.

14. Governor Collins, *Toyota Incentive Plan Announcement*, December 17, 1985.

15. Governor Collins, *Toyota Incentive Plan Announcement*, December 17, 1985.

16. *House Appropriations and Revenue Committee Minutes*, public hearing on Senate Joint Resolution 7, General Assembly, Commonwealth of Kentucky, February 05, 1986, 2.

17. Mary Ann Roser and Jack Brammer, "Senate Approves Incentive Package for Toyota," *Lexington Herald-Leader*, January 25, 1986, A1.

18. Jacqueline Duke, "House Ok's Aide Package for Toyota," *Lexington Herald-Leader*, February 12, 1986, B1.

19. *Acts of the 1986 General Assembly for the Commonwealth of Kentucky*, Chapter 28 (SJR 7), 70.

20. Governor Collins, *Toyota Incentive Plan Announcement*, December 17, 1985.

21. Governor Collins, *Toyota Incentive Plan Announcement*, December 17, 1985.

22. *Minutes of the Kentucky Senate Appropriations and Revenue Committee*, January 22, 1986, Legislative Research Commission, State Capitol, Frankfort, Kentucky.

23. Toyota Motor Manufacturing U.S.A., Inc., *Automobile Manufacturing Complex Schematic*, 1986. The document is on record in the Lexington, Kentucky Public Library, Special Collections, The Kentucky Room, Toyota Folder.

24. Andy Mead, "Scott Panel Approves Toyota Site Plan," *Lexington Herald-Leader*, April 11, 1986, A1.

25. Governor Martha Layne Collins, Speech at the Toyota ground breaking ceremony, May 05, 1986. The speech is filed in the Governor's Economic Development File, 1983–1987, Box 10, Series 00240, Kentucky State Archives, Public Records Division, Frankfort, Kentucky.

26. Cabinet for Human Resources, *Georgetown Labor Force Profile*, December, 1988, 1.

27. C. Theodore Koebel et. Al., *Impact of the Toyota Plant on Scott County, Kentucky*, prepared for the Department of Local Government, Commonwealth of Kentucky (Louisville: Chapman and Company, 1987), 21.

28. John L. Bruce to "All Members of Iron Workers Local Union Number 70," July 10, 1986. The letter is part of the Toyota File, 1983–1987, Box 62, Series 00240, Kentucky State Archives, Public Records Division, Frankfort, Kentucky. The "peace and harmony agreement" to which Bruce refers in his letter is an agreement between a company and contracted workers that strikes or work stoppages will not occur during the contract's period.

29. John L. Bruce to "All Members of Iron Workers Local Number 70," July 10, 1986, 2.

30. John L. Bruce to "All Members of Iron Workers Local Number 70," July 10, 1986, 2.

31. Paul Prather, "Toyota, Union Leaders Fail to Resolve Labor Issues," *Lexington Herald-Leader*, July 11, 1986, C7.

32. Paul Prather, "Toyota, Union Leaders Fail to Resolve Labor Issues," *Lexington Herald-Leader*, July 11, 1986, C7.

33. Paul Prather, "Toyota, Union Leaders Fail to Resolve Labor Issues," *Lexington Herald-Leader*, July 11, 1986, C9.

34. The case, Hammond and Hoffmaster v. The Commonwealth of Kentucky Natural Resources and Environmental Cabinet is recorded as #86-CI-192, and is on file at the Scott County Circuit Court Clerk's Office in Georgetown, Kentucky.

35. The Honorable Judge David L. Knox, opinion on Hammond and Hoffmaster v. The Commonwealth of Kentucky Natural Resources and Environmental Cabinet, case #86-CI-192, 3.

36. Ray Cohn, "Suit to Halt Toyota Plant Thrown Out," *Lexington Herald-Leader*, July 29, 1986, B1.

37. Governor Martha Layne Collins to Dr. and Mrs. Toyoda Shoichiro, June 24, 1986. The letter is filed in the Governor's Correspondence File, 1983–1987, Box 64, Series 00240, Kentucky State Archives, Public Records Division, Frankfort, Kentucky.

38. Alecia Swasy and Michael York, "Unions and Toyota Builder Resolve Hiring Dispute," *Lexington Herald-Leader*, November 26, 1986, A1.

39. Alecia Swasy and Michael York, "Unions and Toyota Builder Resolve Hiring Dispute," *Lexington Herald-Leader*, November 26, 1986, A10.

40. Alecia Swasy and Michael York, "Unions and Toyota Builder Resolve Hiring Dispute," *Lexington Herald-Leader*, November 26, 1986, A10.

41. *Lexington Herald-Leader*, December 07, 1986, A18.

42. C. Theodore Koebel et al., *Impacts of the Toyota Plant on Scott County, Kentucky*, 39.

43. C. Theodore Koebel et al., *Impacts of the Toyota Plant on Scott County, Kentucky*, 46.

44. C. Theodore Koebel et al., *Impacts of the Toyota Plant on Scott County, Kentucky*, 45.

45. Theodore Koebel et al., *Impacts of the Toyota Plant on Scott County, Kentucky*, 16.

46. C. Theodore Koebel et al., *Impacts of the Toyota Plant on Scott County, Kentucky*, 24, 8, 35.

47. The Commonwealth of Kentucky Cabinet for Human Resources, *Georgetown Labor Force Profile*, December, 1988, 1.

48. Martha Kimball's letter, and dozens of others like it, are filed in the Governor's Correspondence File, 1983–1987, Box 64, Series 00240, Kentucky State Archives, Public Records Division, Frankfort, Kentucky.

49. Alecia Swasy, "Line Forming for 3,000 Toyota Jobs as Complex Hiring Process Begins," *Lexington Herald-Leader*, January 12, 1987, D1.

50. Toyota Motor Manufacturing, U.S.A., *Fact Sheet: Hiring Process for Group Leaders, Team Leaders, and Team Members*, 1990. The document is on record in the Lexington, Kentucky Public Library, Special Collections, the Kentucky Room, Toyota Folder.

51. Alecia Swasy, "26 Toyota Workers Leave for Training in Japan," *Lexington Herald-Leader*, July 04, 1987, B3.

52. Governor Martha Layne Collins to Commerce Secretary Malcolm Baldridge, June 16, 1986. Secretary Baldridge to Governor Collins, June 20, 1986. Both letters are filed in the Governor's Correspondence File, 1983–1987, Box 64, Series 00240, Kentucky State Archives, Public Records Division, Frankfort, Kentucky. The application for the foreign trade subzone was filed on June 04, 1986, and is on record as Docket 19–86, Federal Register, Volume 51, 21846.

53. Alecia Swasy, "Trade Furor Snags Toyota's Bid to Cut Tariffs," *Lexington Herald-Leader*, October 18, 1987, E1.

54. Senator Paul Simon, "Hearing Before the Subcommittee on Employment and Productivity of the Committee on Labor and Human Resources, United States Senate," One Hundredth Congress, First Session, Senate Hearing 100–165, March 30, 1987, 2.

55. Representative Marcy Kaptur, Senate Hearing 100–165, March 30, 1987, 72.

56. Representative Marcy Kaptur, Senate Hearing 100–165, March 30, 1987, 77.

57. Alex Warren, Senate Hearing 100–165, March 30, 1987, 98–99.

58. Alex Warren, Senate Hearing 100–165, March 30, 1987, 99–100.

59. Governor Martha Layne Collins, "Public Hearing on Toyota Subzone Application," Department of Commerce Foreign Trade Zone Board, Washington, DC, August 12, 1987.

60. Collins testimony, August 12, 1987, Washington, DC.

61. Federal Register, Volume 53, 46. Toyota's subzone was designated on the records of the Department of Commerce's Foreign Trade Zones Board as Number 29E.

62. Toyota Motor Manufacturing, U.S.A., Inc., *Milestones 1993*, 8. The document is on record in the Lexington, Kentucky Public Library, Special Collections, The Kentucky Room, Toyota Folder.

63. *Lexington Herald-Leader*, August 19, 1989, A10.

64. Alecia Swasy, "Toyota's New Top American Official Says Plant Will be Worth the Cost," *Lexington Herald-Leader*, October 10, 1986, D8.

65. Governor Collins, *Toyota Incentive Plan Announcement*, December 17, 1985.

66. Center for Business and Economic Research, College of Business and Economics, University of Kentucky, *The Economic Significance of Toyota Motor Manufacturing, U.S.A., Inc, in Kentucky* (Lexington: University of Kentucky, 1992), 7. The $993.4 million figure takes into account Toyota's announced expansion plan. The increased revenue stream projected by the study includes taxes paid by Toyota and its employees, as well as taxes generated from companies and individuals that benefit from Toyota's presence in Kentucky.

67. Toyota Motor Manufacturing, U.S.A., *Facts and Figures 1993*, 2. The document is on record in the Lexington, Kentucky Public Library, Special Collections, The Kentucky Room, Toyota Folder.

68. Scott County Judge Executive George Libby, interview with author, September 30, 1994.

69. Scott County Judge Executive George Libby, interview with author, September 30, 1994.

70. Toya Richards Hill, "Toyota, Trades Council Cooperate on Addition," *Lexington Herald-Leader*, June 14, 1993, D5.

Chapter Five

Encountering the Critics

The source of the problem is the inferior quality of U.S. labor. U.S. workers are too lazy. They want high pay without working. [About 30 percent] of Americans cannot even read. So managers cannot convey their orders in written form. Therefore, they get a high ratio of bad parts.

—Sakurauchi Yoshio, 19 January 1992[1]

In January 1992, President George H.W. Bush journeyed to Japan on a trade mission, the primary purpose of which was to encourage Japanese purchases of American automobiles and parts. The president brought with him the top executives from America's Big Three auto companies, assorted representatives from auto parts manufacturers, as well as the usual complement of economic and political advisors. The trip was perhaps the low-point in the Bush administration's conduct of foreign affairs. The American delegation received few concessions from their Japanese hosts, other than a disappointing target to increase sales of U.S. vehicles in Japan to 20,000 units annually.[2] In addition, the Japanese also set a goal to increase purchases of American-made auto parts by $10 billion over the course of the next three years.[3] The Americans were frustrated and angered by the Japanese response. They had come desiring more than vaguely worded goals, and were further insulted to be told by Japanese officials that the American automobile industry had to radically transform itself if it hoped to compete in Japan.[4]

Upon returning from Japan, Chrysler Corporation chairman Lee Iacocca told a group of 5,000 Detroit area executives exactly what he thought of his conversations with Japanese officials.

I for one am fed up hearing from the Japanese, and I might say some Americans, too, that all our problems in this industry, all our problems, are our own damn

96

fault. We do not have idiots running General Motors, Ford, and Chrysler, or our suppliers. And our workers are not lazy and stupid.

They say it's [the trade imbalance] because our stuff is junk. I wonder if there's another reason. Like maybe because my Jeep Cherokee costs $12,000 more in Japan than it does here because they don't accept our certification, and everything has to be inspected, and there's a maze of red tape not designed to protect the Japanese consumer, but to keep us out.[5]

One week after the American delegation returned to the United States, Sakurauchi Yoshio gave his assessment of why American companies had difficulty selling their wares in Japan. He responded to both of Iacocca's main points. The problem, according to Sakurauchi, was not attributable to artificial trade barriers, but rather to the poor quality of American workmanship. His were not the comments of an ordinary Japanese citizen, but rather those of a leading political figure. In addition to being Speaker of Japan's lower house of Parliament, Sakurauchi Yoshio had served as Foreign Minster, Agriculture Minister, Minister of International Trade and Industry, and Construction Minister over the course of his long career.[6] He was a man who knew his words carried weight, and within days they were reported in Japan and the United States. Spokesmen throughout the Japanese government apologized, disavowed the Speaker's comments, or said that he had been misinterpreted. Regardless of their efforts, however, Americans were angry and resentful.

Sakurauchi's criticism of Americans was only one of many that had come from Japanese officials in the 1980s and 1990s. In 1986, Prime Minister Nakasone remarked that, "In the United States, because there are a considerable number of blacks, Puerto Ricans and Mexicans, the [intellectual] level is lower."[7] Two years later another senior Japanese official, in discussing the high level of personal debt in the United States said,

They use credit cards a lot. They have no savings, so they go bankrupt. If Japanese become bankrupt, they think it serious enough to escape into the night or commit family suicide. But among those guys over there are so many blacks and so on, who think nonchalantly: 'We're bankrupt, but from tomorrow on we don't have to pay anything back. We just can't use credit cards any more.'[8]

To American observers the pattern seemed clear. Japanese leaders perceived Americans as lazy, illiterate, and burdened by the presence of racial minorities. And if Japan's leaders held Americans in low esteem, many saw little reason to doubt that the Japanese as a whole shared that opinion.

That the United States came in for criticism from abroad was not in itself new or unaccustomed. Europeans regularly leveled charges of cultural imperialism, developing nations accused the U.S. of economic and political exploitation, and Islamic fundamentalists in the Middle East decried the United States as Satanic. Although in some circles there was agreement with the foreign critics, most Americans simply shrugged off such comments. But criticism from Japan brought a different reaction. Given Japan's powerful economy and its ever-growing trade surplus with the United States, there was a defensive reaction to the charges of laziness, especially in light of statistics that showed American labor was more productive than that of Japan throughout the 1980s and 1990s.[9] With the average worker spending longer hours at work by the end of the 1980s, Americans furthermore knew that they were not shiftless.

The comments of Japanese political leaders became ammunition in the hands of the country's detractors. Among many Americans, it became an article of faith that the Japanese were xenophobic at best, and in all likelihood were blatant racists. By extension, Japanese automobile executives were assumed by some to harbor negative views of Americans in general, and racial minorities in particular. And what of those firms that were locating in the States? Was race a factor in deciding which individuals the firms eventually hired? And what of other considerations? Given Sakurauchi's statement regarding American literacy, it might be inferred that Japanese employers had misgivings about the abilities of American workers. Was this in fact the case, and if so, how did it affect the hiring process at the auto plants? These questions are worth examining. The transplant automakers had an opportunity to start fresh and hire precisely the kind of labor force they desired. They were not constrained by the old labor/management patterns that characterized General Motors, Ford, or Chrysler, and thus could approach personnel matters in their own ways.

THE HONDA WAY

During the 1992 controversy regarding Japanese criticism of the U.S. labor force, Honda of America Manufacturing president Yoshino Hiroyuki weighed in on the matter. Under his leadership, Honda employed nearly 11,000 American workers.[10] Of any Japanese person residing in the U.S., Yoshino had a stake in assessing the quality of his workers. In an article appearing in an Ohio business publication, Yoshino wrote,

> The current debate on the work habits of Americans has generated much heat but shed little light on the subject. Beyond all the rhetoric is the reality of the work place.

At Honda, we believe that in order to understand a situation properly, you must go to the spot and see it first-hand. I have no doubt that those making disparaging remarks about American workers would not do so if they take the time to visit a facility like Honda of America Manufacturing.

Hard work is not a matter of nationality. It is a matter of individual choice enhanced by a good work environment through our business philosophy, which we call the Honda Way. Most people would probably just call it common sense.

The basis for the Honda Way is respect for the individual. Honda is really just a team of individuals working together for a common goal. To reach that goal, an atmosphere of mutual respect among associates [Honda's name for its employees] must exist. Each person deserves to have his or her views listened to and considered, and it is our job to facilitate that process.

One way we do that is our Voluntary Involvement Program (VIP). Through VIP, associates are encouraged to express themselves and suggest ways to improve our work place and our products. Another way we promote the exchange of ideas is the lack of physical barriers between people. There are no private offices at Honda or reserved parking spaces. Everyone eats in the same cafeterias and everyone wears the same uniform. In short, we believe every associate deserves equal treatment as a valuable member of the team, and we have designed our work environment to reflect that belief.

Honda of America's 12-year history has been a series of difficult challenges, and our associates have risen to each of them with enthusiasm. Any person who is treated with respect, given the proper tools, and provided with the opportunity and challenge to do their best will respond with their best effort. And isn't that just common sense?[11]

Of course, Yoshino Hiroyuki had good reason to defend his employees. He could not be recorded as having written that Honda "associates" were indolent or incompetent. Such employees could not be expected to build the reliable automobiles for which the firm was known. Moreover, if Lee Iacocca was quoted as saying that Chrysler workers were not "lazy or stupid," Yoshino could do no less. He went further, however, than merely noting that the associates were good at what they did. In essence, he credited his company and its policies for the work habits of the associates. He did not say that Japanese critics of American labor were necessarily wrong, merely that their assessment did not apply to Honda workers. Honda's superior communication and involvement with its employees inspired them to "respond with their best effort." If his American competitors were accused of employing disinterested and perhaps illiterate individuals, the root of their problems might still be attributable to their labor policies.

Yoshino's championing of Honda's practices clearly had public relations value. The firm's president pointed to the unique relationship between management and labor that did not provide executive perquisites such as special dining rooms or favorable parking spaces. Indeed, it was true that all Honda employees, including Yoshino and his top executives, wore the same white uniforms with patches bearing their names. This was not to say that all Honda associates were equal in responsibility or compensation, nor did Yoshino suggest as much. Nevertheless, the superficial divisions between labor and management that were traditionally featured in American factories were not found in Honda facilities.

The "Honda Way," with its emphasis on programs such as the Voluntary Involvement Program (VIP), was more than just a gimmick for public consumption. Employees, too, were reminded that they had a voice in their work environment. Honda managers constantly reminded associates that they were team members who were integral to the process of automotive manufacturing. To encourage worker participation in VIP, Honda established a reward system to recognize employees for their contributions and suggestions to improve quality and solve production problems. Workers could earn points for their involvement that could be redeemed for items such as U.S. Savings Bonds, a Honda Civic automobile, or the more expensive Accord model. For example, working with fellow employees in a quality circle addressing a complex problem in the plant earned an associate 50 points. Once 2,500 points had been accumulated, an individual qualified for a Civic. Honda estimated that it would take five to eight years before a Civic would be rewarded; instead, it took less than three years after the VIP system was initiated in late 1986.[12] According to Denise Garrison, manager of the material-service department at the Marysville plant, Honda took employee involvement very seriously.

We have a goal here: If you can do it better—do it. If you fail, we'll pick you up and dust you off. You really need to use people and resources. When you ask for their help, it makes people feel that they count. Morale goes up, and quality goes up. We rely on associates to keep quality on target. We want them to feel important. If they don't feel important, then they won't think it's important for them to check for quality.

We are all conscious of quality going out the door. As soon as quality problems are found, we get immediate feedback on what might be wrong. Five or six associates swarm around the problem area and solve the problem on the spo—usually within minutes. The problem is always fixed before the next department receives the part.[13]

Al Kinzer, Honda's vice president and senior manager for administration, likened his job to that of the head of a household when he noted that, "operating a plant is just like running a family."[14] Despite the company's comforting analogies to team spirit and family structures, in reality its workers' tasks were not that different from their counterparts at any other automaker. There are only so many ways to assemble an automobile, and Honda had chosen the established pattern of using an assembly line. Workers performed repetitive assignments in eight-hour shifts, occasionally to be supplemented with overtime production. Indeed, not everybody was willing to accept Honda's portrayal of itself as an organization of united "associates" working together for the common good. As an official of the United Automobile Workers union pointed out,

> Honda workers in Japan are employees, and Honda workers in the U.S. are employees, and no fancy terminology can change that fact.[15]

HONDA AND THE UAW

As the first Japanese automobile company to manufacture in the United States, Honda was a natural target for the United Automobile Workers union. In the face of declining membership due to layoffs in the American automotive industry, the UAW desperately sought to organize the workers at the new Honda plant in Ohio. Although the numeric addition of Honda workers to the overall ranks of the UAW would be small, the factory held great symbolic importance for the union. In part, the union's shrinking rolls were due to vehicle importers such as Honda commanding a growing share of the American market. To organize the firm's American employees would thus enable the union to reassert its role as the representative of all American autoworkers.

Before the UAW could secure the right to represent Honda's employees, however, there was organizing work to be done. As a first measure, the union sent representatives to Marysville in late 1979 to encourage workers at Honda's newly opened motorcycle plant to join its ranks. The union distributed literature, held informational sessions, and provided anybody interested with hats, tee shirts, and buttons bearing the UAW insignia. These were time-honored practices for the union to acquaint workers with UAW activities. As it had hoped, Honda workers picked up union pamphlets left at the company's entrances, and some were soon wearing UAW embossed items. It was over this issue that company and union officials first found themselves at loggerheads.

In 1980, Honda banned workers from wearing either UAW buttons or hats in the work place. The company argued that the paraphernalia violated the firm's dress code of white uniforms. If workers chose to wear a cap, Honda hats were acceptable. Anything other than the standard uniform, however, was said to undermine the "Honda Way." The company argued that team spirit and unity were promoted through the uniforms, and deviations from the standard would frustrate carefully laid out plans. They furthermore said that banning the hats had nothing to do with the UAW *per se*. Any hats other than those bearing the Honda insignia were forbidden, and thus the firm claimed that the UAW was not being singled out. Some workers, however, charged that, to the contrary, people throughout the plant could be seen wearing caps with the logos of various sports teams or consumer products. They alleged that Honda's management did not ask these workers to remove their hats, and that only those who donned UAW hats were cited for dress code violations.

As for buttons or pins, the company said that they were proscribed for fear that the workers wearing such items would scratch or otherwise damage the motorcycles in production. Honda's uniforms were designed so that all buttons and zippers were covered so as to prevent damage as well. Not surprisingly, the UAW rejected Honda's claims and argued that the company was blatantly attempting to frustrate the union's organizing drive.

And so it was that the UAW filed an unfair labor complaint against Honda with the National Labor Relations Board at its regional Cleveland office in June 1980. The union cited in its filing an incident involving Matthew Holzapfel, a boiler operator at Honda's motorcycle plant, who had been asked to remove a cap bearing the UAW insignia.[16] According to UAW representative Joseph Tomasi,

> This is an example of how they [Honda] don't intend to abide by the labor laws in our country. We always rely on buttons and T-shirts with our insignia to promote organizing. We believe we have the right to put our caps in the plant.[17]

In October 1981, the NLRB sided with the union, and issued formal charges against Honda for violating U.S. labor laws. Administrative law judge Thomas D. Johnson decided that Honda's ". . . broad uniform rule would, in effect, deprive employees of their lawful right to wear union buttons and insignia."[18]

Despite Johnson's ruling, the issue was yet to be settled. Honda refused to accept the judgment, therefore prompting the Cleveland NLRB to seek court enforcement through the U.S. 6th Circuit Court of Appeals in Cincinnati. Before the Court acted, however, Honda and the union settled their dispute. On 23 April 1982, Honda and the UAW announced that the company would allow its employees to wear any cap of their choosing, so long as it was not for a competitor's product.[19] In a statement released to the press, Honda also said it agreed to cease any opposition to a UAW organizing drive. For its part, the union acknowledged Honda's need to build high quality vehicles, effectively dropping its demand that workers be allowed to wear buttons or pins bearing the UAW logo.[20] Thus, after nearly two years of wrangling, the cap issue was resolved.

Though the union could claim a victory of sorts in the hat controversy, it was a long way from organizing workers at the Honda plant. In the summer of 1981, the UAW secured the right to represent four employees who worked in the facility's boiler room. This victory was of symbolic significance since one of those four workers was Matthew Holzapfel, the man named in the UAW's 1980 complaint to the NLRB. Nevertheless, the union still did not represent the remaining 380 employees at the motorcycle plant.[21] Moreover, with Honda set to open its automobile plant in the autumn of 1982, the union needed to push its efforts along. If it could successfully organize the motorcycle plant, it would have a great advantage when it came time to do the same at the auto facility. Company officials, however, were not the union's sole obstacle in its organization drive. The Honda work force, young and largely unfamiliar with unions, was not the easiest constituency to recruit. It was going to take more than free baseball caps to bring them into the union fold.

UAW efforts at organizing Honda's workers progressed slowly. Even after the Marysville auto plant was operational and staffed, the union had made little impression upon the "associates." For example, in November 1985, the union held an informational session at which it served free hot dogs and cold beer, along with its usual assortment of literature extolling the virtues of membership in the UAW. At a time when Honda employed over 2,500, however, fewer than two dozen people attended.[22] Union officials were quick to blame the automaker for its organizing woes, claiming that the firm continued to be firmly anti-union, despite its agreement in 1982 to cease its opposition to the UAW's efforts. Honda officials, meanwhile, remained adamant that they were not deliberately foiling the union drive.

Nevertheless, the company's hiring procedures may have thwarted the union's organization drive since it shunned applicants who had previous experience working in the automobile industry. According to Honda vice president Hayano Hiroshi, the company sought, "very fresh people, like blotting paper," who would not bring to their jobs preconceived notions about work in an auto plant.[23] Honda believed that "fresh" workers would be open to its production methods, emphasis on quality, and other matters associated with the "Honda Way." Each new employee received 12 hours of classroom training at the company's Associate Development Center before setting foot on the production line, and received an additional 12 hours training each year there-after.[24] Of course, "very fresh people" were unlikely to have been members of the UAW in a previous job. Whether or not this actually hurt the union's drive at Honda was difficult to measure, but clearly it was possible that Honda spared itself from having workers who were predisposed to the union's confrontational tactics in dealing with management.[25]

Interestingly, Honda also hired "fresh people" for its management ranks. Although the top executives were career company men from Japan, several of its American managers and executives had never worked before in the auto-mobile industry. Moreover, among those people were individuals who had never worked in industrial management. As in the case of production line associates, these executives were also "like blotting paper" and did not have in-grained management habits that might resist the "Honda Way." For example, in early 1985 Honda named a Columbus attorney, Scott N. Whitlock, to be plant manager in Marysville. The Harvard Law School graduate had practiced law in Columbus since 1967, and his career seemingly did little to prepare him for his new role. Although Whitlock's background was different from that of most auto company plant managers, Honda vice president Al Kinzer noted that,

> He's had much experience working with us. He spent three months with us on a sabbatical from the law firm working on special projects related to the expansion and construction program.[26]

Whitlock reportedly was to work in conjunction with Ohkubo Shin, an executive vice president and former plant manager of Honda's Sayiema plant in Japan. Clearly it was Ohkubo's experience as a plant manager in Japan that would have a direct impact upon how the Marysville facility operated.[27]

In order for the UAW to secure recognition as the bargaining agent for Honda's employees, a vote among the workforce had to be conducted. To gauge the outcome of the election, union officials distributed cards asking workers whether or not such a vote should be held. By law, if 30 percent of the respondents signed the petition in the affirmative, the union can demand that such a vote be held.[28] Of course, it did not necessarily follow that those who agreed that a vote should be taken necessarily would vote in favor of UAW representation. A person might agree to an election in order to vote in the negative, thereby keeping the union out. Nevertheless, if the UAW did well in its preliminary petition drive, it would proceed to the balloting process with confidence.

After its 1981 signing of four boiler room operators, the union began its signature drive among plant employees. Since Honda was hiring new workers at a steady pace for its automobile facility, the UAW's drive proceeded slowly. The newly hired workers did not yet know their jobs very well, let alone whether they wanted to join a union. By the mid-1980s, however, the UAW believed that it was making progress. In addition to the four boiler operators, the UAW had won an election in 1984 to represent workers of the Port Services Co., a firm subcontracted to load Honda automobiles onto rail cars for shipment. Though the 26 workers were not direct employees of Honda, they nevertheless worked at the Marysville plant.[29] The UAW thought it hopeful that workers at the facility, even those not directly in the employ of Honda, sought their representation at the bargaining table. Perhaps the time was at hand to step up its drive.

In January 1985, the UAW began a radio advertising campaign aimed at Honda employees. The spots played on popular Columbus area radio stations and were critical of Honda and its working conditions. In one advertisement, for example, an announcer charged that the speed at which the assembly line moved was too fast, and that Honda employees worked three times as hard as their counterparts at General Motors and Ford. The narrator continued,

> When I was 18, 20 years old I worked hard also. But I also had on my mind things to do that night. I hate to see what these people will be like when they are 30, 35 years old. In the UAW you are not a machine. You've got rights and your union will protect them . . .[30]

According to union spokesman Peter Laarman, the strategy of using advertising was nothing new to the UAW.

> It is not at all unusual for the UAW to engage in commercial ads in major organizing efforts. The UAW has never been stingy when it comes to the communication side of the union.[31]

Indeed, Laarman knew of what he spoke. Although he declined to specify precisely how much the local radio advertisements cost the UAW, he told news reporters that it was "in the six-figure range."[32]

As a matter of formality, the UAW asked Honda to recognize it as the bargaining agent for its employees in late October 1985. After the firm rejected the union's request, the UAW asked the NLRB to oversee an election at the Marysville facility.[33] Since the union had gathered the requisite number of signatures from Honda workers, the NLRB approved the UAW's petition, and scheduled the vote for 19 December. With the date of the election set, industry and labor analysts throughout the country monitored events in Marysville closely. At a time when Japanese firms were expanding their direct investment in the United States, including Honda with the addition of its

Anna powertrain plant, a vote to unionize the first Japanese-owned auto factory potentially had ramifications beyond the company itself. According to University of California San Diego labor specialist Harley Shaiken, "It [the union election] really does transcend Honda. If the UAW wins, it is a major trendsetter."[34] Though few would disagree with Professor Shaiken's assessment, the outcome of the election was still far from certain.

In early December 1985, a workers group known as the Associates Alliance began to actively challenge the UAW. Steve Barker, a Honda employee who previously had worked in a union environment, was instrumental in forming the Associates Alliance. When he learned of the UAW's efforts to organize the Honda workers, he decided that somebody had to try to stop them. According to Barker,

> The day I heard that the UAW had petitioned Honda for a vote, I was on the phone all that night getting people together and financial backing. I started with eight key people . . . and it has snowballed.[35]

With a budget of approximately $10,000, raised through contributions and the sale of caps bearing the UAW symbol with a slash through it, the Associates Alliance placed advertisements in local newspapers asking fellow Honda employees to vote against the union at the 19 December election. As another Alliance member told a Columbus newspaper reporter, "We're trying to send the message that we're the younger generation and we don't want anything to do with the UAW."[36]

Just days before the election was to be held, the UAW called for a postponement. As it had done in the past, the union filed charges of unfair labor practices against Honda with the National Labor Relations Board. The UAW said that the election would be on hold until the NLRB had an opportunity to investigate its charges. Specifically, the union listed three major complaints against Honda that it claimed violated U.S. labor laws. The UAW alleged that: 1) Honda set out "to chill employee participation" in union activity by holding a poll on 29 October 1985 to gauge interest in the UAW; 2) Honda recently increased benefits, including an extension of Christmas vacation shutdown time, to discourage union activity; and, 3) Honda supported an employer-controlled labor organization known as the Associates Alliance in order to defeat the UAW.[37] The company denied all charges, and further stated that the union had reasons of its own for filing the complaint with the NLRB. According to company executive vice president Yoshida Shige, "We can only conclude that the UAW has taken this step because it knew it didn't have the votes to win."[38]

By the following March, it appeared that Yoshida was correct in his assessment of the UAW's prospects in an election. In February 1986, the NLRB dismissed the charges that the union had filed against Honda, citing a lack of evidence for the unfair labor practice allegations. Confident of its position, Honda notified the NLRB that it sought a new election date to be set within 30 days of its ruling.[39] But, the day before a hearing was to be conducted to determine a new election date, the UAW withdrew its petition to hold the vote. In a statement released to the media, the UAW said that the climate for an election was poor due to a combination of factors, including anti-union information distributed by the company, and a high number of newly hired employees at the Honda facilities.[40] Regardless of the specific excuses issued by the union, it was clear that the UAW feared they would lose an election for representation.

Over the course of the next year, UAW officials regularly stated that the plants would be organized sometime in the future. In a 1987 speech to the Central Ohio Chapter of the Financial Executives Institute, UAW president Owen Bieber contended that, "We'll organize those plants eventually. It's just a matter of time."[41] Despite Bieber's bravado, however, the outlook for the UAW organizing Honda's workers did not appear to be particularly bright. After devoting years of work at Honda, the union first had to stall the December 1985 election, and then had to bow out of the 1986 election entirely. Since the NLRB found the UAW's allegations against Honda without merit, it appeared that the union's problems in organizing the firm's employees could not be attributed to unfair company tactics.

This was not to say that Honda played no role in the UAW's plight. It was common practice for a firm targeted by union organizers to advance the company's position through literature and other means, just as the union did to promote its message. There was nothing illegal or improper about a company engaging in such activities, so long as it did not try to deliberately prevent workers from joining a labor union. Nevertheless, it would seem incredible that Honda's literature would dissuade workers who were predisposed to union representation. At its most persuasive, it may have had an effect upon workers who were unsure how they felt about the UAW, or reinforced the opinion of those who were staunchly anti-union. The union's difficulties were rooted elsewhere.

Part of the difficulty facing the UAW's organization drive was working conditions at Honda. Even union officials admitted that Honda was not a bad place to work. According to UAW spokesman Peter Laarman in Detroit,

We are glad Honda is doing business in America. The dispute we have is not a bitter dispute at all. It is whether the workers will be better off with an organization of their own. I'm not suggesting Honda is ruthless. It is true that Honda pays well. Their benefit plan is reasonably attractive. But that doesn't mean there couldn't be a bitter fight later on."[42]

Laarman's concession was an important one. If the company paid well and offered good benefits, it indeed was a challenge to convince workers that they would benefit substantially by paying union dues. Clearly the UAW would have preferred Honda to be an abusive employer that exploited its workforce under brutal circumstances. In the absence of oppressive conditions, however, the relevancy of the UAW could be questioned. As for Laarman's prediction that a bitter dispute could emerge at a later date, surely Honda would do what it could to prevent such a situation from arising.

Since the UAW could not rely on the issue of wages and benefits to woo Honda workers to join its ranks, it had to cite seemingly lesser complaints against the automaker. Dick Olsen, a public relations representative from the union, noted that compensation "has not been the cutting issue here. The issue is that there are not enough people on the line to do the work Honda wants."[43] The union therefore was not promising that it could secure better wages or benefits, but rather that it would try to force Honda to hire more people, presumably so that tasks could be accomplished at a more leisurely pace. The matter of staffing levels, however, was something that the employees easily could judge for themselves. If they thought that Honda was severely understaffed, workers should have responded to the union's message more positively. That the UAW canceled its call for an election, however, indicated that the issue of staff levels was not sufficiently compelling.

The UAW's charge that Honda did not hire ample people to accomplish its output was a traditional ploy. Logically, a larger workforce at a given facility translated into more members for the union. Once the UAW secured the right of representation, it also called upon companies to provide very specific job classifications for its work force. A given worker's area of responsibility would be narrowly defined. Should a task fall out of the boundaries of the worker's job description, an additional worker would be required to fulfill the need. By raising such issues at the bargaining table, the union would be able to swell its ranks. Among America's Big Three auto firms, factories typically had dozens of job descriptions that applied to various jobs throughout the plant. While this practice added to the UAW's membership, at the same time it burdened companies with additional workers on the payroll. From management's perspective, narrow job descriptions were an inefficient way in which to manufacture a product. To the UAW, however, the issue was one of fairness. If jobs were not specifically defined, management could take advantage of workers by having them perform excessive amounts of work. Given the gulf between labor and management's view of the issue, job descriptions were a constant matter of contention during labor negotiations throughout the American automobile industry.

Although Honda executives never publicly decried job descriptions or the union's call for additional workers on the assembly line, the two points likely would have been anathema to management. Honda did not have dozens of descriptions that applied to its workers. Rather, the company had only one description for its assembly line workers, that of "assembly associate." By so doing, the company had tremendous flexibility in assigning tasks to workers. Employees could be allocated jobs depending on individual skills or attributes. Moreover, as production schedules fluctuated due to market demand, workers could be reassigned as necessary. For example, in 1991, Honda had a larger inventory of Accords than it could sell for the time being. Instead of laying workers off until supply and demand reached equilibrium, as was the typical practice among the Big Three producers, Honda temporarily reassigned some production workers to perform other tasks in the plant until the sales picture improved.[44] This would have been impossible if Honda's workers were assigned strict job descriptions in a union shop.

Given a combination of factors, the UAW's task in organizing Honda's workers was a difficult one. The workforce was comprised of many young people to whom union membership was unknown. Since even union officials conceded that pay and benefits were good at Honda, the UAW was denied an obvious target in its organizing message. Though some employees might have preferred additional staff at the company to ease the work pace, the issue was not sufficiently compelling as a rallying point. The company had demonstrated its commitment to its personnel during periods of slack sales, something that could not be said by auto companies whose workers were represented by the UAW. With an embarrassing defeat a distinct possibility in the 1986 election, the UAW chose to save face and withdraw.

HONDA AND THE EEOC

Although Honda was able to stave off UAW criticism of its labor practices, charges by the Equal Employment Opportunity Commission (EEOC) were not as easily dismissed. Beginning in 1984, the federal agency launched two separate investigations into alleged discrimination in hiring and promotion practices at Honda. In both instances, the firm was accused of systemic discrimination as defined under Title VII of the Civil Rights Act of 1964. In the first case, Honda was accused of discriminating against 85 individuals on the basis of age, and in the second, discriminating against 377 employees on the basis of race and gender. As in most probes of this nature, events proceeded at a slow and deliberate pace.

That Honda was investigated for allegations of discrimination was not in itself remarkable. In a firm of its size, it could be expected that certain individuals might charge the company with discriminatory practices. Since Honda was hiring people at a brisk pace throughout the 1980s, those who were not hired could conceivably blame their circumstances on discrimination. Likewise, Honda employees who did not receive desired promotions might also cite discrimination as the cause of their fate. What made the Honda case newsworthy, therefore, was not the allegations of discrimination per se, but rather that Honda was the company involved. With Japanese politicians disparaging the quality of American labor and the presence of racial minorities, the EEOC's investigation seemed to confirm that Japanese firms operating in the U.S. harbored racist sentiments. Regardless of the probe's outcome, the mere investigation of Honda and its hiring and promotion policies was sufficient evidence for critics to render the company guilty.

Before the government concluded its investigation, however, Honda opted to reach a settlement with the disgruntled workers and the EEOC. The first case that was brought to a conclusion was the one involving age discrimination. In June 1987, Honda agreed to pay $451,111 in back wages to the 85 employees who alleged that the company discriminated against them.[45] As the basis for their claim, the 85 individuals said that they had been denied jobs in 1984 and 1985 because of their age, but then had been hired at a subsequent date.[46] The financial settlement therefore compensated the claimants for the time that had elapsed between their initial denial of employment, and their later hiring dates in 1986. Moreover, the agreement subjected the company's hiring practices to government oversight for the next three years. Honda also agreed to advertise in local newspapers and on radio stations that it encouraged people over the age of 40 to apply for jobs if any became available in the future.[47]

As part of the agreement, Honda was not formally cited for discrimination by the EEOC. Though a spokesman for the federal agency said that the settlement amounted to a plea of no contest by Honda, company executives were unwilling to admit any wrongdoing. According to Honda spokesman Roger Lambert, the auto maker had not "intentionally discriminated against anybody."[48] In the same briefing that he gave to the press, Lambert noted that, "We were following our usual hiring practices."[49] Of course, such a statement was open to interpretation, but presumably Lambert intended to say that the company had never discriminated.

The $451,111 settlement with the 85 employees meant that each person on average received over $5300 in compensation.[50] Though this sum was considerable, it paled in comparison to the settlement Honda made with 377 black and female employees approximately one year later in March 1988.

Like the earlier case, the EEOC had been investigating Honda for discrimination in hiring and promotion practices involving the 377 employees since September 1984. Though the workers were all on the Honda payroll by the time of the settlement, they alleged that they had been discriminated against when they initially applied for jobs beginning in 1983. The race and gender discrimination charges were more heated than the earlier case due to the sensitive issues involved. Japanese government officials did not make negative comments about older Americans, but as has been discussed, race was a different matter entirely.

The agreement reached with the workers and the EEOC was similar to the one reached in 1987. Honda was not formally charged with any criminal wrongdoing, but it did agree to pay substantial amounts of money to compensate the aggrieved parties in question. According to then-EEOC chairman Clarence Thomas, the settlement between the agency and the automaker,

> resolves an investigation of systemic discrimination under Title VII of the Civil Rights Act of 1964. It provides $6 million in monetary relief and seniority adjustments to approximately 370 specifically identified black and female individuals who applied for jobs at Honda between 1983 and 1986.[51]

Though the wording of the 1987 and 1988 settlements was similar, the monetary expense to Honda was considerably higher in the race and gender case.[52] On average, the 377 individuals in the case were to receive nearly $16,000 in payments, or more than three times as much as the 85 people in the earlier suit. According to sources at Honda, the company agreed to the settlement in order to "bring this [the investigation] to a close."[53]

Since the details of the EEOC's investigation were to remain undisclosed by terms of the agreement between the government and Honda, it is unclear what was uncovered in regard to the company's hiring policies. As to the composition of the employed workforce, a spokesman for the auto company told news reporters that of the firm's 5,430 employees, approximately 3.4 percent were African-American and 25.8 percent were women.[54] Taking into consideration the percentage of African-American employees, the firm's stated figures largely reflected the counties in which its plants were located. In Union County, Ohio, where the Marysville factory operated, 3.4 percent of the population was black around the time that the EEOC conducted its investigation. Logan County, where the East Liberty plant was located, had a smaller number of African-American residents, approximately 1.9 percent of its total population.[55] The residents within these two counties, however, could not fulfill Honda's staffing needs. Therefore, it is necessary to consider the demographic composition of surrounding counties from which Honda would be likely to hire employees in order to gauge how the company's work force reflected the potential applicant pool.

University of Michigan researchers Robert E. Cole and Donald R. Deskins applied the widely used "gravity model" in order to assess the racial composition of the Honda's likely hiring pool. According to Cole and Deskins,

> The gravity model allows us to measure explicitly the location of a specific manufacturing establishment in relation to the diverse location of potential employees by integrating measures of relative distance with measures of relative population size.[56]

In other words, the researchers set out to determine the radius from which Honda's workers commuted, and then used census data to ascertain the demographic composition of that area. They found that on the average, Honda's workers lived within 26 miles of the factory sites.[57] Interestingly, government census data found that most American workers had similar commuting patterns, with only 6.2 percent commuting to work beyond 30 miles.[58]

Although the percentage of African American employees at Honda compared favorably with the black population within the counties in which the company operated factories, Cole and Deskins found that the comparison was not as favorable when considering the black population within the 26-mile radius. Whereas Honda noted that 3.4 percent of its employees were African American, the University of Michigan researchers found that 10.5 percent of the population was black within the typical commuting distance to the factories.[59] Apparently the EEOC reached a similar conclusion during the course of its investigation. According to published reports, Honda agreed as part of its settlement with the EEOC to expand its recruiting base, with specific efforts aimed at hiring blacks. The news was particularly welcome to black civic leaders in Columbus, an area Honda agreed to focus upon, since its unemployment rate among African Americans was nearly 14 percent in 1988, roughly twice as high as the rate for the city as a whole.[60]

Was Honda guilty of illegal discrimination because its percentage of black employees was lower than that of surrounding communities? The debate of course is not new, nor is it restricted to the Honda case. Because Honda's surrounding communities were 10.5 percent black does not necessarily indicate that these individuals were part of the hiring pool. There could be dozens of reasons aside from race why the population in question was not hired for work at the Honda plants. Among the black residents near the company's plants surely were individuals too old, too young, or in some manner physically or mentally incapable of auto assembly work. A Union County official cited one case in point where EEOC investigators were misclassifying certain black residents as part of Honda's hiring pool.

I remember that we [Ernest Bumgarner, Glenn Irwin, and Max Robinson, Union County's three County Commissioners] were having a meeting one day with investigators from the government. They wanted to know all sorts of information about Honda, and of course we told them we would help in any way we could. During the course of our conversation, one guy came up with some astronomical figure as to the number of black people living in the county. I don't remember what that number was now, but it just seemed out of whack. The three of us have lived here all of our lives, and we all have a pretty good idea who lives around here. We just couldn't figure out where he was getting his numbers from. After the meeting had ended, we talked about this matter for quite some time among us. It wasn't making any sense until it dawned on us that his numbers included people from the women's prison that is on the edge of the county. The women there are included in the census figures since they technically live in the county, but obviously they weren't in any position to take up work at Honda. It's things like this that make you wonder sometimes . . .[61]

Although the Union County case may be an error in the extreme, it nevertheless demonstrated how population statistics could be misleading. Moreover, Cole and Deskins could not demonstrate that a significant number of local blacks had applied for jobs at Honda. Presumably the EEOC could not uncover such evidence either, for if it had, it would seem unlikely that it would have reached a settlement with the automaker, but instead would have taken the case to court. If people do not apply for work, is it the company's responsibility to seek them out? And if the question was answered in the affirmative, does that mean that Honda was guilty of discrimination, or rather lax recruiting efforts?

As to the number of women employed at Honda, it was even more difficult to judge the merits of Honda's hiring policies. Without question, the women that comprised 25.8 percent of the Honda work force did not mirror the percentage of women in adjacent communities, nor was there widespread outcry that it should. In part, Honda might have been spared allegations of widespread sexist hiring policies since the percentage of women working there was far greater than the percentage of women at General Motors, Ford, or Chrysler.[62] Nevertheless, the settlement covering the 377 aggrieved employees did include women who charged the firm with discrimination on the basis of gender. Given the thousands of women who worked at the automaker, however, the number of those filing a complaint with the EEOC was statistically modest.

In both local and national press accounts of the settlement, far more attention was given to the charges of racism than was given over to the charges of sexism. The uneven coverage may be attributed to the political sensitivity of racism and to statements from Japanese politicians that appeared racist in nature. While the statements made over the years would seem racist and worthy of American media attention, it was interesting that similar scrutiny was not focused on issues of gender. Although women in the U.S. have had a difficult struggle to make gains in formerly male dominated occupations such as heavy manufacturing, women in Japan had yet to make significant inroads at all. It indeed was rare for Japanese women to work in automobile factories, and rarer still for them to occupy management positions. Therefore, if one were looking for Honda's Japanese executives to bring with them prejudices that affected the company's hiring policy in the United States, one would expect to find few women on the payroll. That this was not the case cast doubt on the notion that Japanese managers could not or would not adapt to American society.

During visits to the parent company, it was clear to women working for Honda of America Manufacturing that they worked for a different employer than Honda Motor Company of Japan. On a business trip to Japan in November 1986, for example, Denise Garrison, the manager who coordinated parts delivery from original equipment manufacturers to the plant in Ohio, saw that job opportunities at the American subsidiary were different from those at the parent company.

> [Japanese managers] really didn't know what to think of me over there at first, so they put me with six or seven Japanese women [employees] who were secretaries, I think. When these women found out what I did, they just couldn't stop asking questions. They asked what I would say if a man tried to boss me around, and I just said that if I was in charge, I would say what to do. They just shook their heads.[63]

If Honda of America Manufacturing provided women with greater opportunities than the Tokyo-based Honda Motor Company, the majority of its female employees still were hourly and not salaried staff.[64] And regardless of one's gender or place in the corporate hierarchy, Honda preferred "fresh" employees with little or no experience in the automotive field. Indeed, it might have been this aspect of the company's hiring policy that resulted in a greater percentage of female employees than at America's Big Three auto manufacturers. For example, like her American male counterparts, Susan J. Insley, the firm's highest ranking woman, came to Honda with no manufacturing experience whatsoever. The company's vice president for corporate planning, Insley had formerly been a partner with the Columbus law firm of Vorys, Sater, Seymour & Pease, the same firm from which plant manager Scott Whitlock had been recruited earlier. And like Whitlock, Insley was not a stranger to Honda. Beginning in 1981, she had been assigned by her firm to work on tax-exempt bonds for pollution-control equipment at Honda's motorcycle plant in

Marysville. Later she worked on the development project surrounding the company's engine plant in Anna, Ohio.[65] Thus, in the case of some of its American executives at least, Honda may have desired fresh people, but not necessarily unknown people.

The question remains if Honda was guilty of intentional discrimination. As noted above, the EEOC did not charge Honda with discriminatory hiring policies. On the other hand, Honda did agree to pay a large sum to the 377 employees that alleged the firm discriminated against them by not hiring them when they had originally applied for jobs at the Honda plants. To some, the payment represented an admission of guilt by Honda, whereas others viewed the settlement as a relatively simple way for the company to put the matter behind them. As to the role of race in selecting sites for American factories on the part of Japanese firms, Cole and Deskins found that demography was a matter of consideration. In an interview they conducted with an official from the Japan External Trade Organization (JETRO), the researches found that,

> The Tokyo office of JETRO provides detailed census tract information for the United States to Japanese companies wishing to invest in this country [the U.S.A.] The official informed us that companies routinely examine these data when weighing possible plant locations. In addition, he said that racial composition of the population near the sites was one of the things that they usually investigated. JETRO's extensive publications discussing the characteristics of the site locations in given states routinely report racial structure (though no specific advice is given to avoid blacks). From the perspective of Japanese managers, these decisions are perhaps not so surprising. As one Japanese executive explained, Japanese managers consider it their job to recreate the successful operations they have in Japan, which implies 'how do we get American workers to act like Japanese.'[66]

The quote from the Japanese executive that managers seek American workers who are likely to accept a Japanese-style workplace might indicate that the managers look beyond race when evaluating the composition of their work force. Although Cole and Deskins did not explore his comments further, a Canadian auto industry consultant found that demographic composition in general, and not just race in particular, figured into the site selection process. According to Dennis Des Rosiers,

> They [the Japanese] ask for profiles of the community by ethnic background, by religious background, by professional makeup. They want to know how many accountants there are in the area versus how many farmers. Those are key variables. . . . There are demographic aspects that they like. They like a high

German content. Germans have a good work ethic—well-trained, easy to train, they accept things. . . . They probably don't like other types of profiles.[67]

While consideration of race thus may enter into the site selection process, it was not the sole demographic characteristic that Japanese managers weighed.

By way of conclusion, Cole and Deskins compared the hiring patterns between Japanese and American manufacturing firms. In short, they explored the issue of whether Japanese companies were more focused on racial composition in site selection than their American counterparts. The matter bore consideration since critics of the Japanese auto firms argued that indeed the Japanese were more racially biased than American auto firms that employed large numbers of blacks.

However, a simple comparison between the Japanese auto companies and America's Big Three was misleading. Many of the blacks employed by the Big Three, for example, had been hired during the tight employment markets of the 1960s and seventies, and were protected by seniority when massive auto industry layoffs became prominent in the 1980s, thereby boosting the percentage of black employees at American auto plants. Moreover, in the rare instances when an American automaker built a new plant during the 1980s, as in the case of the General Motors Saturn facility in Tennessee, it was contractually obligated to offer the new jobs to its employees that had been previously laid off. Indeed, no new workers could be hired at Saturn until *all* laid off G.M. workers across the country had been given the opportunity to relocate to Tennessee. Thus, when critics pointed to new American auto plants and noted that they still employed a higher percentage of black workers than Japanese-owned auto facilities, the comparison was not entirely fair since the employees had been culled from the ranks of the companies' former workers.

This being the case, Cole and Deskins compared the Japanese hiring patterns to those American manufacturing firms that were in fact building new factories that required a new workforce. In so doing, the researchers found that the Japanese companies were perhaps not so different from American firms after all.

If our own companies were growing rapidly and seeking new plant locations, would they not be building them in many of the same places as the Japanese? Indeed, analysis of the data from areas that are experiencing rapid growth (such as the high-tech sector) led researchers . . . to conclude that black share of a metropolitan area's population is negatively associated with high-tech jobs and plant locations. Industrial development specialists in state government report that they are often asked by American firms in a variety of industries to eliminate from consideration plant sites in counties with 30 percent or more black population. All of this ought to provide food for thought for those tempted to use our data for simple Japan bashing.

> Even if Japanese thresholds are lower, all this looks in principle quite similar to the practices we have just been describing. The fact that Japanese managers seem to voice racist sentiments should not be interpreted to mean that they are necessarily more racist than American managers. It is clear that many have yet to learn the American taboos with regard to talking about race. By telling state officials that they don't want sites near minority areas, the Japanese might simply be telling white American state officials what they think these officials would like to hear and what they think is appropriate under the circumstances. White American managers may simply be more subtle in their behavior toward blacks rather than any less racist than the Japanese.[68]

Indeed, given the high profile that Japanese firms had received in the press during the 1980s, it was reasonable to conclude that they were being unfairly singled out for what was, after all, a widespread American practice.

In the end, it is unwarranted to conclude that Honda located in factories in rural Ohio simply as a means of avoiding a black work force. Though race probably was a consideration in the site selection process, it was only one among many factors. Given the company's long struggle against the United Automobile Workers, it was apparent that it was more concerned with the unionization of its employees than with racial or gender issues. The desire for a "fresh" work force open to new ideas about personnel management necessarily meant that Honda would not locate in America's traditional industrial cities that indeed may have had a larger minority population. If it had located in a city such as Detroit, Cleveland, or St. Louis, preconceived notions of employee-management relations could have heavily influenced Honda's pool of potential workers, making a unionized work place more likely. Perhaps more than anything else, Honda feared that its methods of manufacturing would have been hampered in a unionized setting. And if the company could not build cars in the manner it had perfected over the years, could it in fact succeed in transplanting itself to American soil? Corporate executives apparently thought not.

That Honda was charged with union bashing, sexism, and racism was more reflective of American frustration with its own societal conditions than with illegal activities on the part of the automaker. With the declining influence of labor unions, as well as an evident stagnation in the economic advance of African-Americans, the 1980s found various groups disaffected and disappointed with recent trends throughout the country. When the automaker opted to ply its trade in unconventional setting using novel organizational methods, it stood out as an easy target for those looking to advance their causes and vent their anger. The UAW and the EEOC were powerful and resourceful organizations; if Honda had been in violation of American labor laws, the union and the government would have prevailed in the courts. There were simply too many forces arrayed against Honda for it to have escaped justice. In the final analysis, Honda had to ensure that the billions of dollars it invested in American manufacturing facilities accomplished its mission of building high quality passenger cars in the United States. That the company was not a clone of its American counterparts was an intentional choice. Indeed, to the millions of Americans who bought its products, it was a virtue that Honda could pursue its way.

NOTES

1. David E. Sanger, "A Top Japanese Politician Calls U.S. Work Force Lazy," *The New York Times*, January 21, 1992, D1. Sakurauchi's comments were delivered to supporters in Masuda City.

2. David E. Sanger, "A Trade Mission Ends in Tension as the 'Big Eight' of Autos Meet," *The New York Times*, January 10, 1992, A1.

3. Michael Wines, "Export Goal Unmet," *The New York Times*, January 10, 1992, A1.

4. David E. Sanger, "A Trade Mission Ends in Tension as the 'Big Eight' of Autos Meet," *The New York Times*, January 10, 1992, A1.

5. Barnaby J. Feder, "Blunt Talk by Iacocca, Just Back from Japan," *The New York Times*, January 11, 1992, 33, 44.

6. David E. Sanger, "A Top Japanese Politician Calls U.S. Work Force Lazy," *The New York Times*, January 21, 1992, D11.

7. Susan Chira, "2 Papers Quote Japanese Leader on Abilities of Minorities in U.S.," *The New York Times*, September 24, 1986, A12. There was a dispute over the word "intellectual" that was in parentheses in the two Japanese newspapers that originally carried the story, *Yomiuri Shimbun* and *Tokyo Shimbun*. Both newspapers asserted that that Nakasone implied that the intellectual level of Americans was lower because of the presence of minority groups. A spokesman for the Prime Minister later stated that the papers had been mistaken and that Nakasone meant that America's literacy rate was lower because of minorities. In either case, furor erupted in the U.S. over the remarks.

8. Susan Chria, "Tokyo Again Astir Over Racial Slight," *The New York Times*, July 26, 1988, A10.

9. U.S. Department of Labor, *Monthly Labor Review, December 1991* (Washington: Bureau of Labor Statistics, 1991), 114.

10. Steven G. Craig et. Al., *The Economic Impact of Honda's U.S. Operations: Production, Sales and Distribution, and Technology Transfer* (Houston: University of Houston, Department of Economics, 1994), Table 4.

11. Yoshino Hiroyuki, "Honda Way Workers Not Lazy," *Business First: The Business Newspaper of Greater Columbus*, March 16, 1992, 11.

12. Brian S. Moskal, "Supervision (Or Lack of It): How you manage, don't manage, or overmanage may determine other aspects of your business strategy and whether you'll be ranked at the head of the manufacturing class," *Industry Week*, December 03, 1990, 56.

13. Brian S. Moskal, "Supervision (Or Lack of It)," *Industry Week*, December 03, 1990, 56–57.

14. Dale D. Buss and John Bussey, "Japanese Management Confronts U.S. Union in Election at Honda," *The Wall Street Journal* December 27, 1985, 11.

15. "NLRB Will Accuse Honda of Violations, Auto Workers Say," *The Wall Street Journal*, October 07, 1980, 41.

16. Jerry Condo, "NLRB Rules for Worker in Hat Fuss," *Columbus Citizen-Journal*, October 23, 1981, 20.

17. Robert L. Simison, "UAW Blows Its Top Over Ban on the Use of Its Caps at Plant," *The Wall Street Journal*, June 24, 1980, 14.

18. Jerry Condo, "NLRB Rules for Worker in Hat Fuss," *Columbus Citizen-Journal*, October 23, 1981, 20.

19. Robert W. Reiss, "Union Steps Up Pressure on Honda," *The Columbus Dispatch*, March 31, 1985, 3B.

20. "Honda, UAW Reach 1st-of-a-Kind Labor Agreement," *The Columbus Dispatch*, April 23, 1982, 9B; "Honda of America Drops Opposition to UAW's Drive," *The Wall Street Journal*, April 26, 1982, 5.

21. "UAW Wins in Vote at Honda Plant," *Columbus Citizen-Journal*, July 11, 1981, 15.

22. Dale D. Buss and John Bussey, "Japanese Management Confronts U.S. Union in Election at Honda," *The Wall Street Journal*, December 27, 1985, 11.

23. Masayoshi Kanabayashi, "Honda's Accord: How a Japanese Firm Is Faring on Its Dealings with Workers in U.S.," *The Wall Street Journal*, October 02, 1981, 25.

24. Brian S. Moskal, "Supervision (Or Lack of It)," *Industry Week*, December 03, 1990, 55.

25. Honda would be careful, however, not to hire people based solely on the criteria of their views on unions. United States Federal Code Title 29, Chapter 7, Section 158 (3) prohibits employers from screening applicants with regard to pro- or anti-union sentiments.

26. "Honda Names Plant Manager," *The Columbus Dispatch*, January 02, 1985, 6E.

27. Honda Names Plant Manager," *The Columbus Dispatch*, January 02, 1985, 6E.

28. United States Federal Code, Title 29, Chapter 7, Section 159 (e).

29. "NLRB Upholds UAW," *The Wall Street Journal*, July 31, 1984, C7.

30. Bill Atkinson, "Auto Workers 'Air' Grievances Against Honda," *Business First of Greater Columbus*, February 04, 1985, 3.

31. Bill Atkinson, "Auto Workers 'Air' Grievances Against Honda," *Business First of Greater Columbus*, February 04, 1985, 3.

32. Bill Atkinson, "Auto Workers 'Air' Grievances Against Honda," *Business First of Greater Columbus*, February 04, 1985, 3.

33. "Honda Rejects a Request by UAW for Recognition," *The Wall Street Journal*, November 01, 1985, 25.

34. Dale D. Buss and John Bussey, "Japanese Management Confronts U.S. Union in Election at Honda," *The Wall Street Journal*, December 27, 1985, 11.

35. Robert W. Reiss, "Honda Workers Will Vote on Forming Union," *The Columbus Dispatch*, December 15, 1985, 3B.

36. Robert W. Reiss, "Honda Workers Will Vote on Forming Union," *The Columbus Dispatch*, December 15, 1985, 3B.

37. Robert W. Reiss, "Honda Union Election Postponed," *The Columbus Dispatch*, December 17, 1985, 1B.

38. Diane Solov, "Honda Says Union Charges Mask Lack of Votes," *Business First of Greater Columbus*, December 23, 1985, 10.

39. "Unionization Vote at Honda on Hold," *The Columbus Dispatch*, February 11, 1986, E1.

40. Christopher A. Amatos, "Election Canceled at Honda," *The Columbus Dispatch*, March 18, 1986, 1A.

41. Barnet D. Wolf, "Japanese Plants Will be Organized, UAW Leader Says," *The Columbus Dispatch*, March 17, 1987, 1E.

42. Bill Atkinson, "Auto Workers 'Air' Grievances Against Honda," *Business First of Greater Columbus*, February 04, 1985, 3.

43. Robert W. Reiss, "Honda Workers Will Vote on Forming Union," *The Columbus Dispatch*, December 15, 1985, 3B.

44. "Honda Stores 2,000 Accords as U.S. Sales Lag," *The Columbus Dispatch*, March 06, 1991, 1F.

45. "Honda to Pay for Age Discrimination," *The Columbus Dispatch*, June 02, 1987, 1E.

46. David Wagman, "After Settlement, Honda Still Faces EEO Charges," *Business First of Greater Columbus*, June 08, 1987, 9.

47. David Wagman, "After Settlement, Honda Still Faces EEO Charges," *Business First of Greater Columbus*, June 08, 1987, 9.

48. David Wagman, "After Settlement, Honda Still Faces EEO Charges," *Business First of Greater Columbus*, June 08, 1987, 9; "Honda to Pay Back Wages to Settle Age Bias Charges," *The Wall Street Journal*, June 03, 1987, 17.

49. "Honda to Pay Back Wages to Settle Age Bias Charges," *The Wall Street Journal*, June 03, 1987, 17.

50. The exact Details of the settlement remain unknown. As part of the agreement between Honda and the EEOC, the settlement was to remain confidential, and therefore it is unknown if each claimant received identical compensation. In all likelihood, the payment to each individual varied somewhat depending upon when one was initially denied employment, but was then subsequently hired. The average payment of $5300 is therefore intended for illustrative purposes.

51. George Embrey, "Honda to Pay Discrimination Penalties," *The Columbus Dispatch,* March 24, 1988, 1A.

52. Under the terms of the agreement, the EEOC was barred from releasing details of the investigation, the circumstances that led to the complaint, or conditions of the settlement itself. According to a spokeswoman from the federal agency, even the wording of the press release was negotiated between the EEOC and Honda. See Michael McQueen and Joseph B. White, "Blacks, Women at Honda Unit Win Back Pay," *The Wall Street Journal*, March 24, 1988.

53. Michael McQueen and Joseph B. White, "Blacks, Women at Honda Unit Win Back Pay," *The Wall Street Journal*, March 24, 1988, 2.

54. George Embrey, "Honda to Pay Discrimination Penalties," *The Columbus Dispatch*, March 24, 1988, 1A.

55. U.S. Department of Commerce, *1990 Census of the Population: Social and Economic Characteristics, Ohio*, Table 6, 28–32.

56. Robert E. Cole and Donald R. Deskins, Jr., "Racial Factors in Site Location and Employment Patterns of Japanese Auto Firms in America," *California Management Review* 31 (Fall 1988): 12.

57. Robert E. Cole and Donald R. Deskins, Jr., "Racial Factors in Site Location and Employment Patterns of Japanese Auto Firms in America," *California Management Review* 31 (Fall 1988): 12.

58. Bureau of the Census, "The Journey to Work in the United States: 1979," *Current Population Reports*, Special Studies Series P-23 Number 122 (Washington: Department of Commerce, 1982), 5.

59. Robert E. Cole and Donald R. Deskins, Jr., "Racial Factors in Site Location and Employment Patterns of Japanese Auto Firms in America," *California Management Review* 31 (Fall 1988): 12.

60. George Embrey, "Honda to Pay Discrimination Penalties," *The Columbus Dispatch*, March 24, 1988, 1A.

61. Union County Commissioner Glenn W. Irwin, interview with author, June 17, 1994.

62. George Embrey, "Honda to Pay Discrimination Penalties," *The Columbus Dispatch*, March 24, 1988, 1A.

63. Barnet D. Wolf, "Top Female Employee Enjoys Honda Challenges," *The Columbus Dispatch*, June 14, 1987, 2G.

64. Barnet D. Wolf, "Top Female Employee Enjoys Honda Challenges," *The Columbus Dispatch*, June 14, 1987, 2G.

65. Barnet D. Wolf, "Top Female Employee Enjoys Honda Challenges," *The Columbus Dispatch*, June 14, 1987, 2G.

66. Robert E. Cole and Donald R. Deskins, Jr., "Racial Factors in Site Location and Employment Patterns of Japanese Auto Firms in America," *California Management Review* 31 (Fall 1988): 18.

67. Doug Williamson, "Japanese Bias Comes to Light in Hiring Plans," *Windsor Star Special Report: Jobs 2000*, October 29, 1987, 14.

68. Robert E. Cole and Donald R. Deskins, Jr., "Racial Factors in Site Location and Employment Patterns of Japanese Auto Firms in America," *California Management Review* 31 (Fall 1988): 20.

Chapter Six

Selecting the Best

Firms opening new facilities make a point of selecting sites with minimal black populations. This is especially true of foreign-owned corporations, an increasing source of American employment. Thus Toyota located an assembly plant in Kentucky's Harlan County, in which 95 percent of the residents are white . . .[1]

—Andrew Hacker, *Two Nations: Black and White, Separate, Hostile, Unequal.*

Just as Honda came under scrutiny for its hiring policies and the comparatively small percentage of minorities on its payroll, so too did Toyota Motor Manufacturing, U.S.A. In his 1992 diatribe on racial tension and bias in America, professor Andrew Hacker singled out Toyota as an employer that was loath to hire blacks. Like so many others before him, Hacker argued that demographic composition was a decisive factor in Toyota's site selection process. Since employers could not be too obvious in their efforts to exclude blacks lest they invite exhaustive investigations by the EEOC, he maintained that a favorite strategy for employers was to locate their facilities in geographic locations where few blacks lived. Given Hacker's passion and persuasive anecdotal evidence, it is easy for a reader to be taken in by his argument. Upon close examination, however, questions arise about the Hacker proposition.

On the most basic level, Hacker's case against Toyota needs to be scrutinized because of his inaccurate examples. For example, his claim that the company's factory is located in Harlan County is simply incorrect. Toyota's Georgetown factory is located in Scott County, well over 100 miles from Harlan. It is perhaps a small error, but it nevertheless indicates a lack of attention to detail. As for the matter of racial composition, the 1990 Federal census reported that Scott County's black population was 6.3 percent, quite nearly reflecting the 7.1 percent of blacks in Kentucky as a whole.[2] It was therefore not a particularly Caucasian county, but one that was essentially representative of the state. That the Commonwealth of Kentucky spent tens of millions of dollars promoting Scott County to the automaker also escaped Hacker's attention. His focus was to argue that race was the decisive determinant in site selection; perhaps evidence of other factors would have muddied his stance.

In raising the issue of local racial composition, Hacker made an erroneous assumption that Toyota hired primarily from the county in which its plant was located. Unlike Honda, which did in fact hire its employees from surrounding communities, Toyota never established a policy in regard to commuting distances. As noted in Chapter IV, Toyota used the Kentucky Department of Employment Services to initially screen applicants for employment. By so doing, the firm opened itself to applications from throughout the Commonwealth, in addition to those from surrounding states. According to a study conducted by the University of Louisville, the result was that the majority of Toyota applicants did not live in close proximity to Scott County.

Most applicants for these [Toyota] positions (82.9 percent) are Kentuckians. Other states significantly represented are Ohio (4.7 percent), West Virginia (2.6 percent), Indiana (1.9 percent), and Tennessee (1.4 percent). Within Kentucky, the geographical distribution of applicants was concentrated in Scott County and its seven adjacent counties (Bourbon, Fayette, Franklin, Grant, Harrison, Owen and Woodford), and in the state's major urban areas. The local region represented 36.7 percent of applicants for managerial positions, 23.7 percent of applicants for skilled worker positions and 22.5 percent of unskilled worker applicants. Jefferson County represented 10.4 percent of all applicants. Fayette County alone accounted for 25.5 percent of all managerial applications.[3]

As the University of Louisville study demonstrated, less than 40 percent of applicants for managerial positions came from the eight counties surrounding the Toyota plant, and less than one quarter of those applying for skilled and unskilled hourly positions hailed from the local area. The latter figures are particularly important since the vast majority of Toyota's positions were in the hourly skilled and unskilled categories. As for the racial composition of the eight counties in question, on average 7.2 percent of the inhabitants was African American, slightly greater than the Commonwealth's 7.1 percent figure.[4] Despite what critics suggested, most Toyota applicants were not from the counties surrounding the plant, and among those that were, their counties shared the identical racial profile with that of the state.

Regardless of what census data indicated, however, critics were not appeased. By this thinking, there had to be sinister reasons that Toyota chose

Kentucky, and for those interested in emphasizing racial issues, there were always racist quotes by Japanese leaders to fall back upon.[5] Without question, it was true that Kentucky's proportion of blacks was lower than the national average, but surely not sufficiently so as to convince a hardened racist management to locate there.

LOCAL CONCERNS

Not surprisingly, minority groups in Kentucky were interested in monitoring Toyota's hiring policies. While they were not about to decry the company's decision to locate in their community, they did want assurances that the ill-chosen remarks of Japanese leaders were not reflective of Toyota management as a whole. In October 1986, representatives of the Scott County and Lexington chapters of the NAACP, the Urban League, and the Lexington Human Rights Commission conducted a press conference to express their concerns over Toyota's future hiring policies. Although the company would not actually begin hiring employees in large numbers until early 1987, thousands of applications had already been received, and civic leaders wanted assurances that black applicants would be fairly treated.

Interestingly, it became apparent at the press conference that the minority groups were as concerned with the state agency processing applications as they were with the automaker itself. According to Bias Tilford of the Scott County branch of the NAACP, his chief concern was that the Commonwealth of Kentucky exercise fairness in screening black job applicants.[6] State officials were quick to say that they would be absolutely fair in the initial screening process, but that ultimately hiring decisions would be made by Toyota itself. At their own press conference one day later, Toyota executives responded to minority concerns. Company vice president Alex Warren, Jr. insisted that, "Toyota follows all equal employment practices."[7]

Toyota officials were caught off guard by the minority group press conference since they had been in contact with black leaders in Scott County for nearly six months. Toyota's U.S. liaison manager Jeff Smith said that the auto maker had met with about 15 members of the local black community, including Scott County NAACP leader Bias Tilford, and that the firm had considered their dialogue to be open and productive. Smith said that, "The point he [Bias Tilford] brought up was that blacks are not looking for a leg up. We assured him that Toyota has no discrimination in its hiring practices."[8] Regardless of whether or not blacks were "looking for a leg up," Toyota announced that it intended to develop an affirmative action plan at a later date.[9]

On 05 December 1986, officials from Toyota, the state, and representatives of local and state civil rights groups met in Lexington to discuss issues involving hiring practices and race. Although the company had been in contact with African American leaders in Scott County, this meeting included representatives from regional black organizations that had participated in the October press conference. The December meeting apparently did much to address the concerns the black community had about Toyota. According to P.G. Peeples, the director of the Lexington-Fayette County Urban League,

> We are encouraged about the responses and commitments from them [Toyota]. Toyota is committed to providing us with information about their hiring and recruitment process, so that we will be in a position to advocate for and recruit minorities for full participation.[10]

Though Peeples may have been optimistic that Toyota was going to keep his and other similar groups informed about the hiring process, there was always the possibility that he would not be quite as pleased with the details of the hiring process itself.

BUILDING A WORK FORCE FROM SCRATCH

There was a time in the United States when jobs in the auto industry were plentiful. For an automobile company to weed through tens of thousands of applications was unthinkable, and the concept of a "hiring process" was exactly that—a concept. In cities such as Detroit and Flint, jobs on an auto assembly line were easy to acquire. Elaborate screening procedures did not exist. If a job seeker had a friend or relative working in a car plant that could vouch for his character, the chances of being hired were somewhat improved. But on the whole, if there was work available, the auto companies hired people on a first-come basis. As former General Motors assembly line worker Ben Hamper recalled,

> it was not the least bit uncommon for a man to be fired at one factory on a Friday and be given the red carpet treatment at another automotive facility across town on Monday. If this is Tuesday, this must be Buick. If this is Thursday, how 'bout AC Spark Plug. During the sixties there were ten or so factories in Flint workin' three shifts per day and in this kind of boomtown climate even the beggars could afford to be choosers. 'Sign here, Mr. Beerbreath. So glad to have you collapse on our doorstep.'[11]

Though Hamper may have exaggerated the ease with which one could secure work in Flint during the 1960s, his point was rooted in fact. If one could regularly report to the assembly line, there was work to be had in the American auto industry.

Of course, the situation changed entirely during the late 1970s and the 1980s. Over the course of several years, the American auto companies laid off hundreds of thousands of workers. In the rare cases when new plants opened, auto companies rarely hired new workers since they had contractual obligations with the UAW to first offer jobs to workers who had been previously laid off. In the event that workers were rehired, they were called back according to seniority. Quite simply, the opportunities for new workers had severely diminished.

In the case of Toyota, however, the situation was entirely different. Since the firm did not have any agreements with the UAW, it could hire whomever it pleased. This was not an opportunity to be taken lightly. With thousands of employment applications pouring in, Toyota could narrow its applicant pool by means of rigorous screening. In so doing, the automaker could tailor its work force to meet precisely the criteria that it set forth; it did not have to settle for those who showed up at the factory gate. The Toyota hiring process therefore was very different from Hamper's description of Flint in the 1960s.

> Even someone applying for the lowest-paying job on the shop floor goes through at least 14 hours of testing, administered on Toyota's behalf by state employment offices and Kentucky State University. The initial tests cover reading and math, manual dexterity, "job fitness" and, for skilled trades, technical knowledge. Then come the workplace simulations, designed by Development Dimensions International, a Pittsburgh-based consultant to Toyota.
>
> There are also mock production lines, where applicants assemble tubes or circuit boards. The idea is to identify applicants who can keep to a fast pace, endure tedious repetition and yet stay alert. The tube-assembly procedure is intentionally flawed and applicants are asked how they would improve it.[12]

Toyota considered the entire hiring procedure to consist of eight phases, although not every employee was required to be assessed in all 8 areas. According to the company, the hiring process was organized as follows:

Phase I: Orientation/Application
              Fill out an application and view a videotape of the Toyota work
              environment and selection system process (1 hour)

Phase II: Technical Skills Assessment
              Pencil/paper tests

—General Knowledge test (2 hours)
—Job fit inventory (30 minutes)
—Tool and Die or general maintenance test
(6 hours, skilled trade applicants only)

Phase III: Interpersonal Skills Assessment
—Group and individual problem-solving activities (4½ hours)
—Production assembly simulation
(6 hours, production applicants only)

Phase IV: Leadership Skills Assessment
Coaching, scheduling, and problem-solving activities
(6 hours, group leader/team leader applicants only)

Phase V: Technical Performance Assessment
Performing a series of technical tasks
(4 hours, skilled trade applicants only)

Phase VI: Toyota Assessment
Group interview and evaluation (2 hours)

Phase VII: Health Assessment
Physical Exam and drug/alcohol tests (2½ hours)

Phase VIII: On-the-job Observation
Observation and coaching on-the-job after being hired
(6 months)[13]

According to company spokesperson Linda Broadus, Toyota wanted to hire "seekers and problem solvers," not simply people with manual dexterity.[14] That being the case, applicants first had to perform well on the General Aptitude Test Battery (GATB) that was given during Phase II in the hiring process before advancing to the dexterity and technical portions of the test. The GATB was a standardized, multiple-choice examination that was recognized and used throughout the world. The two-hour test was administered and scored by the Kentucky Department of Education Services as part of the incentive package the Collins administration reached with Toyota. The GATB was offered at 27 different sites in Kentucky in order to make it accessible to citizens throughout the state.[15]

Once an applicant took the GATB, the exam was scored at various threshold levels appropriate for different kinds of employment. Toyota insisted that all applicants be graded in a category of scores known as "job-family three" if they were to advance to other portions of its hiring tests. This was a high requirement to set since, according to test coordinator John Hodgkin, job-family three was typically used to evaluate, "the guy on the top who sits in the front office .

. . the guys that make the big decisions."[16] By any definition, Toyota had established a very high standard indeed for its production workers.

Not surprisingly, of the 70,000 applicants who had taken the GATB through 1990, only 20 percent were able to proceed to the next level of tests.[17] Should an applicant perform satisfactorily on the remaining battery of tests, the next stage in the hiring process was an interview with Toyota personnel representing various company departments. Only five percent of applicants ever proceeded to the interview phase. According to Toyota personnel manager Dewey Crawford, by then "we're going to know more about these people than perhaps any company has ever known about people."[18] If the interview went smoothly for an applicant, the final steps toward eventual employment were a physical examination and a drug test. Once a person was hired to come on board at Toyota, there was still a probationary period to ensure that the company and the individual would be a good fit after all.

From the company's perspective, all of these measures made good sense. Though together the tests took several hours to complete, the effort could be easily justified since the people Toyota hired in the 1980s could well be in its employ for decades to come. Because managers throughout the world recognized that it was less expensive to retain valuable employees than it was to face turnover and training of new personnel, it was desirable to hire good employees in the first place. Moreover, the tests Toyota administered were specifically designed to render a quality work force. Some portions of the tests, such as the GATB, were probably not as job-specific as, say, the dexterity tests, but nevertheless served to reveal ability. Toyota needed to sort through the thousands of applicants, and the tests provided a sound and systematic means to do so.

Despite the obvious advantages to administering employment tests, Toyota put itself at some risk. First, there was the consideration of time and money involved in the process. Though Kentucky paid for the administration and scoring of the tests, there remained a significant commitment on the part of Toyota to conduct and evaluate interviews. In the final analysis, the applicants were potential company employees, and therefore the selection of those employees still fell to company executives and department heads. Secondly, and of potentially far greater consequence to the automaker, was that the employment tests could run afoul of federal employment regulations. Beginning in the 1960s, the Supreme Court ruled that at the very least companies had to use hiring policies that were race neutral. There was nothing particularly surprising about the Court's position since it was merely affirming the law as prescribed in the 1964 Civil Rights Act and in the 14th Amendment to the Constitution. What became noteworthy over time, however, was the dampening effect the Court's decisions had on employment testing.

RUNNING THE RISK OF DUKE

Testing job applicants obviously did not originate with Toyota. For decades employers in various industries tested job applicants to ensure that they were suitable to perform tasks that were required of them. Quite typically employers might measure an applicant's manual dexterity or proficiency at conducting a given procedure. If the job in question required a specific skill, such as welding, carpentry, or plumbing, an applicant would often be tested in that area of expertise as well. Of course, testing a skilled worker was a different exercise from testing an unskilled one. It was relatively simple to judge the degree to which a craftsman was a talented welder, but it was another matter entirely to test an unskilled worker. Ideally, an employment test would indicate more than an applicant's dexterity, and might go beyond to help predict an applicant's future productivity. To meet the demand for such predictive tests, the field of industrial psychology blossomed.

Of course, an employment test has little value unless its predictive powers are reliable. By definition, though, the reliability of predictive tests could only be determined after the fact. Did tests actually help employers make informed hiring decisions, or would random hiring yield the same results? As the science of industrial psychology was refined, many employers found that testing applicants was indeed a useful, though hardly foolproof, exercise in which to engage. At the same time, evidence appeared to mount that employment tests could result in the under representation of certain groups in the workforce. In particular, concerns grew that employment tests had a disparate impact upon racial minorities. It was in this regard that court cases were filed to halt, or at least seriously alter, the use of employment tests.

There had long been suspicions that employment tests could be designed to deliberately discriminate against minorities. Different standards could be applied to whites and blacks, or perhaps tests could be devised in such a way to intentionally discriminate against minority applicants. By the provisions of Title VII of the 1964 Civil Rights Act, it became a clear violation of federal law to intentionally discriminate in hiring and promotion. In regard to employment tests, Title VII Section 703 (h) specifically outlined that they were legal, provided that they not be used in a discriminatory manner. According to the Section,

> . . . nor shall it be an unlawful employment practice for an employer to give and to act upon the results of any professionally developed ability test provided that such test, its administration or action upon the results is not designed, intended or used to discriminate because of race, color, religion, sex or national origin.[19]

On the face of it, the law was clear in its purpose. So long as tests were professionally developed and administered in a fair and unbiased manner, employers had every right to use them. Certainly as it pertained to Section 703 (h), Toyota appeared to have had no problem in regard to its elaborate testing procedures. Its tests were professionally developed, widely used, and administered by the Commonwealth of Kentucky at sites throughout the state. Nevertheless, the interpretation of Title VII was not as simple as the language of the law suggested. Over time, the Supreme Court and regulatory officials at the EEOC came to define discrimination very broadly. No longer were employers only guilty when they were found engaging in open and intentional discrimination, but also could be found in violation of Title VII if any of their employment practices appeared to have a negative impact on minorities. If an employer's workforce was found to have a statistical under-representation of a minority group, that employer could be found guilty of discrimination even if there was no harmful intent to damage individuals because of their race. If an employment test resulted in minorities being statistically underrepresented at a given company, the test could be in violation of Title VII. Toyota thus assumed a risk when it established highly competitive hiring requirements. If its resulting work force was not representative of the community in general, it could run afoul of federal employment law.

The most significant Supreme Court decision that impacted the use of employment tests was Griggs v. Duke Power Company (1971). Griggs was a class-action suit brought by 13 African-American employees of the Duke Power Company, a North Carolina electric utility firm. Throughout most of the company's history, Duke openly engaged in discriminatory practices, forbidding blacks from holding all but the least desirable jobs. Prior to 1965, when the 1964 Civil Rights Act became effective, the company restricted blacks to the labor department, "where the highest paying jobs paid less than the lowest paying jobs in the other four operating departments in which only whites were employed."[20] The jobs reserved for blacks were those in maintenance or coal shoveling; in addition to paying poorly, these jobs also held no promise for promotion. Deplorable as the situation was at Duke Power, however, it was hardly unique in the Jim Crow south.

With the passage of the Civil Rights Act and the provisions under Title VII, Duke abandoned its former employment practices and opened all positions to both black and white employees. Since 1955, Duke had required that all job applicants have a high school diploma in order to be hired, but with the enforcement of Title VII, the company furthermore required that applicants pass two professionally developed employment tests. These requirements applied to both blacks and whites, and appeared not to violate the standards set forth in Title VII Section 703 (h). Nevertheless, in the Griggs lawsuit, the petitioners argued that the hiring policies had a disparate impact upon black applicants, and therefore were in violation of Title VII.

Jack Greenberg, the NAACP attorney who managed the case, argued that the Duke requirements had a disparate impact on black applicants since they set standards too high for most African-Americans to meet. He did not argue that his individual clients were incapable of meeting the Duke standards, but that blacks as a group were unlikely to be able to do so. Indeed, Greenberg even acknowledged during oral arguments that he did not know how his clients fared on the tests.[21] The issue was one of group rights instead of the traditional judicial standard of individual rights.

In a unanimous ruling, the Supreme Court accepted Greenberg's argument that the tests discriminated against African-Americans since studies had shown that blacks performed worse than whites on measurements of educational achievement. Greenberg attributed the difference in test results to the inferior education African-Americans received in segregated schools, and the Court concurred. As further evidence, the Court noted statistics from the 1960 census showing that 34 percent of the white population in North Carolina had high school diplomas, whereas only 12 percent of the state's blacks did. The results of the inferior education were said to be reflected in an EEOC finding that showed 58 percent of whites achieved a passing score on the tests Duke used, while only 6 percent of black applicants did.[22] The Court ruled that because of the unequal results, using the test amounted to a violation of the Civil Rights Act. In his opinion on behalf of the Court, Chief Justice Burger wrote that,

> The objective of Congress in the enactment of Title VII is plain from the language of the statute. It was to achieve equality of employment opportunities and remove barriers that have operated in the past to favor an identifiable group of white employees over other employees. Under the Act, practices, procedures, or tests neutral on their face, and even neutral in terms of intent, cannot be maintained if they operate to "freeze" the status quo of prior discriminatory employment practices.[23]

Burger's opinion opened up whole new avenues in the enforcement of Title VII. Though he acknowledged that the Civil Rights Act sought equal employment opportunities, in effect his ruling said that tests such as those used by Duke were discriminatory because they did not show equality of results among the test-takers. Even if Duke was not intentionally discriminatory, the results of its hiring procedures appeared to be so, and thus were in violation of the law. Duke of course was not responsible for the education system in North Carolina, but nevertheless it had to make adjustments to its policies to take into account the flaws of inferior segregated schools. In effect, it was the guilty party for events that were beyond its control since the

> absence of discriminatory intent does not redeem employment procedures or testing mechanisms that operate as "built-in headwinds" for minority groups and are unrelated to measuring job capacity.[24]

In finding for the petitioners, the Supreme Court decision in Griggs v. Duke Power Company dealt a blow to corporate employment testing. The Court said that in order to set education standards and require minimum scores on employment tests, employers had the burden to demonstrate that the requirements were indeed necessary for employees to carry out the duties of the job in question. The touchstone of tests was business necessity. Of course, it would not be difficult for some employers to prove that its hiring policies were justified due to job demands, even if those policies resulted in few minorities being hired. Few would question, for example, that an airline needed to hire competent pilots, regardless of how that standard affected certain groups. For other employers, however, the standard set by the Court would not be nearly as easy to meet.

Companies such as Duke Power, and most manufacturers for that matter, faced great difficulty in proving that an applicant needed a high school degree or a good test score in order to carry out most entry-level jobs. It would be nearly impossible to prove that a high school education was needed to shovel coal or sweep a floor. An employer might rightly believe that in general its interests would be better served by a literate work force, but it was another matter entirely to prove in a court that it was a business necessity. The Griggs decision confronted employers with a variety of unattractive options. At one extreme, employers could abandon standards altogether and simply hire people on a first-come basis. If the resulting work force was still found wanting of significant minority representation, the employer could at least point to the fact it had no standards whatsoever and it could not control who showed up at the employment office seeking work. For most employers, however, this would be an undesirable option that would yield unpredictable results. Another option could be to continue to require tests, but hold different groups to different standards. This concept, known as racial norming, might allow some apparently less qualified applicants to gain employment, but would enable the employer to demonstrate good will toward various groups, regardless of test performance. Finally, employers could opt to have a percentage of minorities on their payroll that mirrored the overall minority population of the location in which their business was located. In combination with racial norming, employers could use this final option as a means to avert lawsuits charging disparate impact. Group rights could not be said to be trampled upon if the work force reflected the racial composition of the community at large.

In establishing elaborate testing procedures, Toyota risked legal challenges similar to those that Duke Power had faced. There were, however, important differences between the two companies that were to the benefit of Toyota. Perhaps the most outstanding difference between the two was that Duke clearly had a record of racial discrimination in its past. Though the company changed its policies once federal law proscribed its behavior, it nevertheless had a well-established history of discrimination. Employees and job applicants alike would be on the lookout for a return to the company's former ways. Moreover, the use of tests and the establishment of standards that did not previously exist served to raise suspicions that Duke was merely searching for alternative ways in which to maintain the status quo without violating the letter of the law. Toyota, on the other hand, was in another position entirely. It had no employment history whatsoever in Kentucky, and certainly had never been a part of the pre-1965 Jim Crow environment. Though its employment tests were daunting, at least it could not be accused of attempting to retain a segregated hiring system.

Unlike Duke Power, Toyota did not require applicants to have a high school diploma. It was unclear, however, if its decision was informed by the Griggs ruling. According to 1990 census figures, the percentage of whites and blacks in Kentucky that had the minimum of a high school education was nearly equal. Of persons aged 25 years and over, 61 percent of blacks had graduated from high school, compared to 65 percent of whites.[25] Though clearly more whites achieved high school degrees, the percentages were much closer than they had been in North Carolina in the 1960s. Thus, the requirement of a high school education would be less likely to have a dramatic disparate impact on Africa-American applicants. Nevertheless, by not specifically requiring a high school degree, Toyota spared itself from accusations that educational requirements had an unfair effect upon any applicant.

Given the rigorous standard that Toyota set in the GATB test, it would have been redundant to require a high school degree in any event. Since the company only selected candidates that scored well on the job-family three portion of the exam, it was nearly assured that at the very least a successful applicant would have a high school degree. According to test coordinators for Kentucky, there was a clear correlation between academic achievement and test performance.[26] Thus, the GATB cognitive section screened candidates quite satisfactorily.

Although Toyota did not require a minimum level of education, it nevertheless assembled a group of employees with a relatively high level of academic preparation. By 1992, Toyota's entire work force was comprised of high school graduates. More impressively yet, over 50 percent of its employees had education beyond high school, and nearly 25 percent had college degrees.[27] This impressive number of educated workers in an automobile plant was not lost on Toyota's public relations department; nearly every document or pamphlet that profiled the company's work force championed the educational data. It was clear that the company placed a value on an educated work force. The promotional literature suggested that literate, competent people were manufacturing the firm's products, not a group of dropouts or miscreants. In reality education might not have had a relationship with quality control, but the image was there to promote, and the company did so.

If Toyota was able to sidestep complications arising from requiring its employees to have a high school degree, the rigors of its testing methods were another matter entirely. To require an assembly line worker to successfully pass hours upon hours of tests and interviews was indeed quite a standard to set. Moreover, the question remained whether Toyota could meet the "business necessity" touchstone established in Griggs. Was it possible to prove that such measures were absolutely necessary in order for the company to do business? It would seem unlikely given that few manufacturers anywhere in the country required so much from its applicants. Nevertheless, Toyota had a few matters working in its favor that could forestall legal challenges to its elaborate hiring policies.

As a new business venture in the United States, Toyota needed to hire thousands of personnel in a relatively short period of time. The coming of the new Toyota plant turned into a major media event, and people from all over the region were ready to apply for work long before the first advertisements were printed. Unlike Duke Power and other existing businesses, Toyota was not adding a few workers to an established work force, but rather had to have a rational set of procedures to screen the tens of thousands of people who applied for work. Toyota also had a tremendous stake in hiring workers that could maintain a high level of quality control. The firm spent decades building a reputation as one of the world's finest automobile manufacturers; it could not risk its prestige by building inferior products in its new, multibillion-dollar American facility.

In Japan, the company recruited students directly from vocational high schools upon the recommendation of trusted guidance counselors. Lower-level managers such as foremen or group leaders often came from Japan's military, known as the Self-Defense Forces.[28] They in turn might recommend friends or family members for a job should one become available but, not willing to risk shame or embarrassment, could be trusted to only recommend those who were unquestionably reliable. Without such recruiting resources in the U.S., however, tests at least provided a degree of reassurance to Toyota's personnel planners.

In theory, it would seem that Toyota's tests would be poorly fashioned to meet the Griggs standard. After all, they were not designed to measure the fitness of an applicant to perform one specific task, but rather to measure one's broader aptitude. For many manufacturers it would indeed be difficult to argue that it was a business necessity for its employees to be broadly capable. The difference in Toyota's case, however, was due to its job descriptions. Like Honda, Toyota only had a few broad job descriptions for its factory personnel: team member, team leader, and group leader. Essentially these descriptions translated to assembly line worker, sub-foreman, and general foreman. An applicant who succeeded in securing a job with the company thus was not hired to perform one function, but would be called upon to perform dozens of different tasks.

These sweeping job descriptions were not merely foils to escape the scrutiny of the EEOC or other agencies concerned with hiring policies. To the contrary, Toyota workers switched jobs with line mates as frequently as every two hours, every day of the week.[29] Toyota noted that such regular changes lessened fatigue and monotony for production workers. This claim indeed made sense. Toyota furthermore required that workers be able to perform a wide variety of tasks, and to adapt to changes quickly. Both of these requirements supported the argument that broad tests were in fact a matter of business necessity.

Another matter working in Toyota's favor was that the tests were administered and scored by Kentucky officials. These were not people who worked for unknown testing firms with questionable credentials, but rather professionals from the State's Education Bureau. This was a useful alliance for Toyota to have struck. Since the state was paying for the tests to be taken at all 27 sites of the Department for Employment Services offices, it was in effect giving its approval of the exams. Although the score standards were set by Toyota, it would be impossible to overlook Kentucky's role in the process.

By September 1989, Toyota had approximately 4,000 workers producing the Camry model on two shifts. Given the number of applicants, and the rigors required by the firm, these individuals were obviously a select group. As far as minority performance on the tests was concerned, Toyota had avoided the challenges that Duke Power faced to its hiring requirements. Excluding its 70 Japanese employees, company figures indicated that approximately 13 percent of its workforce was African-American, nearly twice the average percentage of blacks living in the state as a whole.[30] Though there were thousands of disappointed people who could not meet the company standards, they could not charge that the firm's measures had a disparate impact on

African-American applicants. Interestingly, state figures indicated that of all Toyota job applicants, 13.2 percent were black, nearly mirroring the eventual composition of the workforce.[31] Perhaps more than any single factor, it was Toyota's relatively large representation of minorities on its payroll that spared its testing procedures from legal challenges.

Whether Toyota engaged in affirmative action was difficult to determine. Company representatives maintained that the firm simply hired the best possible candidates, despite the fact that it earlier promised to create an affirmative action plan. What was known, however, was that the company had to scale down the minimum scores that it would accept on the GATB for all candidates, regardless of race. This was not entirely surprising since it had set such an exceptional standard. When Toyota hired its very first employees, Kentucky testing officials noted that the automaker had only taken those applicants whose scores were above the 95th percentile of all test takers. Keeping in mind that Toyota was interested in people who scored well in the cognitive category, those first people to be hired were probably an exceptionally bright group of workers. It was unrealistic to hope that every person on the assembly line would be so talented. As the hiring process continued, therefore, Toyota considered candidates whose scores fell into lower percentile categories. In the final analysis, the company expanded its pool of applicants who were interviewed to those whose scores were near the 60-percentile range.[32] As a matter of privacy, Toyota would not release specific data concerning which employees fell into which percentile ranges.

Since 13 percent of the company's personnel were minorities, there was sufficient evidence to discredit claims that Toyota located in Kentucky so as to avoid minority employees. Perhaps if the company's work force precisely mirrored the percentage of blacks within the state, some question could legitimately remain about its intentions. Of course, hard statistical evidence did not necessarily mean that critics would pay any attention. But it did mean that Toyota was spared the entanglements with the EEOC that plagued Honda in the mid-1980s. It did not face investigations, nor did it pay out-of-court settlements as Honda had done. In the final analysis, Toyota's complicated hiring tests produced the desired results. In addition to providing the company with a qualified work force, it also gave the automaker a solid set of procedures to point to if its hiring methods were questioned.

THE ENDS JUSTIFY THE MEANS

The Toyota employment tests revealed a great deal about the company in general. As Japan's largest auto manufacturer, Toyota had long been noted for its conservative characteristics. While Honda was the company that took risks, be it from getting a relatively late start in the auto business to being the first Japanese automaker to build facilities in the United States, Toyota's reputation lay more with steady progress and attention to detail. It was Toyota that emphasized the concept of kaizen, or continual improvement, that became the industry model. The company was more concerned with product perfection than with technical innovation. In a similar fashion, its hiring procedures indicated a tendency toward risk aversion. Toyota obviously wanted the best possible work force, and long hours of objective tests held out the hope that its goal could be achieved. No other auto manufacturer in the United States, regardless of national origin, had ever approached the thoroughness with which Toyota screened job applicants. It was typical of Toyota; little was left to chance.

Such was the case when it came to hiring the American management team as well. Although Toyota did not screen its managers with the same tests it used for production workers, the firm nevertheless exercised caution. Interestingly, Toyota's approach suggested a very different philosophy compared to Honda when it came to assembling its management staff. Unlike its competitor, whose top American executives came with little industrial experience, Toyota's brass often came from other automotive companies. They were not "fresh people" who had never seen the inside of an auto plant before, but rather seasoned veterans who had spent their careers in the business. Toyota clearly wanted these executives' experience with the American auto industry to help the company in its new venture. Russell Scaffede, the plant manager of Toyota's power train facility, was a case in point. A 17-year veteran of General Motors before signing on with Toyota, Scaffede had seen the problems characterizing labor relations at his former employer that he hoped to avoid in his new post. As Scaffrede noted,

> The automotive industry within the United States is still working with an early 1900s production system. And there are many years of built-up animosities between labor and management that you hear about very regularly, that are very, very hard to try to break down and introduce new systems.[33]

Shortly after Toyota decided on the Kentucky site it hired Michael Dodge as its general manager. As the top ranking American on the production side of the business, Dodge too was an industry-insider with over 20 years experience. In addition to knowledge of auto manufacturing, Dodge had unique credentials that prepared him for a relationship with his new employers. After a 15-year tenure with Chrysler, Dodge went to work for Volkswagen of America in 1980, eventually becoming the assistant plant manager at Volkswagen's

Westmoreland, Pennsylvania assembly plant. There he worked closely with
the company's German executives, even taking a one-year position at Volkswagen's Wolfsburg plant.

In Dodge, Toyota found an executive who thus not only knew the auto
business, but who was also accustomed to working at an American subsidiary
of a foreign-owned automobile manufacturer. As for his new employer,
Dodge was impressed with the company's focus on the individual employee.
In a 1988 interview, he told a reporter for a Lexington, Kentucky newspaper
that Toyota's hiring tests were designed to find people who, "have very high
interpersonal skills." Given such a staff to manage, Dodge said that he was
confident the Georgetown plant would soon be producing the "number one
quality vehicle in the United States."[34] His words were to prove prophetic.

In July 1990, approximately one year after the first shift reached full production, the automotive assessment firm J.D. Power and Associates ranked
the company's Kentucky-made Camry third in its New Car Initial Quality
Survey among all cars sold in the United States. Toyota's Japanese-assembled
Cressida model won the top spot in the Power survey, and the Mercedes-Benz
E-series took second place. Though a third place finish was impressive for a
plant that had only been fully operational for one year, the standing was even
more extraordinary since both the Cressida and the Mercedes were imported
models, making the Camry the best-built car in the United States. With the
new plant churning out over 200,000 Camrys annually, it was clear that the
car's reputation was rewarded in dealer showrooms as well.

The accolades for the Georgetown plant did not end with the July, 1990
J.D. Power award. Later that autumn, J.D. Power and Associates presented
company officials with its Gold Plant Quality Award recognizing Toyota as
having the best auto factory in the country. Clearly any car manufacturer
would have been delighted with the award, but coming as it did to a new venture made the recognition even more gratifying. In addition to being bad news
to Toyota's competitors, the J.D. Power awards were perhaps even worse
news to the United Auto Workers union. Though Toyota experienced some
difficulties with the building trades unions during the construction of the facility, it had remained unchallenged by the UAW to date. With a non-union
company producing the best cars in the country, the UAW would have difficulty justifying its claim that "union makes it better."

It was noteworthy that the UAW had not even attempted to organize the newly
hired workers at Toyota. Though Kentucky was not a traditional big-labor state,
the UAW had a presence in the Commonwealth. It represented workers at both
the Ford Motor Company's truck factory in Louisville and the General Motors
plant in Bowling Green that produced the Chevrolet Corvette. Furthermore,
Kentuckians were not necessarily hostile to unions in general. After all, the coal

miners of Kentucky were among the first in the nation to have union representation. Nevertheless, Toyota's shining new factory was far removed from the coal shafts, just as the rigorously tested factory workers were different from the generations who had risked life and limb in the mines.

Though of course Toyota never publicly denounced possible UAW representation of its employees, it had an interest in keeping the union at bay. As noted in Chapter 5, the broad job descriptions that Honda and Toyota favored were anathema to the UAW. But the lack of UAW initiative could not be explained simply by Toyota's hiring process. Indeed, part of the union's reticence about exploring representation was owed to a string of defeats and setbacks that the UAW had experienced in dealing with workers in Japanese-owned factories. After the union withdrew from the representation vote at Honda, it devoted most of its energies to organizing employees at the new Nissan factory in Smyrna, Tennessee. Although the UAW stayed the course with the Nissan vote, it surely wished that it had not. When the votes were tallied on 27 July 1989, Nissan employees rejected UAW representation by more than a two-to-one margin, a stunning blow for what was once among the nation's most prominent labor organizations.[35] Until it could be more certain of a positive outcome of a vote at Toyota, the UAW dared not risk another embarrassing defeat.

Without a challenge from the UAW, Toyota was able to go about the business of manufacturing cars in its own way. Its employees proved that they could make the most reliable automobiles in the country. By the summer of 1992, Toyota's Georgetown facility was exporting Camry and Camry station wagons to Europe, Taiwan, Canada, and the Middle East. Indeed, the factory even exported right-hand drive Camry wagons to Japan, further proof that its products could compete anywhere in the world. Of course, it was not a matter of luck or chance that Toyota's American manufacturing wing met with success. Toyota had developed the necessary expertise for turning out worthwhile automobiles after many years of experience. But in the final analysis, the key to Toyota's success in the Kentucky plant was its personnel. Though engineering and managerial experience were necessary ingredients, these factors would count for little if the assembly line workers were not successful. And although the company was obviously selective about whom it employed, its hiring procedures were justified by the quality of the cars that rolled off the line.

NOTES

1. Andrew Hacker, *Two Nations: Black and White, Separate, Hostile, Unequal* (New York: Charles Scribner's Sons, 1992), 133.

2. Bureau of the Census, *1990 Census of the Population: General Population Characteristics, Kentucky* (Washington: U.S. Department of Commerce, Economics and Statistics Administration, 1991), 23, 12.

3. C. Theodore Koebel et. Al., Socioeconomic Impacts of Toyota on Scott County," *Impacts of the Toyota Plant on Scott County Kentucky* (Louisville: University of Louisville, 1987), 26.

4. Bureau of the Census, *1990 Census of the Population: General Population Characteristics, Kentucky* (Washington: U.S. Department of Commerce, Economics and Statistics Administration, 1991), 13, 16–18, 22.

5. Throughout the mid–to late-1980s, many Japanese leaders and commentators made disparaging remarks about Americans in general, and racial minorities in particular. See Chapter 5 for examples.

6. "Minority Groups Push Role for Blacks at Toyota," *Lexington Herald Leader*, October 15, 1986, B2.

7. Shelia M. Poole, "Toyota Vows to Treat Minorities 'Favorably' in Hiring for Plant," *Lexington Herald Leader*, October 17, 1986, D11.

8. Shelia M. Poole, "Toyota Vows to Treat Minorities 'Favorably' in Hiring for Plant," *Lexington Herald Leader*, October 17, 1986, D11.

9. Shelia M. Poole, "Toyota Vows to Treat Minorities 'Favorably' in Hiring for Plant," *Lexington Herald Leader*, October 17, 1986, D11.

10. Stephen M. Williams, "Civil-Rights Officials Optimistic about Toyota's Hiring Polocies," *Lexington Herald Leader*, December 24, 1986, C6.

11. Ben Hamper, *Rivethead: Tales from the Assembly Line* (New York: Warner Books, Inc., 1992), 3–4.

12. Richard Koenig, "Exacting Employer: Toyota Takes Pains, and Time, Filling Jobs at its Kentucky Plant," *The Wall Street Journal*, December 01, 1987, 31.

13. Toyota Motor Manufacturing, U.S.A., Department of Public Information, *Fact Sheet: Hiring Process for Group Leaders, Team Leaders, and Team Members* (Georgetown, KY: Toyota Motor Manufacturing, U.S.A., 1990), 2–4. The document is filed in the Lexington, Kentucky Public Library, Special Collections, The Kentucky Room, Toyota Folder.

14. Paul Prather, "Toyota Test Screens Out All But Best and Brightest," *Lexington Herald Leader*, April 03, 1988, A1.

15. Alecia Swasy, "Lines Forming for 3,000 Toyota Jobs as Complex Hiring Process Begins," *The Lexington Herald Leader*, January 12, 1987, D1.

16. Paul Prather, "Toyota Test Screens Out All But Best and Brightest," *Lexington Herald Leader*, April 03, 1988, A16.

17. Toyota Motor Manufacturing, U.S.A., *Facts and Figures* (Georgetown, KY: Toyota Motor Manufacturing, U.S.A., 1994), 6. The document is filed in the Lexington, Kentucky Public Library, Special Collections, The Kentucky Room, Toyota Folder.

18. Richard Koenig, "Exacting Employer: Toyota Takes Pains, and Time, Filling Jobs at its Kentucky Plant," *The Wall Street Journal*, December 01, 1987, 31.

19. *United States Code: Congressional and Administrative News*, Eighty-Eighth Congress, Second Sessions, 1964, Volume 1 (St Paul: West Publishing Co., 1964), 306.

20. Griggs v. Duke Power Company, 401 U.S. (1971), 427.

21. Herman Belz, *Equality Transformed: A Quarter-Century of Affirmative Action* (New Brunswick: Transaction Publishers, 1991), 52.

22. Griggs v. Duke Power Company, 401 U.S. (1971), 430.

23. Griggs v. Duke Power Company, 401 U.S. (1971), 429–430.

24. Griggs v. Duke Power Company, 401 U.S. (1971), 432.

25. U.S. Department of Commerce, *1990 Census of the Population: Social and Economic Characteristics, Kentucky* (Washington: Bureau of the Census, 1993), 85.

26. Paul Prather, "Toyota Test Screens Out All But Best and Brightest," *Lexington Herald Leader*, April 03, 1988, A16.

27. Toyota Motor Manufacturing, U.S.A., *Facts and Figures* (Georgetown, KY: Toyota Motor Manufacturing, U.S.A., 1994), 6. The document is filed in the Lexington, Kentucky Public Library, Special Collections, The Kentucky Room, Toyota Folder.

28. Kamata Satoshi, *Japan in the Passing Lane: An Insider's Account of Life in a Japanese Auto Factory* (New York: Pantheon Books, 1982), xiii.

29. Public Relations Tour, Toyota Motor Manufacturing, U.S.A., Georgetown, Kentucky, October 07, 1993.

30. Public Relations Tour, Toyota Motor Manufacturing, U.S.A., Georgetown, Kentucky, October 07, 1993.

31. Paul Prather, "Most Production Applicants White, Male, Under 40," *Lexington Herald Leader*, March 28, 1988, D8.

32. Paul Prather, "Toyota Begins Recruiting for Second Shift," *Lexington Herald Leader*, Auguest 14, 1988, B3.

33. Paul Prather, "Tremendous Job Awaits Toyota Manager," *Lexington Herald Leader*, August 15, 1988, D3–4.

34. Paul Prather, "Toyota Captain Plays for Team," *Lexington Herald Leader*, March 14, 1988, D3.

35. "UAW" Suffers Humiliating Defeat at Nissan," *The Wall Street Journal*, July 28, 1989, A3.

Chapter Seven

Made in the U.S.A.

Honda and Toyota had the luxury of being highly selective in assembling their respective workforces. The steep decline in American manufacturing meant that there was an ample pool of available labor clamoring for the good wages and benefits that both offered. Indeed, the nation's biggest firm was no longer a manufacturer, but instead was the retailer Wal-Mart. Although auto companies like General Motors and Ford still ranked near the top of the Fortune 500, it nevertheless was telling that the largest company in the world sold discount consumer goods, most of which were made in Asia. By the beginning of the 21st century, the American economy was vastly different than it had been 30 years earlier.

That is not to say, of course, that people were necessarily happy with this state of affairs. Wal-Mart in particular was a lightning rod for disagreement, with detractors decrying its relatively low wages and benefits, but its legions of customers enjoying its low prices. Nary had a day passed when it wasn't the subject of a news report, or when the opening of a new Wal-Mart store brought out both protestors and customers in droves. Whenever Honda or Toyota launched a new factory in the U.S., however, there was precious little controversy. Although there was some contention surrounding early site-selection incentive programs, by the 1990s incentives were viewed as the cost of attracting business to one's locale. If tax packages and offers to prepare industrial sites would woo the automakers, several states were willing to enter the bidding contest. Implicit in such competition was the recognition that the firms represented high-wage industrial jobs with significant macroeconomic benefits. Though some might debate the advantages of big box retail stores, there was broad consensus that good jobs in manufacturing were desirable.

Of course, despite the warm welcome that Honda and Toyota might receive, the two were cautious as they expanded their presence in the U.S. Although they were seasoned vehicle manufacturers, transplanting production to the United States was a foray into uncharted waters. Their strong reputations among American consumers applied to vehicles made in Japan and imported to the United States. Duplicating their high levels of quality control in American factories was another matter entirely. If American-made Hondas or Toyotas were shoddy and unreliable, the consequences to either firm would be serious.

That said, there nevertheless were compelling reasons to manufacture in the U.S. In the post-Bretton Woods currency climate, the steadily rising value of the yen eroded the competitive edge that Honda and Toyota had over their American competitors. Imported Honda and Toyota products were quickly losing their bargain status in the 1980s. Coupled with protectionist threats from within the United States, solutions had to be found lest Japanese imports face shrinking market share. Transplanting production to the United States addressed both problems. American-based production helped to insulate products from currency fluctuations, and at the same time counteracted calls for import restrictions. Although transplant manufacturing was a risky venture, the potential benefits made it worthwhile.

By the early 1990s, Honda of America Manufacturing and Toyota Motor Manufacturing, U.S.A., had proven that transplant automotive manufacturing could succeed. Both companies successfully averted the production disasters that could have befallen them. Their vehicles were well received by consumers in both the United States and abroad. As both companies expanded production and payroll during the 1980s, they exhibited confidence in their operations. Nor were Honda and Toyota merely assembling cars in the U.S. Rather, each invested in complete powertrain and stamping facilities, enabling them to claim that they were truly manufacturing automobiles. Honda and Toyota's success as transplants was particularly striking against the backdrop of events in the American auto industry at large. While their U.S.-based competitors were closing factories and shifting production abroad, Honda and Toyota were taking root on American soil. They appeared to be out of synchronization with the times.

FORTUITOUS TIMING

The old adage that, "timing is everything," applied well to the transplantation of Honda and Toyota manufacturing. Indeed, the overcapacity that afflicted the American automobile industry worked in favor of the two transplants. At precisely the time when factories were closing and unemployment was on the rise, Honda and Toyota were searching for manufacturing sites. The development aid and tax abatements that the State of Ohio and Union County provided to Honda may well have been unavailable when American industrial manufacturing was booming a generation earlier. With the rust-belt moniker becoming a suitable description for the state's economy, however, Ohio officials were eager to accommodate the Japanese motorcycle and automobile manufacturer in exchange for its investment dollars.

As the later arrival in the United States, Toyota benefited even further from state incentives. By the time it was searching for a manufacturing site in 1985, the stakes had risen considerably among states in the competition for investment. Communities had come to see that the transplant manufacturers were only the first step in the process; invariably, their parts suppliers of both American and Japanese origin followed closely behind, thereby yielding additional jobs. When Honda signed its initial agreement with Ohio in 1977, the deal was still something of a novelty. But in the passage of just a few years, Kentucky demonstrated that it was willing to be far more generous in order to attract investment. The incentive package that Kentucky offered to Toyota was unprecedented in the history of the Commonwealth. Toyota's delay in establishing an American manufacturing presence clearly worked to its advantage in securing incentives. If Honda's timing was good, Toyota's was even better.

The woes of American industry helped Honda and Toyota in ways aside from incentive packages. As the availability of good-paying industrial jobs diminished during the 1980s, Honda and Toyota were in the enviable position of having a large labor pool from which to hire. Given the Japanese concerns over the quality of American workers, the weak job market was advantageous. Industrial downsizing among American manufacturers made Honda and Toyota a rare commodity for job-seekers. There were not many industrial employers seeking new workers, and since the arrival of both Honda and Toyota were major media events, job applications came in torrents.

The sheer volume of job applications that came to Toyota provided clear evidence of a weak job market. One reason that the company achieved the high hiring standards it set was due to the scarcity of good-paying jobs. That it had located in a region not known for such jobs helped to intensify popular interest in working at the Georgetown plant. Nevertheless, the prospect of working for Toyota generated such overwhelming interest as to suggest that the choice of region alone could not account for the number of applicants. With so many applicants from whom to choose, Toyota could be very selective about whom it eventually employed. In a different employment market in an earlier era, it may not have been in the position of hiring the strong work force that it did.

Transplanting to the United States during a time of industrial decline had other labor ramifications as well. In addition to having a large labor pool from which to hire, Honda and Toyota were also able to avoid successful union drives at their new facilities. In part, site selection unquestionably played a role in keeping the UAW at bay. That both Honda and Toyota located their facilities in locales with little experience in manufacturing was not accidental. If at all possible, both firms wanted to hire employees who were not predisposed to union representation, and locating in rural communities at least held out the possibility of finding such workers. Nevertheless, a compelling union message could have persuaded Honda and Toyota workers to seek UAW representation even if they had never previously worked in a union environment. Once again, fortuitous timing played a role.

Perhaps more than any other industrial union in the United States, the United Automobile Workers had a strong record of securing good wages and benefits for its members. Without question, the pay levels and working conditions of auto assembly line workers over the years had improved dramatically under the auspices of the UAW. Nevertheless, the union remained relatively powerless in the face of massive downsizing. Though at times it could slow the process, or save the jobs of a few selected workers, by and large it stood idly by as American automobile companies slashed their work forces. Thus, by the time that Honda and Toyota established manufacturing facilities in the United States, the union was at a vulnerable stage. It could not convince prospective new members that it had the ability to safeguard their jobs indefinitely. To the contrary, it was losing members at an alarming rate due to layoffs. Among rural people who were perhaps suspicious of big labor in the first place, the UAW could not offer clear membership benefits.

The frustration that the UAW experienced in its aborted organizing effort at Honda's Marysville facility is instructive. With even union officials conceding that Honda paid well and offered good benefits, its message was severely weakened. It was difficult to justify paying union dues when the return for doing so was dubious at best. Ironically, the fact that the UAW had proven to be such an effective organization over the years in the American auto industry perhaps hurt its cause in regard to organizing the Honda workers. The wage and benefit concessions that it had gained from the Big Three became the standard by which American auto production was conducted. If Honda offered substantially less, it was sure to invite a successful union drive in its factories. But, by providing a competitive compensation package, Honda could thwart a UAW drive while at the same time retain its treasured two-tier job classification system. In essence, Honda's labor and management were each able to achieve desired goals, while the UAW was left on the sidelines.

In its accustomed position of reaping rewards due to its later arrival, Toyota benefited from Honda's dealings with the UAW. After canceling its representation vote in Ohio, and losing the campaign to organize workers at Nissan's Tennessee plant, the UAW did not stage an active drive at Toyota's Kentucky facility. The UAW's reluctance to begin a major effort among Toyota's employees was not attributable to any special qualities concerning Toyota itself. Instead, the union appeared tired after a string of disappointments. Given the on-going concerns of its current members, its energies were perhaps better used elsewhere for the time being. Of course, if it sensed a dramatic turn of events at Honda or Toyota, the UAW certainly would launch an organizing attempt. The very threat of a possible representation drive, however, would likely keep the automakers sensitive to worker demands. Honda and Toyota employees could therefore benefit from the existence of the UAW without becoming members.

MAKING IT HAPPEN

Although Honda and Toyota profited from America's industrial climate, their successful transplantation to the United States was more than a matter of good luck. Both firms relied upon their respective strengths and abilities to make their new ventures viable. They had proven themselves to be formidable competitors as importers, and showed no less skill as American manufacturers. That they were able to produce high quality vehicles in a country that was said to have lost its way in heavy industry flew in the face of convention. Though good timing worked to their benefit, both Honda and Toyota made their goals a reality.

As the first Japanese transplant to arrive in the United States, Honda deserves credit for its foresight. Well before the value of the yen or the threat of import restrictions reached critical stages, Honda of America Manufacturing was operating a motorcycle and an automobile factory. In settling into its Ohio location, Honda executives were adept in dealing with state and county officials. When it could secure favorable land prices, such as its initial 210-acre purchase in 1977 and its later acquisition of the Ohio Transportation Research Center in 1987, it seized the opportunity.[1] Likewise, when tax abatements and development aid were offered by Union County, Honda was quick to accept. On the other hand, when it encountered opposition to subsidized land prices during the course of its expansion in 1980, Honda did not press the issue.[2] It adopted the posture of friendly neighbor until the controversy passed. Honda was shrewd in its political and community relations, a quality that served its interests well.

The company saw early rewards for its vision to establish an American facility. In the early 1980s, when Japan's Ministry of International Trade and Industry adopted voluntary restraints on exporting cars to the United States, Honda was the only Japanese auto company that could sidestep the new regulations due to its production in Ohio.[3] Furthermore, its early start in American production enabled it to significantly shift production to the United States. By 1992, nine years after it produced its first car in Ohio, over 61 percent of all Hondas sold in the U.S. were produced by Honda of America Manufacturing.[4] More than any other transplant, Honda could rightly claim a place as an American auto manufacturer.

Of course, Honda's settlement in the United States was not without certain difficulties. Its early confrontation with the UAW and the National Labor Relations Board proved that it was not easy to begin manufacturing in a foreign setting. Though the cap and pin dispute with the UAW took on certain comic qualities, the issue demonstrated Honda's unfamiliarity with American labor organizations and their recruiting techniques.[5] Though Honda's work force responded positively to the egalitarian concepts regarding work uniforms, parking spaces, and dining areas, company management had not anticipated legal challenges to the dress code. Undoubtedly it served as a reminder that Honda still had lessons to learn about its new work site.

More troubling was the company's encounter with the EEOC and employees alleging discrimination. Although Honda was able to avoid a formal citation from the EEOC by reaching a financial settlement with the aggrieved employees, it reinforced the perception that the firm was discriminatory. Coupled with racist statements from Japanese political leaders, critics pointed to the company's alleged discriminatory behavior as evidence that it was hostile to minorities. Given its high profile as the major Japanese automotive transplant in the United States, Honda's case attracted more attention than if had been a traditional American company accused of the same crime. Honda surely would have preferred to avoid the attention it drew, but its novel status precluded any chance at anonymity.

Given the fanfare surrounding its arrival in Kentucky, Toyota found itself in the media spotlight as well. Although it was several years behind Honda in establishing an American manufacturing plant, when it finally decided to do so, it made a major commitment right away. Not content to acquire a few hundred acres at a time, Toyota arranged to have the state give it 1600 acres as part of its multimillion-dollar incentive package.[6] It was then the world's third largest auto company and its every action underscored this point. Even before its $800 million factory was completed, Toyota announced that it would build a $300 million powertrain plant. Though it had been reticent to pursue transplant operations in the U.S., all hesitation seemed to disappear once the announcement of the company's commitment was made.

Like Honda, Toyota demonstrated deftness in dealing with state and local leaders. But as with its manufacturing plans, the Toyota style was always grand. When it was confronted with opposition to its foreign trade subzone application, Kentucky Governor Collins went to Capital Hill to testify on Toyota's behalf. In response to criticism regarding Toyota's parts procurement procedures, the governor was able to point out the hundreds of millions of dollars that Toyota spent nationally. Toyota was equated with big business, and Collins could provide the evidence.[7] Toyota was quick to address local concerns as well. When Scott County needed to build a new school, Toyota paid its taxes 15 years in advance so that the county could do so.[8] The company had clout and deep financial resources, and it was unabashed about using either.

A willingness to exercise influence and power, however, did not mean that Toyota was recklessly bold. Though it called upon its resources when necessary, Toyota remained conservative in most of its dealings. That it went to extraordinary lengths to hire its work force was a clear example of the firm's character. It was not sufficient that a person appeared eager to work. An applicant had to prove his or her abilities by means of elaborate tests and interviews in order to get hired. Even then there remained a six-month probationary period during which Toyota could decide if it had made the right choice after all. This was not a whimsical procedure. Since Kentucky agreed to pay for the tests as an incentive, it was clear that Toyota's eight-phase hiring process had been planned at an early date.[9] It knew what it wanted in a work force and went to great lengths to see that it achieved satisfactory results.

Toyota clearly had considered the legal ramifications behind its hiring policies. It seems an unlikely coincidence that the percentage of minorities on its payroll mirrored the percentage of minorities that had applied for jobs. Given the attention that Toyota's presence drew, the company was scrutinized for the composition of its work force. It was far easier to avoid charges of disparate impact by hiring a relatively substantial number of minorities than risk EEOC investigations and lawsuits. Toyota's main concern was getting its new facility launched into production, and there was nothing to be gained by inviting legal distractions.

Toyota's single-minded desire to manufacture high quality cars at its Kentucky plant was quickly rewarded. Though it may have entered the fray of American manufacturing later than Honda, it made up for lost time by producing the best-made cars in the country. Its hesitancy to become a transplant manufacturer thus should not be confused with indifference. Toyota made a significant investment in the United States once it was confident of success.

Planning and forethought were evident in its approach to American production, and indeed these plans were well laid.

Having successfully established themselves as transplant automobile manufacturers in the United States, Honda and Toyota journeyed great distances. They operated more efficiently and more effectively than their Detroit counterparts, and they did so on American soil. They demonstrated that efficiency, sound management, good labor relations, and effective relationships with suppliers had little to do with national origin or geographic location. Honda and Toyota were good at what they did, regardless of where they did it.

When Toyoda Kiichiro began his automotive research in the late 1920s by disassembling General Motors and Ford cars to see how they functioned, he would not have dreamed that the company he founded would one day be at the top of the world auto industry producing vehicles in the very realm of those auto giants. And as Honda Soichiro was fashioning his first motor scooters, he too might have been skeptical if told that one day he would live to see his company manufacturing some of the top-selling American-made vehicles.

That is not to say, however, that it was easy for either firm to succeed as transplant manufacturers. Both knew that the stakes were high and that the risks were many. And so it was that both proceeded with caution when establishing manufacturing facilities. Honda tested the waters with its motorcycle venture, and Toyota did so through its NUMMI partnership with General Motors. But as the 20th century drew to a close, both demonstrated that their American operations were viable. Indeed, there was nothing wrong with the American automobile industry. Honda and Toyota showed that the industry could succeed in the U.S. Although the Detroit-based au

NOTES

1. See Chapter 3
2. See Chapter 3
3. See Chapter 3
4. *Ward's 1993 Automotive Yearbook*, (Detroit: Ward's Communications. Inc., 1993), 158.
5. See Chapter 5
6. See Chapter 4
7. See Chapter 4
8. See Chapter 4
9. See Chapter 6

Bibliography

BOOKS, JOURNALS, AND PERIODICALS

Allen, G.C. *A Short Economic History of Modern Japan*. New York: St. Martin's Press, 1981.

Aoki, Masahiko, ed. *The Economic Analysis of the Japanese Firm*. Amsterdam: Elsevier Science Publishers, B.V., 1984.

Aoki, Michiko Y., and Margaret B. Dardess, eds. *As the Japanese See It*. Honolulu: University of Hawaii Press, 1981.

Ballon, Robert J., and Iwao Tamita. *The Financial Behavior of Japanese Corporations*. Tokyo: Kodansha International, 1988.

Belz, Herman. *Equality Transformed: A Quarter-Century of Affirmative Action*. New Brunswick: Transaction Publishers, 1991.

Berry, Bryan. "Automakers Fuel Galvanizing Expansion," *Iron Age* 8 (1992): 38–40.

Bryan, Michael F., and John B. Martin. "Realignment in the U.S. Motor Vehicle Industry," *Economic Commentary*, Federal Reserve Bank of Cleveland, 01 June 1991.

Center for Business and Economic Research, College of Business and Economics, University of Kentucky. *The Economic Significance of Toyota Motor Manufacturing U.S.A., Inc., in Kentucky*. Lexington: University of Kentucky, 1992.

Chandler, Alfred D., Jr. *The Visible Hand: The Managerial Revolution in American Business*. Cambridge, MA: Belknap Press, 1977.

Choate, Pat. *Agents of Influence*. New York: Alfred A. Knopf, 1990.

Christopher, Robert C. *The Japanese Mind: The Goliath Explained*. New York: Simon & Schuster, 1983.

Cole, Robert E. *Japanese Blue Collar: The Changing Tradition*. Berkeley: University of California Press, 1973.

Cole, Robert E., and Donald R. Deskins, Jr. "Racial Factors in Site Location and Employment Patterns of Japanese Auto Firms in America." *California Management Review* 31 (1988): 9–22.

Craig, Steven G., Thomas R. DeGregori, Janet E. Kohlhase, and Michael G. Palumbo. *The Economic Impact of Honda's U. S. Operations: Production, Sales and Distribution, and Technology Transfer*. Houston: University of Houston, 1994.

Cusumano, Michael. *The Japanese Automobile Industry : Technology & Management at Nissan & Toyota*. Cambridge, MA: The Council on East Asian Studies, Harvard University, 1991.

Doner, Richard F. *Driving A Bargain: Automobile Industrialization and Japanese Firms in Southeast Asia*. Berkeley: University of California Press, 1991.

Drucker, Peter. *Concept of the Corporation*. New York: John Day Co., 1946.

Dun & Bradstreet International. *Who Owns Whom, 1991: Australasia & Far East*. Bucks, England: Dun and Bradstreet International, 1991.

Dunning, John H. *International Production and the Multinational Enterprise*. London: George Allen & Unwin, 1981.

Eckes, Alfred E., Jr. *A Search for Solvency: Bretton Woods and the International Monetary System, 1941-1971*. Austin: University of Texas Press, 1975.

Fallows, James. *More Like Us: Making America Great Again*. Boston: Houghton Mifflin and Company, 1989.

Feldman, Richard, and Michael Betzold. *End of the Line: Autoworkers and the American Dream*. New York: Weidenfeld & Nicolson, 1988.

Fields, George. *From Bonsai to Levi's*. New York: MacMillan Publishing Company, 1983.

Flink, James. *The Automobile Age*. Cambridge, MA: MIT Press, 1988.

Flint, Jerry. "The New Number Three?" *Forbes* 145 (1990): 136, 140.

Gelsanliter, David. *Jump Start: Japan Comes to the Heartland*. New York: Kodansha International, 1990.

Graham, Hugh Davis. *The Civil Rights Era*. New York: Oxford University Press, 1990.

Greenwald, Gerald. "Playing in the Global Sandbox." *Directors and Boards* 14 (1990): 14–17.

Hacker, Andrew. *Two Nations: Black and White, Separate, Hostile, Unequal*. New York: Charles Scribner's Sons, 1992.

Halberstam, David. *The Reckoning*. New York: William Morrow and Company, 1986.

Hamper, Ben. *Rivethead: Tales from the Assembly Line*. New York: Warner Books, Inc, 1992.

Hoerr, John, and Leah Nathans Spiro. "Culture Shock at Home: Working for a Foreign Boss." *Business Week* no. 3192 (1990): 80–84.

Honda of America Manufacturing, Inc. *Honda in America: Years of Achievement*. Marysville, OH: Honda of America Manufacturing, Inc., 1992.

Honda of America Manufacturing, Inc. *Marysville Motorcycle Plant*. Marysville, OH: Honda of America Manufacturing, Inc., 1991.

Hunker, Jeffrey Allen. *Structural Change in the U.S. Automobile Industry*. Lexington, MA: D.C. Heath and Company, 1983.

Ienaga, Saburo. *The Pacific War, 1931-1945*. New York: Pantheon Books, 1978.

International Conference on Business History. *Japanese Management in Historical Perspective: Proceedings of the Fuji Conference*. Tokyo: University of Tokyo Press, 1989.

The International Monetary Fund. *International Financial Statistics*. Washington, DC: The International Monetary Fund, 1953.

———. *International Financial Statistics*. Washington, DC: The International Monetary Fund, 1961.

———. *International Financial Statistics*. Washington, DC: The International Monetary Fund, 1979.

Kamata, Satoshi. *Japan in the Passing Lane*. New York: Pantheon Books, 1982.

Kamiya, Shotaro. *My Life with Toyota*. Toyota City, Japan: Toyota Motor Sales, Ltd. 1976.

Kenney, Martin, and Richard Florida. "How Japanese Industry Is Rebuilding the Rust Belt." *Technology Review* 94 (1991): 24–33.

Kirschenbaum, Alan I. "Kentucky's New Icon of Economic Strength." *The Lane Report* 8 (1992): 23–26.

Kline, John M. *State Government Influence in U.S. International Economic Policy*. Lexington, MA: Lexington Books, 1983.

Koebel, C. Theodore, Michael L. Price, Ivan Lee Weir, John P. Nelson, and Julia Ingrid Lane. *Impact of the Toyota Plant on Scott County*, Kentucky. Louisville: Chapman and Company, 1987.

Konosuke, Odaka. *The Automobile Industry in Japan*. Tokyo: Kinokuniya Company Ltd., 1988.

Krueger, Anne O. *Exchange Rate Determination*. Cambridge: Cambridge University Press, 1983.

Kujawa, Duane. *Japanese Multinationals in the United States: Case Studies*. New York: Praeger Publishers, 1986.

Kusayanagi, Daizo. *The Enterprise as Kingdom*. Tokyo: Bungei-Shunju Co., 1969.

Lacey, Robert. *Ford*. Boston: Little, Brown and Company, 1986.

Lincoln, James R., Jon Olson, and Mitsuyo Hanada. "Cultural Effects on Organizational Structure: The Case of Japanese Firms in the United States*." American Sociological Review* 43 (1978): 829–847.

Magnusson, Paul, and James B. Treece. "Honda: Is It an American Car?" *Business Week* no. 3240 (1991): 105–112.

Maxcy, George. *The Multinational Automobile Industry*. New York: St. Martin's Press, 1981.

Mito, Setsuo. *The Honda Book of Management: A Leadership Philosophy for High Industrial Success*. London: The Athlone Press, 1990.

Morita, Akio. *Made in Japan*. New York: Penguin Books USA Inc., 1986.

Moskal, Brian S. "World Class Manufacturing: Supervision, (Or Lack of It)." *Industry Week* 239 (1990): 54–59.

National Governors' Association. *States in the International Economy*. Washington, DC: National Governors' Association, 1985.

Newman, Richard G. "The Second Wave Arrives: Japanese Strategy in the U.S. Auto Parts Market." *Business Horizons* 33 (1990): 24–30.

Odaka, Konosuke, Keinosuke Ono, and Fumihiko Adachi. *The Automobile Industry in Japan: A Study of Ancillary Firm Development*. Tokyo: Kinokuniya Company, Ltd., 1988.

Ohki, Emiko. "Automakers Produce Plans to Buy More U.S. Car Parts." *Japan Times Weekly International Edition* 31 (1991): 18.

Okawara, Yoshio. *To Avoid Isolation: An Ambassador's View of U.S./Japanese Relations*. Columbia, SC: University of South Carolina Press, 1990.

Pegels, C. Carl. *Japan vs. the West: Implications for Management*. Boston: Kluwer-Nijoff, 1984.

Perrucci, Robert. *Japanese Auto Transplants in the Heartland: Corporatism and Community*. New York: Aldine de Gruyter, Inc., 1994.

Program Committee of the Committee for Economic Development. *Foreign Investment in the United States: What Does It Signal?* New York: Committee for Economic Development, 1990.

Pugel, Thomas A., ed. *Fragile Interdependence: Economic Issues in U.S.-Japanese Trade and Investment*. Lexington, MA: D.C. Heath and Company, 1986.

Pyle, Kenneth B. *The Japanese Question: Power and Purpose in a New Era*. Washington, DC: The AEI Press, 1992.

Raia, Ernest. "The Americanization of Honda." *Purchasing* 108 (1990): 50–57.

———. "Just-In-Time, Transplant Style." *Purchasing* 113 (1992): 60–65.

Rehder, Robert R. "Japanese Transplants: After the Honeymoon." *Business Horizons* 33 (1990): 87–98.

Reischauer, Edwin O. *Japan: The Story of a Nation*. New York: McGraw-Hill Publishing Company, 1990.

Reischauer, Edwin O. and Albert M. Craig. *Japan: Tradition & Transformation*. Boston: Houghton Mifflin Company, 1989.

Ress, David. *Harry Dexter White: A Study in Paradox*. New York: Coward, McCann & Geoghegan, 1973.

Richardson, Bradley M. and Uedo Taizo. *Business and Society in Japan: Fundamentals for Business*. New York: Praeger Publishers, 1981.

Rohlen, Thomas P. *For Harmony and Strength: Japanese White-Collar Organization in Anthropological Perspective*. Berkeley: University of California Press, 1974.

Sakiya, Tetsuo. *Honda Motor: The Men, the Management, the Machines*. Tokyo: Kodansha International, 1982.

Sanders, Sol. *Honda: The Man and His Machines*. Boston: Little, Brown and Company, 1975.

Sargen, Nicholas, and Richard Segal. *Japan: The World's Number One Capital Exporter*. New York: Salomon Brothers, Inc., 1985.

Sethi, S. Prakash, Nobuaki Namiki, and Carl L. Swanson. *The False Promise of the Japanese Miracle: Illusions and Realities of the Japanese Management System*. Boston: Pitman, 1984.

Shimada, Haruo, and John Paul MacDuffie. *Industrial Relations and "Humanware": Japanese Investments in Automobile Manufacturing in the United States*. Cambridge, MA: MIT Press, 1986.

Shimokawa, Koichi. "Japan's Keiretsu System: The Case of the Automobile Industry." *Japanese Economic Studies* 13 (1985): 3–31.

Shook, Robert. *Honda: An American Success Story.* New York: Prentice Hall Press, 1988.

Simurda, Stephen J. "When Foreign Owners Boost a Sagging Industry." *International Business* 5 (1992): 46–49.

Sinclair, Stuart. *The World Car: The Future of the Automobile Industry.* New York: Facts on File Publications, 1983.

Smitka, Michael J. *Competitive Ties: Subcontracting in the Japanese Automotive Industry.* New York: Columbia University Press, 1991.

Symonds, William C. "Gunfight at the Customs Corral." *Business Week* no. 3254 (1992): 54.

Tasker, Peter. *The Japanese: Portrait of a Nation.* New York: New American Library, 1987.

Tavlas, George S. and Ozeki Yuzuru. *The Internationalization of Currencies: An Appraisal of the Japanese Yen.* Washington, DC: The International Monetary Fund, 1992.

Taylor, Alexander III. "Japan's New U.S. Car Strategy." *Fortune* 122 (1990): 65–80.

Tolchin, Martin and Susan. *Buying Into America.* New York: Times Books, 1988.

Toyoda, Eiji. *Toyota: Fifty Years in Motion.* Tokyo: Kodansha International, 1985.

Toyota Motor Manufacturing U.S.A., Inc. *Automobile Manufacturing Complex Schematic.* Georgetown: Toyota Motor Manufacturing, U.S.A., 1986.

———. *Fact Sheet: Hiring Process for Group Leaders, Team Leaders, and Team Members.* Georgetown: Toyota Motor Manufacturing, U.S.A., 1990.

———. *Facts and Figures 1993.* Georgetown: Toyota Motor Manufacturing, U.S.A., 1993.

———. *Milestones 1993.* Georgetown: Toyota Motor Manufacturing, U.S.A., 1993.

Trevor, Malcolm. *Japan's Reluctant Multinationals: Japanese Management at Home and Abroad.* New York: St. Martin's Press, 1983.

U.S. Department of Commerce, Bureau of the Census. *1980 Census of the Population: Characteristics of the Population, Ohio.* Washington: Bureau of the Census, U.S. Department of Commerce, 1982.

———. *1990 Census of Population: General Population Characteristics, Kentucky.* Washington, DC: U.S. Department of Commerce, 1993.

———. *1990 Census of Population: Social and Economic Characteristics, Ohio.* Washington, DC: Department of Commerce, 1993.

———. "The Journey to Work in the United States: 1979." *Current Population Reports.* Washington, DC: Department of Commerce, 1982.

Vasilash, Gary S. "How It Is at Honda." *Production* 103 (1991): 54–58.

Vogel, Ezra F. *Japan as Number 1: Lessons for America.* New York: Harper & Row Publishers, 1979.

Von Hassell, Agostino. "Ties that Bind: Working for the Transnationals." *Plastics World* 49 (1991): 66–69.

Ward's 1974 Automotive Yearbook. Detroit: Ward's Communications, Inc., 1974.

Ward's 1975 Automotive Yearbook. Detroit: Ward's Communications, Inc., 1975.

Ward's 1979 Automotive Yearbook. Detroit: Ward's Communications, Inc., 1979.

Ward's 1980 Automotive Yearbook. Detroit: Ward's Communications, Inc., 1980.

Ward's 1985 Automotive Yearbook. Detroit: Ward's Communications, Inc., 1985.

Ward's 1990 Automotive Yearbook. Detroit: Ward's Communications, Inc., 1990.

Ward's 1991 Automotive Yearbook. Detroit: Ward's Communications, Inc., 1991.

Ward's 1993 Automotive Yearbook. Detroit: Ward's Communications, Inc., 1993.

Ward's 1994 Automotive Yearbook. Detroit: Ward's Communications, Inc., 1994.

Wolf, Marvin J. *The Japanese Conspiracy*. New York: Empire Books, 1983.

Womack, James, Daniel Jones, and Daniel Roos. *The Machine that Changed the World*. New York: Rawson Associates, 1990.

World Motor Vehicle Data, 1977 Edition. Detroit: Motor Vehicle Manufacturers Association of the United States, 1977.

World Motor Vehicle Data, 1981 Edition. Detroit: Motor Vehicle Manufacturers Association of the United States, 1981.

NEWSPAPER ARTICLES

Allan, William. "Honda Excels in Marysville." *Columbus Citizen-Journal*, 12 May 1983, 34.

Amatos, Christopher A. "Election Canceled at Honda." *The Columbus Dispatch*, 18 March 1986, 1A.

———. "Honda Drawing Nearer to Self-Sufficiency in U.S." *The Columbus Dispatch*, 18 October 1987, 1A.

Atkinson, Bill. "Auto Workers 'Air' Grievances Against Honda." *Business First of Greater Columbus*, 04 February 1985, 3.

———. "Honda Runs Like Clockwork with Just-In-Time." *Business First of Greater Columbus*, 21 October 1985, 6.

———. "Japanese Suppliers Benefit from Honda's Success." *Business First of Greater Columbus*, 06 May 1985, 7.

Bradshaw, James. "Honda Plans No Immediate Push for Rt. 33 Changes." *The Columbus Dispatch*, 06 February 1983, 1C.

Brammer, Jack. "Collins Signs Final Accord with Toyota on Incentives." *Lexington Herald Leader*, 01 March 1986, A1.

———. "State to Pay Toyota Workers for 6 Months." *Lexington Herald-Leader*, 10 September, 1986, A1.

———. "Toyota Training Fund Request Surprises Panel." *Lexington Herald-Leader*, 07 March 1986, B1.

Brammer, Jack, and John Winn Miller. "Toyota Incentives Legal, Court Rules." *Lexington Herald-Leader*, 12 June 1987, A1.

Brooks, Sylvia. "New Road To Honda Preferred." *The Columbus Dispatch*, 20 July 1983, 1A.

Brown, T.C. "Honda Sets Official Dedication." *Columbus Citizen-Journal*, 31 March 1983, 14.

Buss, Dale D. "UAW Suspends Its Organizing Drive at Honda Assembly Complex in Ohio." *The Wall Street Journal*, 18 March 1986, 2.

Buss, Dale D., and John Bussey. "Japanese Management Confronts U.S. Union in Election at Honda." *The Wall Street Journal*, 27 December 1985, 11.

Bussey, John. "UAW's Unfair Labor Practice Charges Against Honda Are Dismissed by NLRB." *The Wall Street Journal*, 03 January 1986, 12.

Carfagno, Jacalyn. "Georgetown Toyota Plant Sending Axles to Japan." *Lexington Herald Leader*, 10 May 1991, B9.

Chira, Susan. "2 Papers Quote Japanese Leader on Abilities of Minorities in U.S." *The New York Times*, 24 September 1986, A12.

———. "Tokyo Again Astir Over Racial Slight." *The New York Times*, 26 July 1988, A10.

Cohn, Ray. "Suit to Halt Toyota Plant Thrown Out." *Lexington Herald-Leader*, 29 July 1986, B1.

Condo, Jerry. "NLRB Rules for Worker in Hat Fuss." *Columbus Citizen-Journal*, 23 October 1981, 20.

Curtin, Michael. "Saxbe Pushes House Bill to Delay Widening Rt. 33." *The Columbus Dispatch*, 11 March 1982, 5C.

Daykin, Tom. "$800 Million Plant to Build Camrys Starting in Late 1993." *Lexington Herald Leader*, 28 November 1990, A1.

Duke, Jacqueline. "House Ok's Aide Package for Toyota." *Lexington Herald-Leader*, 12 February 1986, B1.

Edwards, Larrilyn. "Hard Work by Two Men Brought Honda to Ohio." *Columbus Citizen-Journal*, 11 July 1980, 7.

Ellis, Mark. "Honda Factory to be Expanded." *The Columbus Dispatch*, 10 January 1984, 1A.

Embrey, George. "Honda to Pay Discrimination Penalties." *The Columbus Dispatch*, 24 March 1988, 1A.

Feder, Barnaby J. "Blunt Talk by Iacocca, Just Back from Japan." *The New York Times*, 11 January 1992, 33.

———. "Foreign Money Spreading to All Walks of U.S. Life." *The New York Times*, 29 December 1985, A1.

Foster, Pamela E. "Honda to Hike U.S. Content." *Business First of Greater Columbus*, 13 May 1991, 1.

Franklin, Peter D. "Honda Dedicates Its $250 Million Investment in Ohio." *The Columbus Dispatch*, 26 April 1983, 6A.

Freeman, David. "Japan + U.S.: A Good Combination." *The Columbus Dispatch*, 21 April 1983, 1D.

Gates, Andi. "Honda Mum on Survey for Japan." *The Columbus Dispatch*, 05 November 1982, 13A.

———. "Trees Grown in Marysville Symbol of Honda's Success." *The Columbus Dispatch*, 20 December 1980, 1G.

Grace, Gary. "Gov. Rhodes' Pal Owns Honda Site." *The Marysville Journal-Tribune*, 27 September 1977, 1A.

Guiles, Melinda Grenier. "Toyota Will Invest Up to $800 Million in Kentucky Plant." *The Wall Street Journal*, 12 December 1985, 17.

Haberman, Clyde. "Labor Peace Reigns and Unions Wither." *The New York Times*, 07 June 1985, A2.

Hill, Toya Richards. "Toyota, Trades Council Cooperate on Addition." *Lexington Herald Leader*, 14 June 1993, D5.

Horgan, Sean. "NLRB Dismisses Charges Against Honda." *The Columbus Dispatch*, 01 February 1986, 7C.

Ingrassia, Paul. "Honda Starts Making Car Engines in U.S." *The Wall Street Journal*, 23 September 1986, 10.

Jordan, Jim. "Area Firms Jockey for Honda Business." *Lexington Herald-Leader*, 17 February 1986, D1.

———. "Toyota Plant Will Put UAW to the Test in Central Kentucky." *Lexington Herald-Leader*, 23 December 1985, D1.

Kanabayashi, Masayoshi. "Honda's Accord: How a Japanese Firm Is Faring on Its Dealings with Workers in U.S." *The Wall Street Journal*, 02 October 1981, 1.

Kastil, Peter. "Europe's Safe for American Hondas." *The Wall Street Journal*, 01 September 1989, A6.

Kimmins, Dick. "Honda Site Pick Was Hush-Hush Affair." *Columbus Citizen-Journal*, 09 March 1984, 4.

———. "New Honda Auto Plant Will Mean $800,000 More to School District." *Columbus Citizen-Journal*, 11 July 1980, 11.

———. "No-Strike Pledge Signed for Building Honda Plant." *Columbus Citizen-Journal*. 23 April 1981, 25.

———. "A Smokestack Chase that Paid Off." *Business First of Greater Columbus*, 19 October 1987, 10.

Koenig, Richard. "Exacting Employer: Toyota Takes Pains, And Time, Filling Jobs at Its Kentucky Plant." *The Wall Street Journal*, 01 December 1987, 31.

———. "Toyota Learns to Live with U.S. Unions." *The Wall Street Journal*, 25 February 1987, 12.

LaRoe, Ross M., and John Charles Pool, "Honda Exports from U.S. Sign of Changing Times." *The Columbus Dispatch*, 09 February 1988, 1F.

Leitzke, Ron. "Honda Aims for Flexibility at New Auto Plant." *The Columbus Dispatch*, 12 April 1990, 1G.

Leonard, Lee. "Honda to Buy State Land for Plant Addition at Market Price." *Columbus-Citizen Journal*, 26 June 1980, 20.

———. "Land Deal for Honda Is Attacked." *Columbus Citizen-Journal*, 20 June 1980, 1.

Levin, Doron P. "GM-Toyota Venture Will Test Ability of Workers in U.S. to Match Japanese." *The Wall Street Journal*, 05 April 1985, 6.

———. "Honda Becoming More of an American Company," *The Columbus Dispatch*, 24 March 1990, 1C.

Lilly, Stephen. "Suggestive Comments Win Cash at Some Companies." *Business First of Greater Columbus*, 12 December 1988, 1.

Limbird, Randy and Julie Brienza. "Honda Tax Break Bid Covers Expansion." *Columbus Citizen Journal*, 04 December 1984, 25.

Lore, David. "Land of the Tax-Free Made Honda Go West." *The Columbus Dispatch*, 23 May 1982, 3C.

Masayoshi, Kanabayashi. "Honda's Accord: How a Japanese Firm Is Faring on Its Dealings With Workers in the U.S." *The Wall Street Journal*, 02 October 1981, 1.

McQueen, Michael and Joseph B. White. "Blacks, Women at Honda Unit Win Back Pay." *The Wall Street Journal*, 24 March 1988, 2.

McVicar, Nancy. "Marysville, State Officials Praise Honda Plan to Build New Facility." *Columbus Citizen-Journal*, 26 November 1981, 26.

Mead, Andy. "Scott Panel Approves Toyota Site Plan." *Lexington Herald-Leader*, 11 April 1986, A1.

Mead, Andy, Cheryl Truman, and Art Jester. "Snags Hit in Completing Land Package for Toyota Plant." *Lexington Herald-Leader*, 05 December 1985, A1.

Melloan, George. "Honda's Cash Goes a Long Way in the U.S.A." *The Wall Street Journal*, 13 October 1987, 35.

Miller, Alan. "Labor Chief Says Honda Sure to Fall." *The Columbus Dispatch*, 06 June 1989, 4B.

Miller, John Winn, and Alecia Swasy. "The Wooing of Toyota: Kentucky Adds Up the Bill." *Lexington Herald-Leader*, 28 September 1986, A1.

Miller, Maureen. "Holding the Line." *Business First of Greater Columbus*, 15 September 1986, 12.

Mollard, Beth. "Japanese Auto Firm Employs Inmates." *Business First of Greater Columbus*, 28 January 1991, 1.

———. "Japanese Executives Face American Independence." *Business First of Greater Columbus*, 16 July 1990, 18.

Nag, Amal. "Toyota Said to be Planning U.S. Plant to Build Midsized Camry Model Cars." *The Wall Street Journal*, 09 July 1985, 2.

Nesbitt, Roger. "Scott Leaders Determined to Control Resulting Growth." *Lexington Herald Leader*, 11 December 1985, A1.

Nesbitt, Roger, Andy Mead, and Art Jester. "Way Appears Clear for Deal on Plant Land." *Lexington Herald-Leader*, 07 December 1985, A1.

Petros, Liz Caras. "Japanese Firms' American Workers Must be Doing Something Right." *Lexington Herald-Leader*, 09 February 1992, E1.

Poole, Shelia M. "Toyota Vows to Treat Minorities 'Favorably' in Hiring for Plant." *Lexington Herald-Leader*, 17 October 1986, D11.

Prather, Paul. "Most Production Applicants White, Male, Under 40." *Lexington Herald-Leader*, 28 March 1988, D8.

———. "Survey: Toyota's Jobs Welcome in Scott County." *Lexington Herald-Leader*, 16 December 1989, C4.

———. "Toyota and Georgetown: the Boom that Wasn't." *Lexington Herald-Leader*, 31 December 1989, A1.

———. "Toyota Begins Recruiting for Second Shift." *Lexington Herald-Leader*, 14 August 1988, B3.

———. "Toyota Captain Plays for Team." *Lexington Herald-Leader*, 14 March 1988, D3.

———. "Toyota Chief Knows People Turn Plant's Wheels." *Lexington Herald-Leader*, 06 February 1989, D3.

———. "Toyota Figures Show Most Workers Live Outside Scott County." *Lexington Herald Leader*, 15 November 1989, B5.

———. "Toyota Test Screens Out All But Best and Brightest." *Lexington Herald-Leader*, 03 April 1988, A1.

———. "Toyota, Union Leaders Fail to Resolve Labor Issues." *Lexington Herald-Leader*, 11 July 1986, C7.

———. "Toyota's Warren May Become Trend Setter." *Lexington Herald-Leader*, 19 March 1990, D3.

———. "Tremendous Job Awaits Toyota Manager." *Lexington Herald-Leader*, 15 August 1988, D3.

Rakowsky, Judy. "Lawyer Takes Helm at Honda Plant." *Columbus Citizen-Journal*, 03 March 1985, 5.

Reiss, Robert W. "He Fought for Slice of Nature." *The Columbus Dispatch*, 02 September 1988, 6F.

———. "Honda Has Won Over Most Critics in Marysville." *The Columbus Dispatch*, 20 September 1987, 3B.

———. "Honda Puts Marysville in Driver's Seat." *The Columbus Dispatch*, 01 April 1984, 1C.

———. "Honda Union Election Postponed." *The Columbus Dispatch*, 17 December 1985, 1B.

———. "Honda Workers Will Vote on Forming Union." *The Columbus Dispatch*, 15 December 1985, 3B.

———. "Union Steps Up Pressure on Honda." *The Columbus Dispatch*, 31 March 1985, 3B.

Roser, Mary Ann, and Jack Brammer. "Senate Approves Incentive Package for Toyota." *Lexington Herald-Leader*, 25 January 1986, A1.

Sanger, David E. "A Top Japanese Politician Calls U.S. Work Force Lazy." *The New York Times*, 21 January 1992, D1.

———. "A Trade Mission Ends in Tension as the 'Big Eight' of Autos Meet." *The New York Times*, 10 January 1992, A1.

Sato, Akihiro. "Toyota and Its Sales Arm Plan Merger to be More Responsive to Market Needs." *The Wall Street Journal*, 26 January 1982, 39.

Schnapp, John B. "Soichiro Honda, Japan's Inventive Iconoclast." *The Wall Street Journal*, 01 February 1982, 20.

Sease, Douglas R. "Nowadays Honda Has Good Things to Say About American Cars." *The Wall Street Journal*, 10 November 1982, 31.

Simison, Robert L. "UAW Blows Its Top Over Ban on the Use of Its Caps at Plant." *The Wall Street Journal*, 24 June 1980, 14.

Simon, W. Viana, and Robert S. Strauss. "Foreign Investment in America: Is It Helping or Hurting?" *The Wall Street Journal*, 17 August 1982, 13.

Solov, Diane. "Honda Says Union Charges Mask Lack of Votes." *Business First of Greater Columbus*, 23 December 1985, 10.

St. Clair, Duane. "Auto Center Sale OK'd in Assembly." *The Columbus Dispatch*, 21 January 1988, 7D.

————. "Honda to Expand Marysville Works." *The Columbus Dispatch*, 25 November 1981, 1A.

————. "Panel Examines Sale of Research Center to Honda." *The Columbus Dispatch*, 07 January 1988, 5D.

————. "Rhodes Urging Honda be Given Break on Land." *The Columbus Dispatch*, 20 June 1980, 1B.

————. "State Negotiating to Sell 400 Acres to Honda Motors." *The Columbus Dispatch*, 26 June 1980, 7B.

Swasy, Alecia. "26 Toyota Workers Leave for Training in Japan." *Lexington Herald-Leader*, 04 July 1987, B3.

————. "Auto Suppliers Oppose Subzone for Toyota Plant." *Lexington Herald-Leader*, 17 September, 1986, B5.

————. "Lines Forming for 3,000 Toyota Jobs as Complex Hiring Process Begins." *Lexington Herald-Leader*, 12 January 1987, D1.

————. "Small Town Mayor Faces Big-City Issues." *Lexington Herald-Leader*, 09 February 1987, D3.

————. "Toyota Deal: Did Kentucky Give Away Too Much?" *Lexington Herald-Leader*, 24 August 1986, A1.

————. "Toyota Executive Seeking Harmony in the Bluegrass." *Lexington Herald-Leader*, 25 August 1986, D3.

————. "Toyota-Union Dispute: Key Battle in National Struggle." *Lexington Herald-Leader*, 11 August, 1986, A1.

————. "Toyota's New Top American Official Says Plant Will be Worth the Cost." *Lexington Herald-Leader*, 10 October 1986, D8.

————. "Trade Furor Snags Toyota's Bid to Cut Tariffs." *Lexington Herald-Leader*, 18 October 1987, E1.

————. "Why the Unions Are Fighting Toyota." *Lexington Herald-Leader*, 16 November 1986, A1.

Swasy, Alecia, and Michael York. "Unions and Toyota Builder Resolve Hiring Dispute." *Lexington Herald-Leader*, 26 November 1986, A1.

Tharp, Mike. "Honda Indicates It's Nearing Agreement with Ohio on Building Motorcycle Plant." *The Wall Street Journal*, 28 September 1977, 2.

————. "Honda's Move to Build $200 Million Plant in Ohio Could Spur Other Japanese Firms." *The Wall Street Journal*, 14 January 1980, 11.

————. "Toyota and Nissan Say They Will Resist Pressures to Build Auto Plants in the U.S." *The Wall Street Journal*, 10 April 1980, 6.

Tharp, Mike, and Robert Simison. "Honda's Move to Build $200 million Plant in Ohio Could Spur Other Japanese Firms." *The Wall Street Journal*, 14 January 1980, 2.

Truman, Cheryl, and Andy Mead. "Analyst Says State Attractive for Toyota." *Lexington Herald Leader*, 28 November 1985, A24.

Truman, Cheryl, and Kit Wagar. "Land Options Sought in Scott for Possible Toyota Site." *Lexington Herald-Leader*, 26 November 1985, A1.

Truman, Ceryl, Roger Nesbitt, and Michael York. "Toyota Land Package Nearly Complete." *Lexington Herald-Leader*, 06 December 1985, A1.

Wagar, Kit. "UK Key Part of Package for Toyota, Source Says." *Lexington Herald-Leader*, 09 December 1985, A1.

Wagman, David. "After Settlement, Honda Still Faces EEO Charges." *Business First of Greater Columbus*, 08 June 1987, 9.

——. "Susan Insley Finds a Perch in Japan's Auto Industry." *Business First of Greater Columbus*, 17 November 1986, 14.

——. "Today, What's Good for Honda Is Good for Ohio." *Business First of Greater Columbus*, 28 September 1987, 12.

Webster, Mary Carran. "Town Time Forgot Prepares for Change." *Columbus Citizen Journal*, 02 April 1981, 7.

——. "UAW Win Expected at Marysville Plant." *Columbus Citizen-Journal*, 08 July 1981, 19.

Weisman, Steven R. "Trade Discord Persists as Bush Arrives in Japan." *The New York Times*, 07 January 1992, A1.

Williams, Stephen M. "Civil-Rights Officials Optimistic about Toyota's Hiring Policies." *Lexington Herald-Leader*, 24 December 1986, C6.

Williamson, Doug. "Japanese Bias Comes to Light in Hiring Plans." *Windsor Star Special Report: Jobs 2000*, 29 October 1987, 14.

Wines, Michael. "Export Goal Unmet." *The New York Times*, 10 January 1992, A1.

Wolf, Barnet D. "$450 Million Expansion Planned for Honda Plant." *The Columbus Dispatch*, 09 January 1987, 1E.

——. "Japanese Plants Will be Organized, UAW Leader Says." *The Columbus Dispatch*, 17 March 1987, 1E.

——. "Top Female Employee Enjoys Honda Challenges." *The Columbus Dispatch*, 14 June 1987, 2G.

Woods, Jim. "Effort to Unionize Honda by UAW Is a Hot Topic." *The Columbus Dispatch*, 22 December, 1985, 3D.

Yocum, Robin. "Honda Tax Revenue Aids School Budget." *The Columbus Dispatch*, 15 February 1980, 6B.

Yoshino, Hiroyuki. "Honda Way Workers Not Lazy." *Business First: The Business Newspaper of Greater Columbus*, 16 March 1992, 11.

"Attorney Named to Honda Post." *The Columbus Dispatch*, 08 April 1985, 9C.

"Civic Now Made in America as Marysville Produces First." *The Columbus Dispatch*, 25 July 1986, 1E.

"Commissioners Grant Honda Tax Abatement." *The Marysville Journal-Tribune*, 01 February 1978, 1A.

"Cost of Ohio's Bait Used to Lure Honda Questioned in Study." *Columbus Citizen Journal*, 10 June 1980, 21.

"County Commissioners Consider Road Changes for Honda Company." *The Marysville Journal-Tribune*, 18 April 1978, 1A.

"GM, Toyota Agree to Explore Joint Output of Small Car, a Proposal Rejected by Ford."*The Wall Street Journal*, 09 March 1982, 2.

"Honda of America Drops Opposition to UAW's Drive." *The Wall Street Journal*, 26 April 1982, 5.

"Honda Boss Praises U.S. Workers." *The Columbus Dispatch*, 21 November 1985, 7G.

"Honda to Build Near Marysville." *The Marysville Journal-Tribune*, 11 October 1977, 1A.

"Honda to Build Plant in Area?" *Columbus Citizen-Journal*, 27 September 1977, 1.

"Honda Hits Production Goals at Marysville." *The Columbus Dispatch*, 03 August 1983, 12A.

"Honda May Locate Plant in County" *The Marysville Journal-Tribune*, 27 September 1977, 1A.

"Honda Motor Posts 49% Decline in Net For the Feb. 28 Year." *The Wall Street Journal*, 29 May 1979, 6.

"Honda Names Plant Manager." *The Columbus Dispatch*, 02 January 1985, 6E.

"Honda to Pay for Age Discrimination." *The Columbus Dispatch*, 02 June 1987, 1E.

"Honda to Pay Back Wages to Settle Age Bias Charges." *The Wall Street Journal*, 03 June 1987, 17.

"Honda Promotes Self-Reliance." *The Columbus Dispatch*, 13 May 1991, 1E.

"Honda Rejects a Request By UAW for Recognition." *The Wall Street Journal*, 01 November 1985, 25.

"Honda Stores 2,000 Accords as U.S. Sales Lag." *The Columbus Dispatch*, 06 March 1991, 1F.

"Honda Talks Should Have Included Commissioners." *The Marysville Journal-Tribune*, 03 February 1978, 4A.

"Honda, UAW Reach 1st-of-a-Kind Labor Agreement." *The Columbus Dispatch*, 23 April 1982, 9B.

"Honda Unit in Dispute Over Plant Organizing is Charged by NLRB." *The Wall Street Journal*, 13 October 1980, 23.

"Honda's Ohio Auto Plant May Open Early." *The Columbus Dispatch*, 06 July 1981, 1A.

"Land for Honda Offered at Cost." *Columbus Citizen-Journal*, 29 September 1977, 1.

"Marysville Rolls Out First U.S.-Built Honda." *The Columbus Dispatch*, 01 November 1982, 6B.

"Minority Groups Push Role for Blacks in Toyota." *Lexington Herald Leader*, 15 October 1986, B2.

"More Countries Set to Cash In On Oil Shortage." *The Wall Street Journal*, 17 December 1973, 2.

"NLRB Upholds UAW." *The Columbus Dispatch*, 31 July 1984, 7C.

"NLRB Upholds UAW." *The Wall Street Journal*, 31 July 1984, 7.

"NLRB Will Accuse Honda of Violations, Auto Workers Say." *The Wall Street Journal*, 07 October 1980, 41.

"Nissan Is Latest Auto Firm to Study Starting Assembly Operations in the U.S." *The Wall Street Journal*, 12 July 1973, 15.

"Roaring Yen Hits Honda's Profits." *The Columbus Dispatch*, 22 January 1987, 1G.

"Senate Swiftly Approves Bill to Sell Land to Honda Corp." *Columbus Citizen-Journal*, 27 June 1980, 10.

"State Draws Japanese Car, Food Companies." *The Columbus Dispatch*, 10 February 1980, 13C.

"Toyota Auto Sales in U.S. Up 74% in August from 1970." *The Wall Street Journal*, 03 October 1971, 3.

"Toyota, Honda Raise Car Prices in U.S., Citing the Decline of Dollar Against Yen." *The Wall Street Journal*, 25 November 1977, 12.

"Toyota and Nissan Are Wary of Building in U.S., Fearing Losses, Small-Car Glut." *The Wall Street Journal*, 28 February 1980, 12.

"Toyota Organizes Team to Study Possibility of Production in U.S." *The Wall Street Journal*, 05 December 1979, 18.

"Toyota Plant Produces 100,000th Camry." *Lexington Herald-Leader*, 19 August 1989, A10.

"UAW Faces Honda Fight." *The Columbus Dispatch*, 05 November 1985, 5B.

"UAW Pushes for Honda Vote." *The Columbus Dispatch*, 24 May 1984, 9E.

"UAW to Renew Push for Honda Employees." *The Columbus Dispatch*, 25 October 1985, 7E.

"UAW Wins in Vote at Honda Plant." *Columbus Citizen-Journal*, 11 July 1981, 15.

"U.S. Step Would Give Break on Import Fees to New Toyota Plant." *The Wall Street Journal*, 17 November 1987, 27.

"Union Official Sues to Stop Toyota Work." *Lexington Herald-Leader*, 18 July 1986, B1.

"Unionization Vote at Honda on Hold." *The Columbus Dispatch*, 11 February 1986, 1E.

GOVERNMENT DOCUMENTS, REPORTS, AND TESTIMONY

Auditor of Public Accounts, Commonwealth of Kentucky. *Scott County Sheriff's Settlement—1987 Taxes*. Frankfort: Commonwealth of Kentucky, 1988.

——. *Scott County Sheriff's Settlement—1988 Taxes*. Frankfort: Commonwealth of Kentucky, 1989.

——. *Scott County Sheriff's Settlement—1989 Taxes*. Frankfort: Commonwealth of Kentucky, 1990.

——. *Scott County Sheriff's Settlement—1990 Taxes*. Frankfort: Commonwealth of Kentucky, 1991.

——. *Scott County Sheriff's Settlement—1991 Taxes*. Frankfort: Commonwealth of Kentucky, 1992.

——. *Scott County Sheriff's Settlement—1992 Taxes*. Frankfort: Commonwealth of Kentucky, 1993.

Baldridge, United States Commerce Secretary Malcolm to Governor Martha Layne Collins, 20 June 1986. Governor's Correspondence File, 1983–1987, Box 64, Series 00240, Kentucky State Archives, Public Records Division, Frankfort, Kentucky.

Bass, Gwenell L., and Lenore Sek. "Foreign Trade Zones and the U.S. Automobile Industry." *Congressional Research Service Report for the United States Congress*, 14 October 1988.

Bieber, Owen. "Statement Before the U.S. International Trade Commission Hearing on the Internationalization of the Automobile Industry and Its Effects on the U.S. Automotive Industry." Detroit, Michigan, 04 December 1984.

Bruce, John L. to "All Members of Iron Workers Local Union Number 70," 10 July 1986. Toyota File, 1983–1987, Box 62, Series 00240, Kentucky State Archives, Public Records Division, Frankfort, Kentucky.

Collins, Governor Martha Layne. Speech announcing Toyota's arrival in Kentucky, 11 December 1985. Governor's Economic Development File, 1983–1987, Box 10, Series 00240, Kentucky State Archives, Public Records Division, Frankfort, Kentucky.

———. Speech at the Toyota Ground breaking Ceremony, 05 May 1986. Governor's Economic Development File, 1983–1987, Box 10, Series 00240, Kentucky State Archives, Public Records Division, Frankfort, Kentucky.

———. "Testimony Before the Public Hearing on Toyota Subzone Application, Department of Commerce Foreign Trade Zone Board." Washington, DC, 12 August 1987.

Collins, Governor Martha Layne to Dr. And Mrs. Toyoda Shoichiro, 24 June 1986. Governor's Correspondence File, 1983–1987, Box 64, Series 00240, Kentucky State Archives, Public Records Division, Frankfort, Kentucky.

Collins, Governor Martha Layne to United States Commerce Secretary Malcolm Baldridge, 16 June 1986. Governor's Correspondence File, 1983–1987, Box 64, Series 00240, Kentucky State Archives, Public Records Division, Frankfort, Kentucky.

Collins, Governor Martha Layne. Toyota Incentive Plan Announcement, 17 December 1985. Governor's Economic Development File, 1983–1987, Box 10, Series 00240, Kentucky State Archives, Public Records Division, Frankfort, Kentucky.

Kaptur, Representative Marcy. "Testimony at the Hearing Before the Subcommittee on Employment and Productivity of the Committee on Labor and Human Resources." United States Senate, 100th Congress, First Session, 30 March 1987.

Kentucky. General Assembly. House. House Appropriations and Revenue Committee Minutes, 05 February 1986. Frankfort, Kentucky, 1986.

Kentucky. General Assembly. Senate. Minutes of the Kentucky Senate Appropriations and Revenue Committee, 22 January 1986. Frankfort, Kentucky, 1986.

Kentucky Cabinet for Economic Development, Division of Research and Planning. *Resources for Economic Development, Georgetown, Kentucky.* Frankfort: Commonwealth of Kentucky, 1989.

Kentucky Cabinet for Human Resources. Georgetown Labor Force Profile. Frankfort: Commonwealth of Kentucky, 1988.

Kentucky Commerce Cabinet. Deed: Commerce Cabinet, Grantor, Toyota Motor Manufacturing, U.S.A., Inc., Grantee. Frankfort: Commonwealth of Kentucky, 04 September 1987.

Kimbell, Martha to Governor Martha Layne Collins (undated.) Governor's Correspondence File, 1983–1987, Box 64, Series 00240, Kentucky State Archives, Public Records Division, Frankfort, Kentucky.

Ohio Bureau of Employment Services. *Ohio Labor Market Information, County Profiles, Shelby County and Union County*. Columbus: The State of Ohio,1989.

Ohio Department of Development. *1977 Statistical Guide*. Columbus: The State of Ohio, 1977.

——. *Ohio's Economic Development Incentives*. Columbus: The State of Ohio, March 1984.

Ohio Development Financing Commission. *1982 Annual Report*. Columbus: The State of Ohio, 1982.

Peterson, Gerald D. "Cost Analysis of State Incentive Programs for Industrial Development." *General Accounting Office Report to the United States Department of Commerce*, 09 June 1980.

Simon, Senator Paul. "Testimony at the Hearing Before the Subcommittee on Employment and Productivity of the Committee on Labor and Human Resources." United States Senate, 100th Congress, First Session, 30 March 1987.

Union County Auditors Office, Marysville, Ohio. "Community Reinvestment Area Tax Exemption Program Application by Honda of America Manufacturing, Inc." 16 November 1981.

Union County Auditors Office, Marysville, Ohio. "Community Reinvestment Area Tax Exemption Program Application by Honda of America Manufacturing, Inc." 14 December 1988.

——. "Community Reinvestment Area Tax Exemption Program Application by Honda of America Manufacturing, Inc." 18 December 1990.

——. "Community Reinvestment Area Tax Exemption Program Application by Honda of America Manufacturing, Inc." 16 December 1991.

Union County, Ohio. "Resolution Adopting Agreement Between Board of Union County Commissioners and the City of Marysville, Ohio (Honda)." *Commissioners Journal 33*: 26–27.

——. "Resolution Authorizing County to Enter into an Agreement with Honda of America Mfg., Inc." *Commissioners Journal 34*: 254.

——. "Resolution Establishing and Describing the Boundaries of a Community Reinvestment Area." *Commissioners Journal 32*: 575–576.

——. "Resolution Establishing the Boundaries of a Community Reinvestment Area—Honda." *Commissioners Journal 36*: 119–120.

——. "Resolution Initiating Procedures for the Vacation of a Portion of Benton Road (Honda)." *Commissioners Journal 33*: 14–15.

——. "Resolution Regarding Widening U.S. 33." *Commissioners Journal 34*: 299.

U.S. Congress. House. "Japanese Voluntary Restraints on Auto Exports to the United States." Hearings Before the Subcommittee on Trade of the Committee on Ways and Means. 99th Congress, First Session, 28 February and 04 March 1985.

U.S. Congress. Joint Economic Committee. "Measures Concerning the Export of Passenger Cars to the United States." Submitted by the Ministry of International Trade and Industry to the Hearings Before the Subcommittee on Economic Goals and Intergovernmental Policy. 98th Congress, Second Session, 01 May 1981.

U.S. Congress. Senate. "MOSS Talks/U.S. Auto Parts Industry." Hearing Before the Subcommittee on Employment and Productivity of the Committee on Labor and Human Resources. 100th Congress, First Session, 30 March 1987.

U.S. Department of Commerce. *Attracting Foreign Investment to the United States: A Guide for Government*. Washington, DC: U.S. Government Printing Office, 1982.

———. "Grant of Authority to Establish a Foreign Trade Zone in Scott County, Kentucky." *Federal Register 53*: 45.

U.S. Department of Energy. *1982 Annual Energy Review*. Washington, DC: U.S. Government Printing Office, 1983.

U.S. Department of Energy. *1987 Annual Energy Review*. Washington, DC: U.S. Government Printing Office, 1988.

U.S. Department of Labor. *Monthly Labor Review*, December 1991. Washington, DC: U.S. Government Printing Office, 1991.

U.S. General Accounting Office. *Foreign Investment: Growing Japanese Presence in the U.S. Auto Industry*. Washington, DC: U.S. Government Printing Office, 1988.

U.S. International Trade Commission. *Harmonized Tariff Schedule of the United States, 1993*. Washington, DC: U.S. Government Printing Office, 1993.

———. *Summary of Trade and Tariff Information: Automobiles, Trucks, Buses, and Bodies and Chassis of the Foregoing Motor Vehicles*. Washington, DC: U.S. Government Printing Office, 1984.

———. *U.S. Global Competitiveness: The U.S. Automotive Parts Industry*. Washington, DC: U.S. Government Printing Office, 1987.

U.S. Securities and Exchange Commission. "Facilitation of Multinational Securities Offerings." *Federal Register 50*: 9281-9284.

Warren, Alex. "Testimony at the Hearing Before the Subcommittee on Employment and Productivity of the Committee on Labor and Human Resources." United States Senate, 100th Congress, First Session, 30 March.

Index